D1431326

THE
GREATEST OF THESE
IS LOVE

A Novel By

Dody Myers

Best Wishes Dody Myers

BHouse
BHouse Publishing
Brunswick, Georgia

Volume One

Written By: Dolores H. Myers

ISBN# 0-9653831-1-3

Published By:

BHouse Publishing Co.
716 Fancy Bluff Road
Brunswick, Georgia 31523
E-Mail: bhouse@darientel.net
(912) 265-2490
(912) 264-0660

Dedication

To my husband, Jim
who is my editor, faithful critic,
and best friend,
who tirelessly and patiently pushed
me to complete this novel.

And now these three remain:
faith, hope and love.
But the greatest of these is love.

2 Corinthians 13:13 NIV

AUTHOR'S NOTE

For readers such as myself, who like to know which part of a story is fact or fiction, I offer the following:

All of the facts about the Civil War, its politics and battles, are based on extensive historical research.

Hanover, Pennsylvania was the scene of the first battle between the North and the South to be fought on Northern soil. The cavalry battle at Hanover, in accordance with the views of some military critics, was the turning point of Lee's invasion of Pennsylvania in 1863. The conflict of arms at Hanover compelled the Confederate General, Jeb Stuart, to make a large detour and thus prevented him from communicating with General Lee, who was then concentrating his forces around Gettysburg, preparing for the impending battle.

Details of the Battle of Gettysburg and its aftermath were taken from the books "We Never Expected a Battle," by Robert L. Bloom, published by Pennsylvania History 55, October 1988 and "Gettysburg," by William Frassanito, published by Charles Scriber's Sons, 1975.

Christ Church, the Mother of Reformed Churches in North America, really does exist and sits proudly, as depicted, on its little knoll along the Littlestown Pike—Edward Rebert's handsome granite monument a dominant feature of its intriguing graveyard.

For information about the Pennsylvania. Dutch culture I found Frederick Klees excellent book "The Pennsylvania Dutch", published by The MacMillan Company, 1950, to be my bible.

The novel, however, is a work of fiction. Names if real, are based on oral history and used fictitiously.

Dody Myers

PROLOGUE

The tan Mercuy slowed to a crawl. Four Mennonite children played stick ball in their front yard and a woman gazed intently from the automobile's open passenger window, not at the children, but at the imposing brick farm house sheltered by a huge maple tree. The rural mailbox read "GROVE".

"Go down to the stream and turn around at the bridge. I want to get another look," the woman said softly to her husband.

A farm lane entered the road just above the bridge and her husband turned in its entrance and started back toward the house. "Slowly now, I want to see it all," the woman directed.

The children, three girls and a boy, pretended not to notice the creeping automobile. The oldest, a girl of about twelve, took a swing at the fat ball, bouncing it across the ground to her younger brother who quickly glanced at the car to see if its occupants had seen his catch.

"I think we should stop and tell them what we're looking at," the husband said nervously. "They're liable to think we're up to no good."

The woman frowned, but didn't object as he pulled the car into a driveway that separated the two story brick farmhouse from a large bank-barn.

The oldest girl laid down her bat and approached the car, while the others stood apart watching intently. The girls all wore straight calico dresses that reached to their ankles revealing black cotton stockings and high top shoes, their hair plaited into fat pigtails tied with Sunday hair ribbons. The lone boy wore trim black trousers with black suspenders that spanned a crisp white shirt. All the children were bare-footed.The woman smiled at the girl from the open window.

"My husband thought we should stop and tell you why we're staring at your house," she said quietly. "I believe my great-great-grandfather may have lived here at one time, way back in the eighteen hundreds."

The girl puckered her forehead, then gave the woman a tentative smile. "What was his name, do you know?"

"Rebert. Edward Rebert. We're not sure this is the place. We've been looking for it, off and on, for the past year."

A broad grin spread across the child's face and her blue eyes crinkled with excitement. "Edward Rebert! Oh, you must come inside and talk to my Mama."

The woman felt the hairs on her arm prickle and her breath quickened. "Do you recognize the name then?"

"It's printed in the rafters of our attic."

The other children had moved closer to the car, smiling and bobbing their heads up and down.

"Come, Mama's in the kitchen," the girl said. She stood back to allow the woman to exit the car, then ran toward the back porch, chickens flying from her path, pigtails bouncing, calling to her Mother.

"Go ahead," the man said with a grin. I'll walk around; maybe investigate the barn."

Mrs. Grove was standing on the porch listening to the child, while looking toward the woman making her uncertain way toward her. The other children trailed the woman, giggling when her high heeled shoes stuck in the soft grass and their dog enthusiastically leaped against her good silk skirt.

After introductions were exchanged the woman explained her mission. She told Mrs. Grove what she knew about the history of the farm, her eyes eagerly climbing the brick walls, imagining the rooms and the people who had once lived there.

The invitation she had been hoping for finally came. "Would you like to come inside and see the house?"

"I hate to impose. . . but yes, I would love to see it."

After examining the roomy farm kitchen with its large open fireplace they toured the dining room and double living room before climbing a central stairway to the five second floor bedrooms. "Your little girl mentioned that Edward Rebert's name was printed somewhere in the attic. Could I possibly see it?"

Mrs. Grove hesitated briefly. "The attic stairway's cluttered with things I haven't had time to store away. I don't know as how we could get up there." She apparently noticed the disappointment on the woman's face because she quickly added, "we can try if you want."

They picked their way up the narrow steps and crossed to a far corner of the hot, musty attic. And there on a sloping wall under the rafters the woman saw it:

E. Rebert.

S. Fine - 1863

Probably a stencil, faded now, but used to identify flour sacks in the grist mill Edward operated during the Civil War. The wall bore other initials, haphazardly carved in the grey wood, initials she recognized as those of Rebert children—Alex, Edwin, Annie, and Emma.

Mrs. Grove busied herself moving some items from the stairwell and gave the woman time to gaze somberly at the wall. With a lump in her throat she studied the aged inscriptions, reminders of the human history of this house, of children that had been conceived here, had played, and laughed, and fought, and grown into adulthood in its rooms. Edward Rebert lived his life here during the agonizing war years, had loved, and worked, and died here.

The woman stepped to a tiny window, set in the sloping eaves, covered with dust and lacy cobwebs. She stood quietly and turned her head slowly to absorb the view that Edward would have seen—lush Pennsylvania fields sloping to a meandering stream glimmering in the sun. The grist mill was gone, but the land had not changed since Edward trod the faint path to the water's edge. She could almost feel his presence.

A gaggle of geese were crossing the grass, one out in front, the others following. Barnyard ducks, she had noticed, did the same thing. And sons their fathers.

She watched the geese cross the meadow heading toward the edge of the cut cornfield. The leader paused, his head high, listening for danger while his followers waited patiently until he proceeded into the stubble of stalks.

The geese would head south soon. But spring would find them back in this same breeding place, with nests well under way. No matter how far the journey the need to return home is instinctual, basic.

Was it that same instinct that had drawn her to find this place? It was only a house, wasn't it? An old brick farmhouse, with a barn and several acres of farm land. What was this powerful need she felt to see tangible proof of her beginnings, an anchor with her past? Was it the basic need of all humanity to feel a kinship with the past? To know that the people who came before them placed an indelible stamp on their genes, making them the person they were. Like the stencil on the wall behind her.

I, of course, was the woman. I had found the house. Now I had to know more. I had to know the whole story.

Part 1

North Codorus,
York County, Pennsylvania

1836

Chapter
-1-

Edward Rebert hated his father's distillery. Sometimes, heaven help him, he even hated his father.

The revival tent, pitched in Enoch Oberholtzer's cow pasture, was filled for the evening service despite the unexpected April heat. Oil lanterns flickered in the deepening gloom, casting dancing shadows on canvas walls the color of earth. Over a hundred Pennsylvania Dutch farmers in their black Sunday-go-to-meeting clothes murmured, shifting and swatting at buzzing flies, while cardboard fans with pictures of a praying Jesus fluttered in the still air. Men moved about the sides of the tent to pull back heavy flaps and let in whispers of humid air. Thunder rumbled in the distance and jagged streaks of lightning illuminated the tender Pennsylvania countryside.

Sixteen-year-old Edward Rebert sat on a rough oak plank, squeezed between a buxom Mennonite woman and his best friend, Patrick McPherson.

The woman smelled of clothing hung in the sun to dry; Patrick smelled of clean saw dust. Edward liked their smell and worried about his own. The odor of sour mash from the distillery never left him, it clung to his hair and skin, impossible to wash away.

The evangelist was late and Edward rutched, his emotions as chaotic as the brewing storm. He had no stomach for work in the dark confines of the distillery, disliked the denial of his desire to be a simple farmer, and resented his father, whom he held accountable for both. There were times when he wished he and Patrick could run away, could escape from Pa and the distillery and his overwhelming discontent. But the farm was his heritage. Generations of Reberts had tilled the fertile Codorus valley.

He glanced at Patrick, slouched in his seat. Patrick had an itchy heel. He'd go for sure.

Edward strained forward, his gaze sweeping the crowd. His brother, J.J., sat with a possessive arm around his girl, Rebecca Hoke. Next to Rebecca was her younger sister, Katie.

His gaze passed over them, then swung back to young Katie and traveled down the front of her plain dress. He quickly looked away.

Katie seemed to sense his gaze and turned to give him a smile. He pretended he didn't notice.

A hush swept like a wave from the front of the tent. Edward looked up and saw the black-clad evangelist pause between the tent folds, then enter.

Edward felt a shiver of excitement. The Reverend John Geiselman mounted the stage, slammed his Bible on the makeshift pulpit and grabbed the edge of the wobbly lectern with his knobby fingers. Without a word he stared at the farmers who squirmed in their seats. All about him the silence grew.

"My sermon tonight will be *The Evils of Demon Rum.*"

"Oh God," Patrick muttered.

"*Chust* listen, already. He's started to talk," Edward whispered, his eyes warm and optomistic.

Geiselman's rich voice carried to every corner of the tent. "Oh Mighty God, your people have turned from you and walk in wicked ways. They fill themselves with demon rum and in their stupor break your commandments. They..."

Edward leaned forward and stared at the evangelist, an impressive man with a voice to match his size. A shock of white hair crowned his stern face; his side-whiskers were black and luxurious. He wore a flowing black tie and a broad-brimmed black hat. His shout brought Edward upright in his seat. "YOU!" Geiselman bellowed, pointing at the rapt audience with a long hairy finger. "Sinners all of you. YOU, YOU, AND YOU!" He read from the gospel while he paced back and forth across the shaky platform to proclaim the sins of all present. The crowd hung on his every word, electric tension mounted, fans waved, and lightning streaked through the black night.

Edward's skin tingled, flushed with the excitement of the crowd. He wiped wet palms on his pants and felt the sweat drip inside his shirt.

When the evangelist called for prayer, Edward bowed his head. People prayed and swayed all around him. He let his mind wander and peeked at the face of Katie Hoke. There was a femininity about her that caused him to feel uncomfortably warm. Her head was bowed, hands clasped under her chin, thick auburn braids lying softly on her back. A fly landed on her nose and she broke her prayerful posture to give it a sharp swat, then glanced sideways to see if she had been observed. Her eyes met Edward's and she smiled. Edward's heart gave a queer lurch and in confusion he dropped his gaze to his lap, attempting to concentrate on the prayer.

"Hallelujahs" and "Amens" filled the tent.

Reverend Geiselman lifted his head, then slowly raised his Bible into the air and shouted, "Whiskey - it's a plague on our land! There are those interested only in the almighty dollar who sell swill to our unsuspecting people, young and old, ruining their health and their lives. Distillers! Tavern Keepers! Woe to them!"

Edward shuddered. The evangelist's eyes, black as licorice, seemed to glare straight at him. Edward's face flushed with heat. Did Geiselman know his family owned the local distillery?

The sermon gained momentum, the condemnation

scalding, every word burning him like hot coals.

Deep in his pocket, Edward worried the coin he'd brought for the collection. His nose itched from the dust of the straw covered floor. A sudden breeze moved through the tent, stirring smells of damp earth, cow dung, and musty canvas.

The evangelist pleaded with the people. "Repent! Come forward! You must be saved! Come! Come!" His voice dropped to a warm whisper, the harsh planes of his face softened by golden light from the flickering lanterns. "I'm not talking of men who deliberately defy God. I'm talking of simple men who've fallen prey to the devil. I'm talking of men who are helpless . . . yea, helpless in the clutch of the evil spirits that lurk in the bottle. You must confess your sin of drunkenness, your sin of distilling the evil brew. Come!" His voice trembled with emotion, his face was wet and shiny and several droplets of sweat dripped off the tip of his nose. "Come, throw yourself on the mercy of the Lord. You must be saved! Don't worry what your friends will think. Come . . . come!"

Edward squirmed in his seat, the hypnotic voice of the fiery evangelist tugged at him with a mysterious force. Did he need to be saved? He was only obeying his father's vision for him. A shattering thought shook him. And what of his divine Father's vision for him. Was it that of a distiller? He doubted it.

He edged forward.

"Oh, no, you don't," Patrick muttered. He grabbed Edward's arm and jerked him from the bench. "That's it. I've heard enough. We're leaving."

Reluctantly, Edward followed his friend and struggled to regain control of himself.

They left the thundering evangelist and the normally staid, serious German farmers now waving their arms in excitement and strode into the quiet Pennsylvania countryside, across trampled pasture and fallow fields awaiting the spring plow. Dark hills covered with whispering blue-black hemlocks and emerald firs loomed on the horizon, swaying in the breeze quickened by the approaching storm. The smell of rain was heavy in the air.

"Don't ever do that to me again," Patrick said, stopping so suddenly Edward banged into him. "I've never seen such a put-up act in my life. Why that old geezer just plain hypnotized everybody, including you."

Edward stood toe to toe with Patrick and glared at him.

The silence stretched. Edward took the first steps back, then spoke. "Ei,yi,yi. Chust once you could have waited yet. The preacher was about finished." Heat flushed his face; he hated it when he failed to speak proper English. He took a deep breath before continuing. "What the evangelist preached wasn't a lie, Patrick. Liquor puts the devil to work, and working for Pa at the distillery is wrong . . . dead wrong."

"Aye, an' you think the devil is working on me, don't you? I bet you knew what the sermon was about tonight and got me to go on purpose. You've become a cussed saint, Edward Rebert. A real pain-in-the-neck!"

Edward clenched his fists and stepped forward. Patrick's words riled him. He wasn't a saint! He never pretended to be. Patrick had the real problem; he drank more than he should, then got mean and nasty.

"You're the one always first at the cider barrel and last to leave," he shouted. "You're the real pain-in-the-neck, Patrick McPherson!"

A sharp clap of thunder interrupted their angry exchange. Dark clouds scudded across the full moon and a sudden gust of warm air ruffled Edward's hair. Fat drops of rain slapped his head. The full fury of a spring storm would soon be upon them and he began to run, Patrick following. Streams, already running full to overflowing from the winter break-up, would flood quickly if much rain fell.

Within minutes the wind picked up and the storm broke.

They ran faster, heads down against the rain, hair dripping, boots squishing in the mud. "We've only a mile to our farm," Edward panted. "Head for the distillery . . . it's closest . . . and I was supposed to check the mash barrels anyhow."

"Your Pa's gonna be mighty upset with you if he finds you were at the revival instead of working the still."

"He's always upset with me regardless of what I do," Edward said simply, with no trace of self-pity.

He and Patrick ran across Patapsco Road and dove into the woods where sweeping pines offered protection from the driving rain. By cutting through the thick wood lot they'd be able to ford Codorus Creek at its shallowest point, just where it was diverted to the millrace that served Pa's grist mill and distillery. With luck they could get across the creek before it flooded.

Edward slowed to catch his breath and grinned at the spectacle Patrick presented. Rain rivulets flowed from his springy red curls and dripped off the end of his beard, while his overalls sagged from the weight of the rain. His physical appearance reminded Edward of a huge male lion and made him look far older than his eighteen years; yet despite his size, his voice was so soft Edward usually had to strain to hear what he said. He and Patrick had been fast friends since childhood.

They peered into the darkness to get their bearings. Edward cocked his head toward the sound of rushing water and pointed toward a huge hemlock several feet ahead. They pushed through its rain-laden pine branches and resumed running.

Leaving the protection of the trees, they approached the bank of Codorus Creek. Water frothed and swirled around rocks imbedded in the river bottom. Edward paused and looked across it in dismay. "I don't know, Patrick. It looks mighty treacherous," he shouted.

"Tis our only chance and this storm's getting worse."

Edward looked through the mist rising from the creek toward the distillery a short distance ahead. The distillery would offer protection from the driving rain, they could wait out the storm there.

Patrick was already wading across the stream and without hesitation Edward followed, sloshing up water that filled his boots, his attention centered on keeping his footing in the flooding water.

He leaped for a flat rock protruding from the surging stream and momentarily gained a foothold before his right foot began to slide. He tumbled forward. His chest hit the rock and he landed face down in the cold water. He gasped for breath, but drew in only water.

Caught by the swirling motion of the flooding creek he found he could not right himself. Frightened, he tried to yell for Patrick, but instead choked on a mouthful of muddy water.

His panic rose as the water swept him downstream. He felt he would suffocate with fear. He was going to drown!

Limbs from a large tree hung low over the water. He had to grab hold of a limb . . . had to right himself. He flung his arm high, but his fingers clutched only wet leaves. In desperation he tried to hold onto the slippery branch, but the surging water flung his flailing body against another rock and he lost his grip.

Terrified, he thrashed his arms and legs in a frantic effort to regain his footing. He tried to direct his arms toward a boulder imbedded in the stream-bed, but a sudden swirl of water turned him around and his head bounced off the rock.

Stunned, he felt strong arms lift and cradle him like a baby. Patrick struggled through the raging creek. He staggered once, and almost fell, but his powerful legs fought the currents and in minutes he reached the far bank.

They both lay in the mud fighting for calm, Edward retching muddy water, Patrick shuddering in the aftermath of danger.

"Never saw that stream come up so fast. The Lord must be angry at somebody tonight," Patrick said, shaking his rugged head and throwing sprays of water in all directions. Edward smiled in spite of his discomfort, and fingered the swelling lump on his forehead. "That was mighty close. Thanks Patrick, I would've drowned for sure."

Patrick took his hand and Edward felt a wave of brotherly love for the burly redhead. Despite his size, Patrick had a softness that he tried hard to hide.

Patrick rose to his feet. "Aye, t'was a moment or two I was scared myself. Come now, lad, before we catch our death of cold. The distillery is close and a slug of Rebert whiskey is just what we need to take the chill from our bones. Can you walk?"

"I think so."

They took off through the heavy rain, a wobbly Edward trailing the faster Patrick. Patrick reached the mill first and waited, huddled under an overhang. Edward fumbled in the pocket of his soaked pants for his key. He unlocked the iron padlock and pushed the massive doors across a heavy metal track just as thunder shook the building and a bolt of lightning tore through the sky.

Inside, they stood for a few minutes, each catching his breath. Then Patrick started to laugh.

"A fittin' end to ole blood and thunder's sermon," he chuckled. "Bet this storm was part of his plan."

Edward pulled the suspenders from his shoulders and unbuttoned his sodden shirt. "Grab one of them feed sacks and dry yourself off, you Irish heathen," he said, fighting to hide a smile.

After he wiped his dripping head, Patrick ambled over to one of the huge still kettles in the center of the mill. "Any whiskey left from today's run?" he called.

"Might be a little sampling whiskey in that bucket."

Patrick shook the bucket and stirred the contents with a dipper before raising it to his mouth. "Want some?" he called.

"Nein."

"Don't know what you're missin'."

Patrick helped himself to another dipper of the potent brew. "That's the best . . ."

His voice trailed off as a small 'possum ran unsteadily across the floor and banged headlong into the wall. It staggered, then shook itself fiercely and scurried through the open doorway. "I swear, Edward, I think that crazy possum is drunk," Patrick said, his eyes wide with disbelief.

Edward laughed. "Probably is. We've lots of drunken critters 'round here. They crawl up into the mash vats and have loads of fun. Some of them get so drunk they fall right in. Rats, snakes, even a skunk one time."

"No wonder Rebert Whiskey has such a kick." Patrick slapped his thigh, his green eyes slitted in a grin.

"Ei, and that's not the best of it. You know how Pa hates crows. Well, he puts mash out in the barnyard where they can eat it 'cause they're easier to shoot if they're tipsy." Edward chuckled at the mental picture of Pa and the drunken crows while searching for something to say to get Patrick's mind off the contents of the still kettle.

"There's a barn-dance Saturday night at the Petersons. You planning to go?"

"Guess so."

"My brother was telling me the Petersons have a new indentured girl that'll be at the dance. J.J. says she's right pretty and doesn't have a fellow."

"She got a name?"

"Inger Andreasen."

"Sounds Swedish. How old is she?"

"Sixteen, I think. Just the right age, Patrick. Bet she's never been kissed."

"Aye, an 'tisn't right for a girl to miss out on kissin'," Patrick said, with feigned seriousness. He looked at Edward, eyes shining with mischief. "You stillin' tomorrow?"

"Yeah."

"Bring a pint to the dance. We'll get them gals all warm and cozy."

Edward smiled tolerantly at Patrick, who was sometimes friend, sometimes adversary. Since childhood, Edward had alternately loved, admired, and resented his best friend. He often wondered at the strange nature of their friendship—giving and taking—each needing the other. Patrick—two fisted, sometimes profane, always carefree, fond of girls and fonder yet of whiskey—a lifestyle certainly in conflict with his own.

Edward's parents were far too busy to communicate much with him, and they exhibited typical German reserve. What he learned of life he learned from Patrick.

The storm still raged outside and Patrick wandered back to the still for another sip of whiskey while Edward's thoughts drifted back to the revival they'd left earlier.

The evangelist had struck a chord in his spirit; this day had changed him in a way he barely understood. He didn't want to be a distiller, wouldn't spend the rest of his life in a sinful trade he detested. Could he ever drum up the courage to leave the family farm and head West? He'd always thought about being a soldier. Maybe he and Patrick could join up with Sam Houston in Texas to fight the Mexicans. Edward threw back his shoulders, visualizing himself in a colorful uniform, astride his mighty horse, charging the enemy with sword extended.

He sighed. That wasn't what Pa saw for him. All Edward really wanted from Pa was love and understanding, but Pa insisted he take his place in the family business and he had to obey—didn't he? He was afraid of Pa, pure and simple.

Vague longings and shadowy dreams seemed to float like foggy mist rising from the warm, wet earth. He stood by the open door watching the storm, breathing air thick with the smell of sour mash and fresh rain. Patrick wouldn't be afraid to run away. *What would Patrick say if I told him what I want to do?* Edward wondered, shivering from his wet clothes and the enormity of his growing desire to break free.

His reverie was interrupted when Patrick joined him in the doorway. "The storm's about spent, I'm gonna run for it. Meet you here Saturday night and we'll go to the Petersons together."

"Ei,"

"And don't forget the whiskey."

Chapter

-2-

Saturday evening, after bathing in the big wooden tub placed in the middle of the kitchen floor for everyone's weekly bath, Edward dressed for the Peterson barn dance. Carefully he tucked a crisp shirt of bleached linen into his black trousers and buttoned the suspender loops to his pants.

He stood in front of a cloudy mirror that hung from a nail beside the kitchen door and took his straight razor to shave the soft fuzz from his face, careful not to nick the deep cleft in his chin, then slicked down his hair with a generous amount of bear grease, turning it a deep honey color. After a final glance in the mirror, he put a wide-brimmed straw hat on his head and adjusted it to a rakish angle. Satisfied, he hurried out of the kitchen and ran toward the distillery.

Patrick waited for him, perched on the seat of the old spring wagon. Brandy, Pa's new bay colt, pranced in his traces and whinnied a gentle greeting.

"I helped myself to a pint," Patrick said, lifting a small bottle in the air. He grinned at Edward and gave him a sly wink. "Didn't trust you to bring it along."

Edward leaped onto the narrow wooden seat with a smile and took the reins. This was a grand evening; he felt something unforgettable was about to happen. He looked at Patrick, spiffy in black trousers and green calico shirt, red beard neatly trimmed, bright unruly hair slicked back and tamed with grease. Whispers among the girls had Patrick rugged and handsome, and Edward thought him all of that.

"Gidup," Edward said, snapping the reins smartly.

They bounced along the deeply rutted dirt lane in the gentleness of the April evening, past budding maples, pink redbud, and blossoming dogwood. Robins were everywhere and a red-winged blackbird flashed by. Edward hung onto the reins with one hand and his new straw hat with the other until they entered Porter Road where he turned the horse north toward Menges Mills.

The fiery sun had begun its descent and the air, fresh and sweet from an earlier thunderstorm, was turning cooler. They followed a grassy lane that ran through fragrant orchards where wide-spread cherry trees hung heavy with white blossoms. A white board fence stretched in the distance and on the horizon, silhouetted against the darkening sky, two horses touched noses over the fence rail.

Edward finally broke the easy silence. "You're not wearing a hat tonight."

"Can't find one of a size to fit this big head of mine."

"If you'd cut off some of those red curls, a hat might fit."

"Aye, but all the gals like my red curls. And I don't want to do anything that'd upset the gals."

"Speaking of girls, are you gonna dance with Inger, the girl I told you about?"

"I might if she's pretty enough. What about you, though? Seems like you're the one in need of a partner."

"You know I don't have a girl," Edward said.

"Well it's time you did. That Sally Stremell is right pretty and I noticed her giving you the eye at the picnic last month."

"She's kinda fat."

"Just well rounded and she's got it where it counts most."

Edward tried to hide a grin. He ran his hand across his chin, a habit he'd acquired when he needed more time to form an answer. He decided to ignore Patrick's comment. "Last I knew she was Amos Finkelberger's girl."

"Maybe, but Amos won't be there tonight. He's over in Gettysburg with some woodsmen, cutting timber from a hill called Little Round Top. Cotton up to her; see what happens." Patrick poked Edward in the arm. "Besides, I hear she's pretty free with her favors. Just the girl you need to get things goin'."

Edward shifted uncomfortably, aware of what Patrick was referring to. "Well then, why don't you cotton up to her, you're the experienced one."

"Ain't me we're working on. Cripes, Edward, it just ain't right, a good looking Dutchman like you, still in the dark about such important matters."

Edward felt the heat rising in his face. "It's not for lack of trying," he muttered. "I just haven't found a girl to fall in love with."

Patrick hooted. "You're plum crazy. You don't hafta love 'em. You're a farm boy. Look around you. The animals don't love one another. They just do what nature tells 'em to do."

Before Edward could think of a witty reply they were within sight of the brightly lit Petterson barn.

He could hear the happy music long before they pulled into a field behind the barn and hitched Brandy. Loud shouts of laughter and clapping filled the night sky. With quickened footsteps he and Patrick climbed an earthen barn bridge and walked through massive swinging doors into the barn.

Edward felt a throb of excitement at the festive sight before him. All four walls were banked with people and in the center of the floor dancers waited for the music to begin. They were all ages, all sizes and shapes. Boys and men on one side, dressed in black trousers and white shirts, and women and girls opposite them, with long dresses of plain blue, green, or purple; calico's of bright yellow and red; and the always serviceable black broadcloth.

Soon the floor was crowded with gliding, whirling dancers, a mass of swirling colors. The thump, thump,

thump of the bass blended with the whine of the fiddle and the twanging banjo. Skirts swished, energetic boys twirled their partners, and the voice of the caller became quicker and lustier.

Patrick stomped his foot to the beat, and Edward saw his gaze rake the crowd until it settled on a pretty girl standing alone at the end of the table.

"That's Inger Andreasen," Edward commented. "The girl I was telling you about."

"Tis a fact she's a bonny lass. And she looks lonely. I'll fetch her some refreshment."

Patrick refilled his mug of cider, filled a second cup for Inger and sauntered toward the girl, leaving Edward to his own pursuits.

Sally Stremell, in a bright pink dress, was standing beside her brother and Edward felt a moment of panic when she spotted him. She approached with a smile of welcome.

Sally was short and blond, her face round with rosy cheeks, her mouth wide with full lips. Her grey eyes met his, but before he could talk to her, she was pulled into a circle of giggling girls.

Was it his imagination or did Sally deliberately turn so she was facing him? She was pretty, in a plump sort of way.

The dance ended and Patrick returned Inger to her friends and rejoined Edward.

Hearing snickers and muffled laughter from the boys nearby, Edward turned in time to see Patrick pour the contents of his pint bottle into the cider barrel.

"Didja hear 'bout that fiery revival meeting over at Oberholtzer's farm last week?" a young farmer from nearby Jefferson was commenting. "People was shouting and falling down all over that dang tent. Dozens was saved and signed the pledge to give up their drinking ways."

"Yeah," young Christian Stambaugh said with a laugh. "They say old Jake, the town drunk, fell into a trance and never came out of it till the evening service was plumb over.

"They's a new Temperance Society holdin' meetings in the basement of the Reformed Church in Jefferson," a freckled faced young man with a shock of curly black hair interjected. "I hear they get real riled up at times. You get angry women and bellowing preachers fightin' against something and you got yourself a powerful combination."

Everyone nodded agreement.

Patrick stood with a second cup of the spiked cider in his hand. "Aye, but they don't stand a chance of gettin' a Prohibition Law passed. Too many folks depend on havin' some spirits handy." He took a large gulp of his drink and winked at Edward. "Like me!"

The young farmer turned to Edward. "Ain't your Pa worried 'bout them new taxes the Feds are puttin' on spirits? People are talking 'bout another Whiskey Rebellion like the one near Pittsburgh back in '29 when they tarred and feathered a bunch of tax collectors."

Edward felt himself flushing as six pair of eyes swung in his direction. He shifted from foot to foot. "I guess he is, though he don't say much." He laughed trying to hide his discomfort.

"They say the Whigs "Hard Cider" campaign is bound to get Harrison elected President next term," Christian said thoughtfully.

Edward nodded. "There's a cagey old distiller from Philadelphia named E.G. Booz, handing out whiskey in little bottles shaped like log cabins, getting men all liquored up, and turning political meetings into drunken brawls. That's where folks go wrong and don't use good sense."

"Don't go gettin' on your soapbox," Patrick growled, shooting a sour look in Edward's direction "A more lively subject, I should think, is William Garrison's call for the abolition of slavery."

That got everyone talking at once.

"I heared they captured a runaway slave over at

Zimmerman's farm last week. Poor bugger was probably sent back to his mean southern master."

"Just ain't right to send 'em back. Ain't human to hold another man slave."

"Constitution says..."

Edward turned from the group, glad the conversation had turned from whiskey, but not in the mood to debate slavery. He looked across the crowded barn floor, searching for his brothers. Henry was talking to several farmers, young John was stuffing his mouth with cookies, and J.J. was standing at the far end of the refreshment table talking to Rebecca and Katie. Edward ambled towards them, a little surprised to see the girls at a dance. The Hokes were Mennonite and he didn't thik Mennonites held with dancing. He frowned, watching them. J.J. was sweet on Rebecca and that could only spell trouble. Mennonites weren't as strict as Amish, but they were Sect people nevertheless. The Reberts belonged to the German Reformed Church. Sect people didn't often marry Church people.

Rebecca greeted him warmly and he looked down at Katie. She had an impish face, with soft brown eyes and a generous sprikling of freckles across a pug nose. Her fiery auburn hair was pulled back from her face into two plump pigtails, tied with green satin bows. She wore the traditional plain dress of young Mennonite girls, ending at slender ankles which revealed black stockings and high top shoes.

J.J. always said Katie had a crush on him. He had to admit she was cute and she watched him now with a look of hero worship.

"Hi, Katie," he said, feeling warm and uncomfortable with her admiration. "Or should it be Catherine, now that you're older?"

"Oh, no, please call me Katie. I think every girl in this whole country must be named Catherine . . . an' I like Katie ever so much better."

Edward smiled. Katie suited this laughing child much

better than the formal Catherine. And she is just a child, he reminded himself.

"Katie fits you. You're growing up fast. How old are you now? Eleven . . . twelve?"

"Almost twelve." A wide grin spread across her face and her brown eyes crinkled at the corners. "My birthday is next month."

"Are you liking the dance?"

"I am, oh, I am. Listen, Edward. They're playing Turkey in the Straw, one of my favorites. I do hope someone asks me to dance." Little tendrils of hair curled around her face as she tilted her head to look at him, her face alight with hope.

Edward didn't know what to say. He'd be kidded something awful if his friends saw him dance with such a young girl. And Patrick would never let it be. He fingered his chin, then with a nervous laugh he reached over and tweaked one of her pigtails. "I see my little brother John, over there against the wall, hasn't taken his eyes off you since we started to talk. I'll bet he'll ask you to dance the minute I leave."

Katie giggled and looked toward John.

"Don't you have a partner tonight?" J. J. asked, poking Edward in the arm.

"Nein. Thought I'd just spread my charms around to all the girls." He smiled at Katie.

Suddenly he couldn't think of anything else to say. He felt his face grow hot as Katie continued to look up at him with those soft brown eyes. *She was a child really. A child!* But there was something so dreaming, so soft in her expression he felt a kind of melting sensation in his chest. He had a funny feeling that Catherine. . . Katie. . . Hoke was going to grow into quite a woman.

In confusion he walked back to his friends.

Katie watched his retreating back and shook her head in

exasperation. He treats me like a child, she thought. If only Mamma would let me undo these childish braids and wrap my long hair in a bun at the nape of my neck I wouldn't look like such a baby.

She thought Edward Rebert was the handsomest boy she had ever seen. He was tall . . . all the Reberts were tall and blond and blue-eyed . . . and he had been her secret hero as long as she could remember.

Their grandfathers, Kasper Hoke and Johann Rebert, had crossed the Atlantic on the same ship and both settled in the Codorus Valley. The families had been close friends ever since and now it looked as though they might be joined by marriage. J.J. had been courting Rebecca for well over a year.

"Isn't he beautiful?" she whispered to Rebecca.

"Don't call a man beautiful, honey," Rebecca said placing an affectionate hand on the top of her head.

"Oh, but he. is. When he smiles he has the cutest little crease in his chin. And his eyes! They're as blue as the wild bluebottles that cover our fields in the spring."

J.J. listened to the exchange with a smile pulling at his lips. Now he laughed out loud. "It sounds like you have more than a passing fancy for my brother, Katie."

She tilted her head to look up at J.J. "Someday I just may marry him." A smile appeared at the thought of it. "That is, if he'll wait for me to grow up . . . and if he'll become Mennonite."

Edward watched couples drift out onto the floor, forming sets, while Fiddler Sam tuned up his fiddle and his sidekick thumbed the bass. Patrick was already there with Inger and had a firm hold on her waist, laughing into her flushed face.

Edward stood talking to his friends, but he couldn't get Katie's image out of his mind. He kept glancing in her direction and when he did he saw her watching him intently.

She turned to look at the dancers, eyes sparkling, cheeks flushed, tiny feet tapping to the music. His brother John had disappeared. Maybe he should ask her to dance. No, better not. She was too young.

Sally flashed a smile at him and, encouraged, he approached her. "If you don't have a partner, I'd like to dance with you."

"Thank you, Edward," she said with just a hint of appealing shyness, her cheeks growing pinker and her blond eyelashes dropping to cover flirting eyes.

With a boldness he didn't feel he took her hand and led her onto the floor. Her hand was cool and soft, but his own felt hot and sweaty.

"All join hands and circle to the right. Greet your honey then with a grand right and left," the caller shouted.

Edward abandoned himself to the dance. Funny how he felt so bashful around girls when he had to stand and talk to them, but when he was square dancing he was able to relax and lose himself to the beat of the music.

It was close to ten when the musicians played their final dance of the first half and everyone headed for the tables Mrs. Peterson had spread with pies and cakes.

Edward felt awkward and shy. Dancing was one thing, but eating together—that was something else. Mustering courage, he cleared his throat and looked straight into Sally's grey eyes. "Will you eat supper with me?"

"I'd be glad to, Edward."

He smiled happily.

They made their way along the long table, filling their plates with ham, baked beans, biscuits, honey, doughnuts, and pie. He took a gourd, ladled two mugs of the spiked cider from the large wooden tub, and led Sally outside where Patrick and Inger were sitting on the edge of the earthen bank leading to the barn. The swish of Sally's gown, the warm pressure of her arm on his, made him feel ten feet tall . They dropped down beside Patrick and Inger, balancing plates of food on their laps.

In contrast to Sally, Inger was slim and dainty. She had the smooth, pale complexion of Swedish girls with a delicate rose blush in her cheeks, and long yellow hair that was held back with a simple velvet bow. Her hands kept twisting a lace hanky and when she spoke it was in a soft, almost inaudible voice. She seemed to be quite taken with Patrick.

Patrick, in high fetter, kept up a steady stream of banter that had both girls laughing. Edward looked at his food, his thoughts racing in confusion. Say something, he thought desperately. Something smart, funny. . .

He stuffed another donut into his mouth.

Why couldn't he be clever like Patrick? When Patrick, whose slurred voice revealed the large amount of whiskey laden cider he'd consumed, poked a few jokes at him, trying to draw him into the conversation, he only felt worse.

Patrick's teasing, however, relaxed Sally and she drew Edward into laughing conversation. Soon they were chatting about music, county fairs, and sulky races.

He polished off his plate and loaded it up again. With mocking eyes, Patrick put another cup of cider in his hands. He downed it in a single gulp.

As they ate and drank he felt more self-confident. Everything Sally said was funny; he liked the way she tilted her head when she laughed and she suddenly seemed to be the softest, prettiest thing he had ever seen. When Sally's finger tips accidently brushed his it was as though he had been touched with a hot wire. Heat came to his face and a warm glow to his belly.

Shortly before eleven, the supper was finished and the caller announced the next set. Edward laughed as he observed quite a few men, who had been making frequent trips to the barrel of cider, enter the floor with a little extra zip to their step. He took Sally's soft hand, ready to lead her onto the dance floor, when he felt Patrick's restraining hand on his arm.

"I've been telling Inger about Mr. Peterson's new filly, the one that won the harness race at York last week. 'Tis down in the stables and Inger allows as how she'd like to see it. Would you two like to come along?"

Edward's eyes locked with Patrick's and he saw the hidden meaning there. To hesitate would show his nervous youth, and more than anything he wanted Patrick's approval. He felt hot and confused; yet he was glad the suggestion had been made.

Sally giggled and looked at him coyly. "Oh, let's have a look, Edward. I just love horses."

He took her arm possessively and strutted off the crowded floor.

They followed Patrick and Inger to the back of the barn where a steep ladder descended to the lower barn, housing cattle, sheep and horses. Patrick went first and lit a kerosene lantern which he carefully hung on a hook protruding from the wall. It swayed, dancing their silhouettes along the grey stone walls. Horses poked curious heads from their stalls and nickered softly. Edward felt his way to an outside double door and threw open the upper half, letting soft moonlight flood the barn, partially dispelling the gloom.

They converged on the stall of Mr. Peterson's winning filly. Sally stroked the horse's soft muzzle and talked to her softly. It nuzzled Sally's sleeve, responding to her caress.

Edward stood speechless at the sight of the magnificent animal. He stared at the black fire that burned in the velvety eyes, intelligent and alert, and inhaled the strong scent of horse and hay, then raised his hand to smooth the long black forelock on the filly's forehead. "Someday, I want to raise trotting horses," he said, staring lovingly at the young filly, voicing a desire he'd never before expressed.

Sally looked at him in admiration and he squared his shoulders, hooking his thumbs in his suspenders. "My Pa just bought a new bay colt, a trotter with pure bloodlines. We call him Brandy and have him entered as a yearling at

York Fair next year. Pa promised I can help with the training, " he finished importantly. The training part wasn't quite true, but it seemed to make an impression on Sally.

Patrick looked at him with a grin and a wink.

The girls fussed over the filly until finally Patrick put his arm around Inger and pulled her aside. "There's another horse I want you to see," he said leading her toward the dark shadows ahead. "We'll be back in a few minutes," he called over his shoulder, his voice soft and urgent. Within seconds they had disappeared into the liquid darkness.

Edward went into action. There were several bales of straw beside the ladder and he led Sally toward them. "May as well be comfortable, while we wait," he said, pulling her down beside him.

"I don't want to get mussed. People will notice when we go back upstairs." Sally smoothed her skirts primly.

Edward slipped his arm around her waist. It was unbelievably round and comfortable. He drew her to him. She smelled like warm apricots. "You're awful pretty," he said, rubbing his cheek against her shinning hair.

Sally looked at him through narrowed eyes, and for a moment the smile left her face. But then she answered coyly, "and you're mighty handsome. I think I could like you a lot."

"I always thought you were Amos' girl."

"He don't own me."

Edward found himself looking at her lips as she talked. She had full, pale pink lips and she kept licking them with her tongue. He imagined himself kissing them. "Would you be my girl, then," he asked his voice wavering between falsetto and bass.

"You can call on me, if you like. We'd have to get to know one another better for me to promise that."

He reached down, touching his lips to hers, tentatively, before pulling away. She giggled softly and rested her head against his shoulder. He turned to face her and this time he kissed her harder. Her lips seemed to change, they became warm and yielding and he increased the pressure of his mouth. He was getting excited and he ground his lips into hers so hard his teeth cut the inside of his lip. He backed off, afraid he might be hurting her. He hadn't had much experience with this kind of kissing. His own inexperience made him feel hot with shame.

Sally smiled up at him. "Not so hard, Edward," she whispered, running a finger down the crease in his chin. He cupped her face in his hand and this time he kissed her more slowly, trying to keep his lips gentle. He could feel her heart drumming against his chest and her eyes were closed.

His right hand moved across her dress to the mound of flesh straining the bodice. He'd never touched a girl there. This was better than any fantasy he'd ever had.

Sally shifted in his arms. He suspected she was no stranger to this kind of petting. A burning sensation began creeping over him; shivers shot through his body. He felt an irresistible urge and roughly fastened his lips back on hers.

She suddenly pulled back and pushed his hand away. In the glow of the lantern her face looked flushed and little beads of perspiration dotted her upper lip. "No, Edward," she whispered. "I'm not that kind of girl."

"I promise I won't think badly of you," he pleaded, trying to draw her back into his arms. He was a little bewildered.

"Your friends could come back at any time." Sally had a determined look on her face and began to pat her tousled curls into place.

Edward bit his lip in disappointment.

"Come with me. Someplace where we can. . ."

"No, no. I won't do that." She straightened her clothes and stood up.

"When can I see you again? Can I . . .?"

They both froze as scuffling noises emanated from the end of the barn where Patrick and Inger had disappeared.

Edward had been so absorbed in his own affairs he had not realized the passing of time. He strained to hear further sounds from the other end of the barn. Something was not right. Suddenly he heard what sounded like sobbing and Patrick's voice. What was happening back there?

Sally pressed her fingers to her mouth and looked at him, her grey eyes dark with distress.

He pulled her to her feet and brushed himself off, still uncertain what to do, when he heard approaching footsteps.

Patrick and Inger appeared out of the gloom. Inger stared at the floor and she clutched her torn dress, trying to hide her exposed bosom. Her yellow hair was disheveled, her eyes wet and round in apprehension.

Patrick headed for the ladder. Inger ran out the open door and Sally ran after her. Edward stared in spite of himself. In the flickering light of the lantern he thought he could see blood on the back of her skirt.

The horses, alarmed by all the fuss, were turning in their stalls, blowing loudly, and shaking their heads in excitement.

"Wa . . . what happened?" Edward asked.

Patrick swayed, a hangdog look on his handsome face, as he turned to face Edward. "Darn girls are bold enough with their eyes and mouths, but sure put on that innocent act when things start getting serious. 'Tis enough to drive a man crazy."

"Sounded to me like you made her do something she didn't want to do," Edward said, thrusting his hands deep into his pockets and curling his fists.

"She was willing enough."

"How did her dress get torn, then?"

Patrick looked away. "The whiskey might'a made me a little rough."

Edward felt sick on his stomach, the cider rising sour in his throat. He started to tremble.

Patrick went on talking, as though unaware of his

reaction. "She isn't really hurt. She..."

"Shut up," Edward shouted. He grabbed hold of the ladder and heaved himself up. "I'm leaving! Alone! You get home the best way you can."

Chapter

-3-

Black clouds that promised more rain hung low in the spring sky, matching Edward's mood perfectly. He squatted beside Codorus Creek and swished his hand back and forth in its icy waters. A splinter, deeply imbedded in his left thumb, hurt like thunder.

The silvery creek chuckled and splashed over grey rocks, breaking the silence of the surrounding woods. Edward leaned back, looked up at the cranky sky, and gave a deep sigh. He couldn't seem to get Saturday night out of his mind. Nothing had gone right since the dance. Problems just seemed to keep coming his way. If he hadn't been so shushly dressing the grinding wheel yesterday he wouldn't have this nasty metal splinter in his throbbing thumb. There was a Dutch saying that the flecks of steel in a stone dresser's hands showed the "metal of the man." Pa said Edward's hands only showed his clumsiness. And now, on top of all that, he'd let a vat of fermenting mash intended for this afternoon's still, turn sour. Pa was going to be mad as a March hare. This would be just one more failure in his eyes. Edward sighed. Would he ever get anything right?

"Verdammte dunnerwetter!," he muttered. He stuffed his painful hand into his trouser pocket and hitched up his muddy trousers. With downcast eyes he started glumly toward the distillery, following a tiny stream through grassy meadows carpeted with Quaker ladies. The sun peeked through the menacing clouds and glimmered on spring daisies and yellow dandelions shimmering in the soft light of the cool morning. Along the fence row cherry trees blossomed, their fleecy white startling against the indigo sky. Hillsides wore colorful carpets of spring flowers: late anemones, hepaticas, Dutchman's-pipe, and violets. He started to whistle, his steps quickening.

A skein of Canada geese flew overhead. Their call left him with a strange thrill in his heart and a wild desire for something, wings maybe, so he too could be free to soar across the clouds. He watched them, honking and trumpeting their way through the currents that buffeted them about, heading, who knew where. But the geese knew. Wasn't their journey predestined? Wasn't his?

He headed toward the old mill built by his grandfather, Johann Rebert, in the late 1700's to provide flour to feed his family of eleven children and now used to distill grain into whiskey. His bare feet dawdled in the wet grass. Soon he'd have to explain to Pa how he'd left the mash turn sour. His feelings for Pa were so muddled. Love most of the time, hatred when he was angry. Hatred? How could he even think such a horrible thing. He shuddered. Surely his emotions weren't that strong. How could he love and hate at the same time? Maybe resented was a better word. Ei, that was better.

Pa, steeped in old-country German tradition, stern and demanding, was determined to send him in a direction he didn't want to go, but he didn't doubt Pa's good intentions. If only Pa'd let me be myself, he brooded, and not try to make me a copy of himself and my brothers.

Edward ambled along a stone-strewn path, admiring the beauty of the valley around him. He passed a birch tree, just beginning to unfurl its baby leaves and broke off a twig to chew its bark, feeling the clean, tangy juice trickle down his throat.

The mill was just ahead, and so was Pa.

The stone mill with its slowly turning water wheel looked peaceful on the bank of the creek, its beauty spoiled only by the black column of vile smoke rising from its tall chimney like an angry finger pointing to the heavens. He wrinkled his nose. The stringent odor of sour mash hung heavy in the air. Its stench seemed to collect and linger on the leaves of nearby trees and the entire countryside smelled of mash and the pigs that roamed free, growing fat on their diet of mash and corn.

A wooden sign hanging above the double door of the old mill read REBERT'S GRIST MILL AND DISTILLERY. The word distillery, lettered in red paint, appeared newer than the other faded letters. The sight of it triggered fresh anger.

His steps faltered at the sound of a ringing hammer. Pa crouched in the stream working on a rotted section of gate that controlled the mill race. Edward wasn't ready to face him yet so he headed for an entry at the rear of the mill. He unlatched the seldom used door, cut into the massive stone wall, and pushed it open on creaking hinges, stepping from the warm sunshine into the dark cavernous room.

Once inside he hesitated, letting his eyes adjust to the gloom, before starting across the wooden floor toward his brother Andy. Musty flour dust hung in the air mingling with the earthy sour smell of fermenting grain and the acrid odor of charred wood from cold fireplaces. He kicked at a chunk of oak lying beside one of the copper still kettles. *God, how he hated it all!*

Andy, raking a pile of grain, looked up at the sudden noise.

"About time you showed up," he grunted, leaning against the cumbersome wooden rake. "You're late, as usual. I'm gonna need help soon as this still starts runnin'. And we gotta get the fires goin' under those other kettles for this afternoon's batch."

" 'Fraid we won't be making any more whiskey today, except what you got brewing," Edward replied, kicking at a clump of rye. "I let the mash go bad. It plum turned to vinegar."

"Ei,yi,yi! Does Pa know?"

"Not yet, but he will soon enough."

"Scheiss! What happened? We've tole you time and time again you gotta keep a close eye on that mash after it's fermented a coupla days. I swear Edward, sometimes I think you try to rile Pa on purpose. We're gonna lose over a hundred gallons of whiskey, already."

"I did watch it. I checked it last thing before I went to bed. Seemed to me it wasn't near ripe enough. Then this morning I stopped on my way to the mill to check on Sassy. She was in the woodshed, having an awful time birthin' her pups, so I stayed to help her. It took longer than I figured and when I got back to the mill it was too late."

Andy brushed the flour dust from his hair with a grimy hand and shook his head. "When you gonna learn to be trusty? Pa keeps givin' you another chance, but this time he's gonna be mad . . . really mad."

"I try, Andy. I try hard." Edward chewed fiercely on the piece of birch bark he still held between his teeth, searching for words to express himself. He studied Andy, two years older, lean almost to the point of skinniness, but with a deceivingly wiry strength. And feisty! Boy, was he ever feisty. Still, of his seven brothers, Andy was the one he always turned to for help and friendship.

Edward pushed his hair back from his forehead and spoke softly. "I want Pa to think good of me like he does the rest of you. I just don't have a nose, or an eye, for stilling like you and Pa do. Guess it's cause I don't like doing it very much."

"Why? Why're you so agin distilling?"

Edward shrugged. How could he explain when he hardly understood himself? And he didn't want to bring up the subject of sin and be called a "cussed saint" again. Those words of Patrick's still bothered him.

"I guess I just don't want to get old and have nothing to

look back on but a life making whiskey."

"Sounds rewarding enough to me."

"Well, not to me. And it's plain that whiskey's bad for some folks. Look at Patrick. He's always hanging around here pretending to help, but I know he's after sampling the brew. Besides, Reverend Geiger's sermons last winter set me to thinking pretty hard."

"You been sneaking off to those Temperance meetings in Jefferson?" Andy asked with a quizzical frown.

"Chust one or two. It's mostly women and reformed drunks go to them." He hesitated. "I was some taken by that evangelist that preached over near Jefferson last week."

"Balderdash. Does Pa know you went to that revival?"

"Nein."

Unable to meet the disapproval in Andy's eyes, Edward moved toward the three copper still kettles that squatted in the middle of the cave-like room against smoke blackened chimneys. They reminded him of giant turnips. One of them had a slow, even fire burning in its firebox and he picked up a few pieces of dry oak and added them to the fire. "How long before this one starts to run?"

" 'Bout half an hour. Grab a rake and help me pull this pile of rye apart. Check it careful, now, an' make sure it's not sprouting. It ain't grass we need."

Edward worked silently beside Andy, their wooden rakes rasping on the plank floor. Suddenly a squeaking rumble announced the heavy double doors at the front of the mill were opening on their metal track. Bright sunlight silhouetted Pa's burly figure.

Pa was a big man, barrel-chested, with muscular arms and stocky legs, and no neck at all. His ears seemed to sit squarely on his broad shoulders. Grey hair, cropped short, lent a look of fierceness to his broad Germanic features. Full, bushy eyebrows framed piercing blue eyes that seldom smiled, at least at Edward.

He watched Pa cross the room to the tub of mash. It

wouldn't take long for him to discover it was sour.

Pa let out a bellow and charged toward him. "You dumkopf! Nothing can I trust you mit. All that mash is gude for now is pig feed," he shouted, his heavy Dutch dialect always more pronounced when he was angry. "PIG FEED!"

Edward clutched the rake. "I'm sorry, Pa."

"Sorry, I don't vanna hear sorry. I vanta hear vye."

"I thought I was watching it close enough. It got clean ahead of me."

"Ach, vell close enough you didn't vatch it. You're no child anymore, Edward Rebert. You're accountable for vhat you do."

Edward bit his lower lip. Pa always made him doubt his manhood. "You know I hate this stinking, sinful business. It goes against my nature."

Pa raised to the balls of his feet, clenching his fists, a wave of crimson moving up his face. "Sinful... sinful? You vould talk back to your Pa this vay?" he yelled. "You vill do chust as I say. No argument."

Edward was taller than his father, and more powerfully built, but he had no doubt Pa could best him in any fight. He shifted from foot to foot, and stared at the floor.

"But, Pa," he said, attempting to conceal his anger and divert the conversation, "all the farmers are complaining about the new taxes the Feds are putting on whiskey. Mister Stambaugh says he'll close their stills and go back to shipping raw grain rather than pay more taxes. And the temperance societies keep stirring up new trouble. They're talking some new law called prohibition. Distilling don't seem worth all the trouble." Edward looked to Andy for help, but Andy avoided his eyes, raking with renewed vigor.

"Don't change the subject, young man. It's talking about your job on this farm ve're doing, not the rights and wrongs of making whiskey. In the distillery, that's vhere you vork, vhere you're needed. These sinful stills you're talking about make plenty good money. You got clouds in your head.

Grow up and put your shoulder to the yoke like your brothers."

Edward tossed the rake to the floor, confused and angry, envy a knot in his stomach. He was sick of hearing about his brothers. *Look at me*, he longed to say. I'm not just one of your eight sons. I'm Edward. He swallowed a sob and closed his eyes to hold back the tears. *Why couldn't he say that to Pa?*

Pa grabbed a sack of grain and with an angry grunt threw its contents into an empty barrel. "Git back to vork, now . . . no more talk about the sin of making good money. Evangelists and jabbering women got this country all riled up. Ach, sin, my foot!"

Just then a loud hello rang out from the front of the mill. Edward sighed in relief as his brother-in-law, Moses, strode across the floor.

Pa thrust gnarled hands into the pockets of his faded overalls and cleared his throat. He turned to Edward and Andy. "Moses vants to learn distilling. Vhiskey for the hired hands during harvest he needs, already. Let him vork mit you. Green as corn, he is, about stilling, but quick to learn if you teach him right."

Tall, lanky Moses Senft reached his father-in-law and shook hands heartily.

"Catharine sends her love," he said, a warm smile on his somewhat homely face, distorted as usual with a huge plug of tobacco puffing one cheek.

"Send her mine, and her Mamma's," Jonas answered brusquely, his anger cooling noticeably at news of his only daughter. "How's she feeling today?"

"Pretty uncomfortable, but cheerful as always. She thinks the baby will come soon. Next week's the full of the moon."

"Gude, gude! Tell Catharine she's in our prayers." His face hardened once more. "The boys know vhy you're here. They'll tell you how things vork, but you'll have to come back tomorrow. Edward here, let the mash meant for this afternoon's run go sour."

Pa fixed Edward with a tight lipped glare before turning on his heel. As he strode briskly away, Edward watched his retreating back and let out a sigh of relief. He looked at Andy who still leaned on his rake in silence.

"Could have been worse, I guess," Edward said.

Andy winked in reply.

Moses ambled over to the vat of sour mash bubbling thickly in a large cyprus tub and looked at it with interest.

Andy joined him, a good natured grin spreading across his dirty face. "What you're seeing there is the start of things. The rye's been fermenting for about three days and it's turning into what we call "distillers beer" . That means it's about ready to distill into whiskey."

"Don't you sometimes use corn instead of rye?"

"Whiskey's best made from rye. We only still with corn when there's an especially good crop." Andy took a stained, faded piece of paper from a nail on the wall, and handed it to Moses. "Here's Pa's recipe, given him by an old-timer when we bought the first still."

Moses read it aloud:

RECIPE FOR MAKING FINE WHISKEY, Friedrich Heinrich Gelwicks—Shoemaker and Distiller Accounts - 1760-1783

A still can be set up so that one can obtain up to 5 gallons of high proof spirits from 1 bushel of grain. The art is to give the spirits an aged flavor and color so that it is strong and of high proof, and to assure that the spirits do not weaken in the barrel.

Most important to making good whiskey is good

water. The water must be cold in summer and warm in winter. A warm spirit is already in it which the heat of the fire will evaporate and expel into the whiskey.

Make mash by finely grinding 1 bushel rye malt, 1 bushel-3 pecks wheat, and 1 bushel rye grain. The wheat gives the whiskey a pleasant taste.

Bucket mash into still kettle and start fire in firebox. The fire must be of oak wood, even and gentle, otherwise the mash will scorch. If the steam builds up too fast the still can explode.

After mash begins to cook watch the worm carefully. Just before the whiskey starts running from the worm, you'll see some steam blown out ahead of it, like pipe smoke if the temperature is just right. From the end of the worm will come a gush of steam followed by a surge of liquid. Wait for second surge. This is the start of whiskey.

Moses shook his head and handed it back. "Sounds kinda knotty."

"Naw, it ain't hard, Moses. Stillin's simple once you get the picture. It's just a way of converting liquid mash to alcohol by boiling it, collecting its steam, then changing the steam back to liquid again by passing it through cold water."

"You're a good teacher, Andy. That don't seem so hard."

Edward listened in silence. How sad that Moses would soon corrupt his pretty farm with the hateful stills.

Moses stuck his nose close to the tub and sniffed the steamy, beery vapors.

"Don't go breathing it in, Moses. It'll knock your head clean off. The sugar in that stuff is pure alcohol and carbonic acid," Andy said with a sly grin.

"A man could git dronk, just standin' here." Moses chuckled, shifting his chew of tobacco from side to side.

Edward laughed. He liked Moses.

Pointing toward one of the copper pot stills resting on the base of a stone firebox, Andy continued his lesson. "When it's ripe the "beer" is bucketed from the tub into this copper pot and brought to a boil. Its vapor raises into that long tube you see on top, the one that looks like the spout on a teapot. Then it passes into a worm in that tub of cold water over there at end of the firebox."

"What in tarnation is a worm?"

"Just a long, skinny, copper tube twisted into a coil so it'll fit in that tub . . . looks just like a wriggled up old worm. The tub's kept filled with cold water from our spring and the cold water around the worm causes the alcohol steam inside to condense into liquor."

A loud hiss interrupted their talk and puffs of steam, like pipe smoke, shot out of the end of the worm. Andy rushed over to steady the collection jug as a surge of liquid followed the gush of steam.

"There she comes," Edward interjected. "That's the start of our whiskey. The first run's got a lot of water and oil in it, so we double it back in one of the other stills to purify it and make it nice and clear. Sometimes we have to run it back two or three times to get the strength right."

"How do you know when it's powerful enough?"

"Pa throws a pine splinter into the kettle and if it floats, it's strong enough," Andy said, with a hearty chuckle. And that's only one of his secrets. "

"Secrets?"

"It's pure white when it comes from the worm so Pa cooks up a special brew of sugar and water till it's like molasses and adds it to the whiskey to make it look old. Then he flavors it with some good Corsica wine and gives it that famous Rebert "bite" by adding ground ginger. Just how much is his secret, but believe me that whiskey is pure, fiery, and strong."

Andy watched the clear liquid flowing from the end of the worm. "Shame we don't have a fresh batch of mash ready so's you could help run it from start to finish."

Moses shot a stream of tobacco juice onto the floor and wiped his mouth on his sleeve. "I kin come back tomorrow. I'll go on home and get the milking done afore Catharine tries to get down to the barn. She's so big she can hardly see the teats on the cow for her belly. See you boys in the mornin'."

Edward turned to Andy and rolled up his sleeves. "I'll slop the pigs and get some barrels ready for tomorrow's run while you run the liquor back through." At Andy's nod of agreement, he took the grain left on the bottom of the mash barrels outside to the pigs. Contented pigs they were, contented and slightly drunk most of the time.

Good whiskey had to be aged in charred oaken barrels and the longer it "stayed in the wood" the more mellow it became. Edward washed the wooden casks with a strong solution of hot water and lye then wiped them dry with sulfur rags and added some ginger to keep them from smelling sour. He dropped the rags in a pile beside the still and started to stack the empty casks along the long wall, two high.   Tomorrow he and Andy would fill the barrels with whiskey and roll them down the hill to a vaulted cave behind the barn where they would be left to age.

Edward paused to take a deep breath and wipe the sweat from his forehead. His shoulder muscles trembled with weariness. One more cask should do it. He lifted the cask high and jammed it on the top row.

Leaning his aching back against the cool stone wall he waited for Andy to finish. The mill was cloaked in shadows now, with only small patches of fading sunlight filtering through windows etched with silvery cobwebs. He began to relax, soothed by the rumbling of the water wheel as it rotated the ponderous millstones with creaking wooden pulleys and leather belts.

"That's it for today," Andy said, walking toward him out of the gloom. "I'll help you lock up."

Edward moved toward the massive oak doors at the entrance. He swung them shut and Andy slipped the iron locking bar into place.

Edward looked back over his shoulder as they strode across the field toward home. Mist shrouded the mill in the distance; the setting sun tinting the old grey stone walls with velvety lavender shadows. The ends of the mill, made of wood fashioned from axehewn chestnut timbers, had weathered and mellowed with age. The huge water wheel, fed by the nearby creek, turned slowly in the gathering twilight. Too bad, he thought, such a handsome building had to house a whiskey distillery.

Chapter

4

Edward stretched lazily under a light quilt, rubbing sleep from his eyes and wiggling his toes. Dawn assailed the clear night sky and in the farm yard below a cock crowed lustily while outside his window a thrush heralded the morning with an energetic song.

He stretched once more, flexed the muscles in his long legs, and yawned noisily. The tiny room, illuminated by the first weak shafts of light, was airless and stuffy. He sniffed. A tantalizing aroma of bacon was coming from the kitchen. Breakfast must be well under way. His gaze flew to the bed where Andrew and Michael slept. It was empty! He jerked upright, cracking his head against the headboard. "Ach," he mumbled, rubbing his head gingerly. He was always doing that of late; he had grown far too tall for his childhood bed.

He swung his legs over the side of the rope bed and stripped off his nightshirt. Quickly he donned yesterday's work clothes of coarse homespun, stuffed his feet into worn leather boots, splashed cold water on his face from the basin, ran a comb through tangled hair, and hurried to the kitchen. He slid into his seat at the table, trying to attract as little attention as possible. Andrew, William, J.J., and Michael were heaping bacon and fried cornmeal mush onto their plates while John was busy with a bowl of oatmeal. Samuel and Jacob were on the side porch, already finished with breakfast, ready to leave for the fields.

Pa looked up from his plate with an angry scowl. "Late to the table you are," he growled, pushing a thick hunk of bread around his plate to soak up the grease.

"I'm sorry," Edward said, taking the platter of bacon from Michael's outstretched hands.

"Alvays sorry. Chust like yesterday vhen you left the mash go the vay of winegar. A day's stilling gone, thanks to your *schioppiness*." With a jerk Jonas pushed his empty plate away, and turned to Ma, busy at the stove. "Today Moses comes back. Edward I can't trust to teach him right. Moses can vork mitt Andrew. Chust use Edward vhere you vant."

Ma turned from the stove where slow-sizzling slabs of cornmeal mush rested in a pan of hot lard and looked sadly toward Edward. "After morning chores he can take the wagon into Jefferson for some things I need and I can surely use him in the garden," she said. She moved to the table with a fresh plate of mush. "I'm sure Edward's sorry, Jonas. It's hard you are on the boy."

Pa shot her a warning look and she turned quickly back to the stove, busying herself with the mush.

"Any job is better than working in the distillery," Edward said, a muscle quivering in his jaw while he fought to sound unconcerned.

"Ei-yi-yi. That a man must be burdened with a son who dares to talk back. No more vords vill I hear from you! Leave the table!" Pa yelled, banging his heavy fist on the table.

Michael kept his eyes on his plate, busily shoveling mush into his mouth, but Andrew looked with interest from Pa to Edward. William opened his mouth to speak, but received a warning look from Andrew and shut it quickly. An embarrassed silence descended on the table as they all studiously ate their breakfast and avoided looking at Edward.

Humiliation turned to anger. He shoved the chair away from the table, striking it against the wall, and ran out of the kitchen, slamming the back door. *I hate you, hate you,*

hate you, he thought wildly, running towards the barn.
It was unheard of to abandon morning chores without
first asking permission, but he set his jaw grimly, grabbed
an old hat and jacket from a peg just inside the barn door,
and ran to the stall where Dolly, his mare, watched him with
interest. Edward led Dolly from her stall and saddled her
quickly.

They took off across the fields at a fast gallop. Astride
Dolly, he felt less angry, more in control. "Let's go up to my
thinking rock," he called out to the little mare. He always
talked to animals as though they were human; and, much to
Pa's disgust, treated them as friends.

He crossed Porters Lane and headed up a steep hill.
Newly plowed fields stood ready for planting, and robins
hopped on stiff legs to pull plump worms from the rich
red-brown furrows. High in a maiden-blush, a rose-breasted
grosbeak sang to his mate and bobwhites whistled merrily
from fence posts. Edward guided Dolly along a winding
trail, following a low stone wall which formed the southern
boundary of the farm, then rode beside a tiny brook through
woods fragrant with hemlock and wild cherry. Reaching the
knoll of a high ridge overlooking the farm, he headed for his
special rock, a huge granite boulder that commanded an
unobstructed view of the valley below.

He left Dolly free to graze and climbed onto the rock,
scrunching his backside into a slight depression worn
smooth over the years by wind and weather. It was a rare
morning, and he took a deep breath of the sweet clean air,
looking down on his home.

A small plot of grass extended a short distance on each
side of the house, but Pa didn't abide by much land being
given over to things "chust for nice", and the tiny lawn was
bordered closely by a cornfield on one side and Ma's
vegetable garden on the other side. Behind the garden stood
the bank barn and barn-yard, and beyond that, along a run
feeding Codorus Creek, the mill. A neat walk led from the

barn to the front porch of the two-story frame home. Every shutter facing the road was closed and a stranger, ignorant of their Pennsylvania Dutch custom of living in the kitchen and shutting off the "best rooms" to use only on Sunday, might have thought the house empty. "Austere," he muttered, rolling the fancy word around his tongue. "Just like the whole Rebert family."

He gave a deep sigh and relaxed against the rock. He felt better already. He loved this farm, it was his home, the only home he had ever known. The original log house, built by Grandfather Johann over fifty years ago, had been sided over, and expanded as grandfather's family grew. Edward could still picture his grandfather, sitting in an old rocker on the side porch, a woolen afghan over his arthritic knees, spinning tales of his arrival in America to anyone who would listen. And Edward had listened eagerly.

In 1759 Johann Rebert had emigrated from the Palatinate, a large German-speaking province lying along the Rhine River in southwestern Europe. It was a fair land, and his grandfather spoke reverently of its fertile fields and vine clad hills, but its very lushness had raised the envy of Louis XIV of France and his colossal ambition. The French army went through the land destroying cities and villages, stripping the people of their homes, leaving the land scorched and plundered.

Grandfather, along with other Germans wishing to escape the poverty brought on by the Thirty Years War, listened to the golden promises of William Penn, a shrewd Quaker wishing to attract good settlers and farmers to his large land grant, Pennsylvania, in America. When, at the age of nineteen, Johann faced forced conscription into the army, to fight off another invasion of the Vaterland by the French, he fled the Palatinate and headed for America, the land of promise.

He brought his entire life with him in a simple wooden chest, his Bible, a few items of clothing, some seeds, and a few precious tools. His ship, the Neptune, landed in the busy port of Philadelphia and after buying a horse and cart to haul his chest and bedding, he headed west toward the Susquehanna River, full of dreams and optimism. Even in the Old Country he'd heard stirring accounts of the fertile limestone farmland of Lancaster County, with top soil said to be fifteen feet deep under the roots of mighty oaks and hemlocks.

After weeks of lonely travel he crossed the Susquehanna at Columbia and when he saw the serenely beautiful Codorus Valley he fell to his knees in prayerful thanks. The familiar Rhine-like appearance of steep wooded hills spoke to him of home. The valley was bordered by a small mountain range called the Pigeon Hills and watered by Codorus Creek which flowed eastward to become part of Susquehanna River system. Johann staked out his claim and before the first snow fell he had erected a crude log cabin beside a good spring and near the banks of the lovely little creek.

In the spring Johann applied to William Penn for a warrant deed to purchase three hundred and fifty acres and sold his cart to buy a plow and a bucksaw. He improved the hastily constructed cabin from trees he felled, working alone from dawn to dusk all that first hot summer of 1750. That fall his garden and ten acres of corn were destroyed by a fierce hail storm.

He was penniless and discouraged, but so were most of his neighbors, other Pennsylvania Dutch farmers. At church he met Catherine Eyster, daughter of another emigrant German. He married her the next spring and that year he cleared ten more acres, planted rye and wheat, bought a milch cow, and fathered his first son, Jonas.

Johann's crops were lusher than he'd ever dreamed possible, and his old voice would grow soft as he spoke to Edward of those years. Natural pastures of knee-high grass provided prime grazing land and he built a sturdy barn for his fat animals and a stone grist mill to provide for his family of nine children, cutting and laying each stone by hand, The mill shared the sweet water of Codorus Creek with plentiful wildlife—white-tailed deer, red fox, turkey, hedgehogs, and the occasional black bear. Locust trees and drooping willows were home to chattering squirrels and trilling birds, while rabbits, raccoon and grouse found cover in the thickets of wild gooseberries growing in profusion along its deep cut bank.

Edward remembered vividly the day Grandfather Johann pulled him onto his skinny knees, folded Edward's soft childish hand into his gnarled, calloused fingers and in a halting voice, half German and half English, spoke of his passion for the land. "Edward," his grandfather had said, "don't ever forget, that God gave man life in a garden. Treat this land with love and respect, as God's garden. You can never truly own it. It's yours only to tend and care for during your stay on this earth."

Edward sighed. He wondered what Grandfather Johann would think of the conversion of his grist mill, built to provide bread for his family, into a money making distillery.

He hitched sideways, trying to find a more comfortable spot on the hard rock. Rolling fields sloped away toward the blue-green Pigeon Hills on the east and, through a stand of towering oaks, he could see the graceful steeple of Lischey's church. Down in the meadow cow bells tinkled. Tiny villages ringed the valley:

Hanover, Littlestown, and Gettysburg in the west; Jefferson, Spring Forge, Red Lion, and rapidly growing Yorktown to the north and east. The Codorus Valley seemed more lovely than he had ever known it, bathed now in sunshine, now in shadow, as fleecy clouds scudded across the sky.

Stone walls, covered with wild roses, marked the boundaries of Jacob Bollinger's farm called "Acorn Hill", Andrew Hershey's "Garden Acres", and Peter Stambaugh's

"Plenty". Pretty names they were. He wondered why Pa had never named their place. He loved this valley; had learned how to fish and swim in its creeks, mastered ice skates on its frozen ponds, and learned to ride a horse across its lush pastures. Could he really leave it? Leaning against the warm rock, his hat tilted over his eyes, a favorite piece of scripture came to mind.

> *For He, when times of trouble come,*
> *Shall hide me in his secret place*
> *And set me high upon a rock*
> *Above my foes and keep me Safe.*
> Psalm 27:5-11

What did he want to do, really do with his life? He stretched out his legs and yawned. His ambitions seemed vague, no stronger than the haze covering the distant hills.

But there was the exciting idea of heading west. He was still mad at Patrick, but they would probably make up soon. And he just knew Patrick would be willing to go. Edward's breath came more quickly. That was what he really longed to do. Prove his manhood; fight with Sam Houston in Texas, become a hero. Pa'd be proud of him then!

He sat hunched on the rock, resolve settling over him like a warm cloak. That was it. He wanted adventure, he wanted to be a soldier. He'd talk to Patrick first chance he got and they'd start making plans.

The sun was high in the sky by the time he got back to the farm. He stopped by the springhouse and lifted a tin cup from a stone ledge just inside the door. The spring gurgled between large grey crocks of yellow-skimmed milk, waiting to be churned into butter and he dipped a cupful of the sweet water, smiling down at his reflection in the crystal clear water.

Sky blue eyes, Rebert blue, smiled back at him. Straight blond hair, bowl cut, fell forward around a broad face. A deep furrow creased his chin, a gift everyone said, from his Grandfather Johann. Edward cupped his hands and splashed water on his warm face, his image disappearing in wavy ripples.

After quenching his thirst, he strode toward the barn, resolved to get the chores done quickly. He worked extra hard and finished by the time the sun was directly overhead, then headed for the house.

Ma was sitting in a high-backed rocker on the side porch, a granite dish-pan in her lap filled with dandelion greens, her busy hands cutting the roots from the fresh greens as she washed and sorted them. Her preoccupation gave him an opportunity to study her.

Ma was not heavy, but substantial; warm and solid, with a soft chest to nestle against. Long after he became too old for it, Edward had longed to snuggle on her lap—to be soothed and comforted—like the younger children.

Today Ma wore a long grey calico dress, patterned with tiny sprigs of yellow flowers, covered by a spotless white apron, starched stiff and tied around her neck. Always spotlessly clean, her clothing smelled of lavender, and her skin of rosewater. Grandfather Johann had once said that Ma was refined, of good stock, beautiful as a young bride, but Edward guessed that eleven children, one every two years from the day of her marriage, had taken their toll. Deep wrinkles criss-crossed her face and wire spectacles shielded faded blue eyes. Fair hair, now liberally streaked with grey, was pulled back into a neat bun, and her hands were bent with arthritis; crooked hands that were always doing. Ma's work never ended.

Caring for everyone, and working the farm, left her little chance to enjoy any luxuries in life. Her whole life had been spent within the boundaries of the valley, and except for an occasional trip to a county fair, she seldom left the farm.

The sad part of this, as Edward saw it, was that this life of hardship was unnecessary. They were not poor; Pa was considered well-to-do by his neighbors. They could afford to get some hired help for the kitchen. But Ma had let herself become a slave to earlier habits of thrift and industry, no longer necessary, a slave to the needs of her family and Pa's unsmiling dominance.

Edward vowed this would not happen to him.

As Ma's hands flew over the greens he lowered himself to the porch stoop, feeling oddly protective of her. "I always know summer's commin' when we have a mess of dandelion greens for supper," he said, stretching his legs and giving her a wide grin.

She smiled at him fondly. "Next to sassafras or wormwood, it's the best spring tonic I've found for you younguns." She laughed when he wrinkled his nose. "I was out in the field early this morning and found a pretty sheltered spot where the greens were nice and leafy. I dug enough for us, and extra for the Hoke family, if you want to take some over later today. With Mrs. Hoke sick with milk fever, I imagine they'd take kindly to some fresh greens. Besides, little Katie is always glad to see her young hero!"

Edward felt the color rise in his face and laughed self-consciously. "I'll be happy to, Ma. I can drop it off after I finish your shopping in Jefferson."

He watched her plump fingers fly in uncommon rhythm. Bless her, she hadn't said a word about this morning's fuss with Pa. But then Ma had always been a steadying influence for him, a buffer in the constant battles with his father.

His shoulders sagged and he frowned. Ma noticed and looked worriedly at him, her fingers pausing in their work. "Edward, you seem so troubled lately, so discontented. Always quarreling with your Pa."

"Seems like Pa is the one always quarreling with me."

"But, son, he's only trying to teach you right and help

you grow up proper. I know he seems stern at times, but that's just his way. Discipline is a father's duty. Jonas is doing what any loving father does for his children. Pa loves you deeply, just as he does all his family."

"He takes a funny way of showing it."

"I don't like that kind of talk, Edward."

He flushed. "I'm sorry Ma." Then, words started coming so fast they tumbled over one another and he blurted, "Pa's life's all church and hard work. There's no joy in him; he never laughs or makes light of things. Everything's got to be done the old way, the German way. He decides who and what each one of us should be and that's the way it is. Nobody should have to respond to a callin' not his own. Doesn't it matter what I want?"

"What do you want? Have you ever talked to him of it?"

"I don't know what I want . . . not yet. He never listens to me anyhow." Edward got up and walked to the edge of the porch, looking across the field to the distillery. "I know that someday I want to be somebody people look up to. I wanted to finish school so I could learn to speak good English, not this dumb Dutchy dialect that sets our people apart."

"Who we are doesn't limit us, Edward. It sets us free."

"But people call us backwards, always poking fun and telling those stupid "dumb Dutchman" stories about us."

Ma looked at him, her blue eyes filled with concern. "I wish I had an answer for you, Edward. I'm sure . . ."

Edward interrupted, "But Ma, that isn't all that's troubling me. Pa's always findin' fault with me. He don't . . . doesn't . . . fault the other boys like he does me. I'm always working against my brothers for the smallest compliment. It's bad for all of us." He stopped and thought about what he had just said. Finally he had admitted, not just to Ma, but to himself, the real problem. He didn't want to be disrespectful, to feel hostility toward Pa or to hurt Ma, but anger and resentment were festering in him, coloring everything he did.

He raised his head and his eyes met hers. It had to be said. "I've thought and thought about it, Ma. I want to head West; make a place for myself out there where land is free for the taking. When Pa's done farming, this place will go to one of the older boys, and I want no part of the distillery. It's best for me to go."

Ma put the basin of greens on the floor and rose quickly to her feet, her face suddenly pale. She seemed to stagger and stopped suddenly to catch her breath. Edward looked at her in alarm. Was she bilious? Or worse yet, was there something wrong with her heart?

He rushed to her side and took her arm, then led her back to the rocker and eased her onto its seat.

"What's the matter, Ma?"

"I just felt a little woozy, just for a moment."

"Has this happened before?"

"A few times," she admitted.

"Have you told Pa? Have you seen Doc Hambaugh?"

Ma fell silent, her hands twisting together in her lap. Finally she looked up at him and a tear slid down her lined cheek. "Your Pa knows, but the boy's don't. The doctor says my heart isn't good. I mustn't work so hard . . . musn't get excited or worry." She gave a soft sigh and settled back, the tremor in her body sending a fresh ache of concern through Edward.

By the time Ma started to rock herself gently to-and-fro, Edward felt himself beginning to resist the knowledge of her illness. He strode to the edge of the porch and looked out across the small yard. Tulips and jonquils crowded against the fence bordering Ma's garden. Almost without seeing, his eyes traveled across the bare soil, last year's withered tomato stalks still covering the ground. He'd have to see to the spading; it was clear Ma shouldn't be handling a shovel.

"I can see I've upset you, Edward," Ma said, speaking to his back, "and I didn't mean for you to see my infirmity."

Her voice began to tremble, despite her obvious effort to control it. "It would grieve me greatly, were you to leave. Especially if you were to leave feeling anger toward your Pa. Bitterness such as that can serve no purpose."

Edward returned to her side where he dropped to one knee beside her chair. She reached down and placed her small hand on his tensely knotted fist, pressing it gently. "I pray that God will take you down the right path, Edward, and that He will give you the wisdom to understand your Pa. I know he's gruff and demanding, even severe at times, but underneath all that bluster he's a caring man. A good man. You'll feel differently about him when you're older."

"Ei, Ma, in my heart I guess I know that. I'll . . . I'll try Ma. I'll stay here and aim harder to be the son he wants." Edward held himself motionless, his mother's illness raging in his mind. He felt too trapped to trust himself to speak further. The golden West would have to wait. There was no adventure in causing his mother pain.

Suddenly a loud explosion rent the quiet. They both jumped to their feet and looked toward the mill where a black cloud of smoke was beginning to billow in the cloudless sky.

"Dear God," Edward cried, running out into the yard. "The distillery's on fire!"

Chapter

-5-

Edward raced across the yard, past the barn, vaulted a low stone wall, and tore across the meadow which sloped to the creek and distillery. His legs flew across the uneven ground, his heart jumping against his ribs. Behind him the air echoed with the clanging dinner bell that Ma was furiously ringing to summon help.

He reached the front of the distillery and paused, gulping thick air. Black clouds of smoke billowed through the door, blown off its hinges by the explosion. Pa was shouting instructions to several running figures barely visible in the murky interior. Bright points of flame danced in the darkness.

Andy came around the corner of the mill, a large bucket of water in his hand, and almost collided with Edward.

"What happened?" Edward gasped .

"Darn fool, Moses, got the fire too hot. Blew the still to smithereens. The fire is spreading across that old floor." Andy paused, looking toward the meadow and the sound of approaching horses. "Help is coming. Grab a bucket and form a water line at the mill race." Andy fled into the mill, precious water slopping from the top of his wooden bucket.

Charles, J.J., and two hired hands, who had been plowing in the north field, galloped into the clearing and sprang from lathered horses. Frantically Edward shouted to them. "We need water. Grab some buckets from along the wall and follow me."

He sprinted to the mill race and dipped his bucket in the

water. The men fell in beside him and started to fill their pails. Edward took his overflowing bucket and ran to the open doorway where Andy had reappeared. Andy grabbed the bucket from him and passed it to the men inside.

Edward dashed back to the mill race. Thank God, neighboring farmers were arriving on horseback in response to the pealing bell. Peter Stambaugh rode in with his two sons and Jacob Bollinger with one of his hired hands. Soon a dozen men were part of the bucket brigade and were racing back and forth from the mill race to the burning building.

Inside the distillery several of the men joined Pa, Moses, and Andy, and formed a wide circle around the ruptured still. They grabbed the slopping buckets from the men and doused the floor in a frantic attempt to keep the flames from spreading.

Edward prayed that flour dust from the milling operation, housed along the outside wall, wouldn't explode. Flames shot higher, licking across the tinder dry floor, and water hissed loudly, raising clouds of steam as it hit hot embers. The acrid smoke from the burning still and sour mash gave off a repulsive stench that left the men gagging and gasping for breath.

"Keep vater coming," Pa shouted, stomping his boots viciously on a pile of burning rags next to the still. "Avay from us it's getting!"

Edward darted back to the bucket brigade. His legs trembled, his nose burned, and his throat was raw.

He gave a few hurried instructions to the men and again dipped his empty bucket into the rushing water. Muscles strained and sweat poured down his aching back as he whipped around and ran once more toward the burning mill.

Much as he hated the distillery he didn't want to see it destroyed. The fire might set him free, but this old mill was a part of his heritage. He had grown up with the sound of the splashing water wheel, he and Patrick had played among the sacks of grain, his grandfather Johann had guided his hands as he learned to operate the mammouth grinding wheels. He had to fight to save the mill.

His shoulders knotted with effort as he tried to keep the water from slopping out of the bucket and he ran faster.

Inside the mill, Pa bellowed instructions in rapid German, his carefully mastered English forgotten in the stress of the moment. "It's chust about out. A few more buckets of vater here, on these rags yet. Ja! Gute, Gute!"

Edward handed his pail of water to Charles and paused to have a look. His arms quivered with exhaustion and he brushed sweat-soaked hair off his forehead with a trembling hand. Clouds of ashy smoke and steam rose from the smoldering floor, but the fire seemed to have been confined to an area around the ruptured still kettle, and the flames were slowly flickering out.

Pa slumped against the wall. He wiped a grimy hand across his sweat-drenched face, streaking it with soot and ash. "Rest once," he croaked to the men still passing pails of water through the open door of the distillery. "And someone run up to the house and tell the Missus she can stop ringing that danged bell!"

Moses was leaning against the side of the building, a bloodsoaked rag wrapped around his hand. Edward hurried over to him.

"How bad are you hurt?" he asked, taking Moses' injured hand in his own.

"Darn near blew my finger off," Moses groaned as Edward gingerly pulled back the sodden rag to assess the damage. "Ow, that hurts like the devil." He looked at Edward, his face pasty white. "Besides, I swallowed my cud of tobacco, and it's making me terrible sick."

Fighting to keep a straight face, Edward led Moses to an overturned whiskey keg and pressed him down. He unwrapped the bloody bandage and prodded the injured hand. "Looks awful," he admitted with a shudder. "You better have the Doc take a look at it. Here, take my bandanna and soak it in some whiskey, then wrap your finger good and tight. I'll take you in to Jefferson, to Doc Hambaugh, soon as everything is safe here. And," he added, the grin breaking through, "stick one of your good fingers down your throat and vomit up that dang wad of tobacco."

He left Moses and joined Pa and the knot of men surveying the boiler which had been split wide open, top to bottom. Pa stood in mute despair, stocky legs spread wide, hands planted on hips, eyes blazing, while he angrily looked over the damage. His heavy eyebrows were singed, his grey hair stood in wet spikes and black soot streaked his flushed face. Edward felt a tug of sympathy.

"Schloppiness, that's vhat caused it," Pa muttered. "Darn fool schloppiness. First Moses he gets the fire too hot and the still blows apart, then the fire catches that pile of sulfur rags some fool left in a heap on the floor." He cast eyes dark with suspicion at Andy and Edward, but said no more, then turned and stomped toward the door.

With a pang of guilt Edward remembered dropping the rags on the floor after wiping out the whiskey kegs the day before. Dang it all, he hadn't thought of any danger. He glanced at Andy, slouched against the ruptured still, watching him. "Guess Pa doesn't rightly know who to blame for the pile of sulfur rags," he said.

"You better hope he doesn't ask," Andy replied, a grin spreading over his dirty face. "Anyhow they didn't cause the explosion and the damage from the fire doesn't seem to be too bad."

Edward poked Andy's arm in gratitude and took a final look around the smelly, smoking room. The copper kettle of the ruptured still was ruined, but the other two stills were unharmed. The fire had not eaten through the heavy plank floor, although it was heavily charred and would probably smolder for hours. The danger appeared to be over and Moses waited for him outside.

Moses was still perched on the bucket talking to Pa, who

was examining the torn finger. Pa gently rewound the bandanna and gave Moses a reassuring pat on the shoulder, then hastened over to his neighbors who were preparing to leave.

"Danke schon! Danke Schon!" he said, grasping each man's hand firmly in his own, tears of gratitude glistening in his eyes.

"Glad we could be of help, Jonas. Good thing the fire didn't take hold of that floor or the whole mill might have gone," big Jacob Bollinger offered.

"Ja, the Lord vas mit us today," Pa said, a tear cutting a channel through the soot on his weather-lined face while he clasped Jacob tightly on the shoulder.

Edward, standing beside Moses, observed the exchanges between Pa and his neighbors. Pa looks old, Edward thought with surprise. Funny he had never noticed that before, the face a map of deep lines, like a newly furrowed field, the eyes, once a bright "Rebert blue," faded and watery.

At that moment he loved Pa so much it hurt. And then he remembered the morning and turned away, anger and rejection more easily accommodated than love.

* * *

As Spring heated up, everyone's attention focused on getting crops in the ground. The fields were plowed and worked smooth, and Edward hurried to get Ma's garden fertilized and ready to plant. It was the dark of the moon. Time to get root crops—potatoes, carrots, and radishes—planted. Lettuce and spring onions were already set out and doing well.

Pa seemed content to clean up the mess created by the fire, but made no attempt to replace the damaged still. Edward pondered that.

He visited Sassy and her new pups every day. This

would probably be her last litter. The dog was getting old and her productive days were about over. Sassy was a tenth generation working collie with a natural herding instinct, but she was also good at chasing rabbits and better yet at grabbing a rat darting from corn crib to wood pile.

There were lots of cats and working dogs about the farm, but Edward longed for a dog of his own, one he could have as a friend. He'd always had pets of some kind. Turtles, a small orphaned lamb, and once, to Pa's disgust, a baby crow that had been knocked from its nest soon after hatching. The little crow adopted Edward, following him around, ignoring other crows, acting as though he were its mother. It was a cute little fellow and Edward even taught it to say a few words, but having a crow for a pet wasn't the same as having a dog.

Dogs on the farm were considered workers, not to be coddled and made lazy. Pa'd promised him a pup from this litter, if he trained it to herd sheep, then refused when he learned Edward was helping Sassy instead of tending the mash barrels. He said Edward needed to learn more responsibility, that dogs knew how to give birth on their own. But Ma intervened and Pa had relented.

Edward hunched down beside the new mother, on her nest of old burlap sacks in the tool shed, and gingerly picked up one of the puppies. He'd known from the beginning which one he wanted. A chubby little male, with beautiful black, white, and tan markings, had licked his hand eagerly the first time he held it. The puppy was old enough to be weaned and today Edward intended to take him along while he did chores and get him used to being away from Sassy.

The little dog seemed to know him and quivered with delight, nestling its warm little body in his arms. The pup's lean face tapered to a trembling black nose, and silken ears of tan and black pricked in alert interest. Edward rubbed the fat tummy and the little dog groaned in ecstasy. Edward hefted the wiggling puppy up to his face, touching noses. "I gotta find a name for you. Now what would be a good name for a boy's best friend?" The little dog looked straight into Edward's eyes and yipped with excitement, almost as though he could understand his new master, and wanted to help with this important decision.

"Maybe Frisky, or Wiggler, or how about Cold Nose?" Edward asked, laughing. "No . . . something very special for a very special dog. I think Duke would suit you. That's a fine upstanding name for such a handsome fellow."

Edward placed Duke on the ground and walked out of the tool shed. "Come along little friend, we've chores to do and it's about time you started to mind your new master." He laughed softly, watching the small puppy bound ahead of him, tail wagging so furiously his whole rear end moved back and forth.

* * *

June is summer at its best; warm, but without the humid heat of July and August. Strawberries are ripe, trees are still fresh and green, and in the fields it is time to make hay.

Edward rose at dawn and after a hearty breakfast followed Pa into the fields along with J.J., Andy, William, and Charles. Each carried a scythe, freshly honed to a razor sharp edge. The grass in the south meadow was waist-high, thick and luxuriant, swaying gently in the slight breeze.

Andy considered haying one of the most irksome jobs on the farm, but Edward secretly enjoyed the test of skill and strength required by the cutting. He'd worry about the nasty jobs later, cleaning the field with a wooden-toothed hay rake and later the sure misery of an aching back and blistered fingers when he had to pitch the hay into the hay-mow using the heavy pitch fork with its rough hickory handle and tines half an inch in diameter. The cutting was different. It presented a challenge to his strength and manhood. It was an exercise in precision teamwork and he was tense with anticipation.

They lined up according to age, five abreast, facing the vast field of waving grass. Charles, first, then J.J., then Andy, then Edward, and finally William. Pa fell in last so he could keep an eye on everyone.

"Touch your stones to the blade another time, yet, and make ready," Pa ordered in a gruff voice, looking critically down the line. He wore heavy patched trousers, with a long ragged tear beneath the knee from a previous haying. The pants were held in place with a length of worn leather and a wide-brimmed straw hat sat firmly on his head.

Edward took a final sweep along the gleaming, curved blade with his whetstone. He grasped the highly polished oak handle of the big scythe and rested the tip gently on the ground, flexing the muscles in his shoulders. He was ready.

Charles stepped out first, his arm rising high in the air, taking the first sweeping cut of the tall grass. He advanced, leaving four great swaths of cut timothy behind him, then J.J. started forward, his arm raising and falling in the same pattern as that of Charles. Andrew watched, and at the proper moment joined the forward moving group.

Finally it was Edward's turn and he grasped the handle of the heavy scythe. The muscles in his arm knotted in anticipation. Carefully he watched Andy, four paces ahead of him, and when Andy's blade swept skyward Edward's arm followed the same high arc. Both gleaming blades rose and fell in the same sweeping motion.

SWISH, SWISH, SWISH.

The hay fell in great swaths, scythes swinging in perfect unison. The slanting line moved slowly forward, the felled grass lying in perfect rows as they advanced down the field, side by side, each four paces behind the one to his left.

The sun was hot and Edward's shirt clung to his body, his arms moving rhythmically back and forth. He was covered with sweat, yet not uncomfortable, working in a steady rhythm. The sweet smell of the freshly cut hay, the swishing of the blades, and the shimmering heat lying upon the open field were almost hypnotic. The sun glinted on the curved metal blade and he clasped the smooth wooden handle of the scythe firmly, swinging it high in a smooth swinging arc.

A frantic little field mouse, suddenly deprived of his home, darted away from the sharp blade and Edward faltered, almost losing his swing. That will never do, he thought, increasing his stride. Pa would be angry if he broke the harmony of the perfectly swinging scythes.

Up and down the field they moved, stopping now and then to pass their whetstones across the blade for a sharper edge.

Only the soft swish, swish, of the blades cutting through the tall grass and the chirring of insects broke the quiet of the summer morning. The field shimmered in the heat, the sun glinted on the steel blades as it rose higher in the cloudless sky.

Edward's arm began to ache and his hand became slippery with sweat, yet he felt strong and happy. This was the life he wanted. He felt like a man, doing a man's work in a man's world. Swish, swish, swish—the grass fell at his feet.

His body and arms were moving without conscious thought and his mind drifted. Pa had been strangely quiet about his reasons for not replacing the damaged still after the fire, saying only that the increasing taxes and growth of commercial distilleries were making it less profitable to operate. Edward suspected that there were other reasons, but Pa wasn't one to discuss his personal feelings with his children. Especially him.

Henry had spoken to him again about apprenticing at the tannery and Pa said he was free to go after the fall harvest if that's what he wanted. Living in Jefferson was an exciting thought. There were lots of girls living in town and more chance to keep company with them.

Charles reached the end of the meadow and threw up his left arm, a signal to the others to stop when they reached that spot. Ma was there, busily uncovering large jugs of fresh spring water from the wagon parked under a stand of sheltering willow trees.

Edward finished his cut smoothly and rested the scythe gently on the ground, waiting for Michael to catch up.

"Ei,ei,ei, it's hotter than blazes," Michael said, wiping his nose across his sleeve and fumbling with the buttons on his pants. "And I have to pee something terrible. With Pa right behind me I didn't dare stop."

Edward grinned in sympathy. He remembered only too well the strain of having Pa behind him when he was the youngest in the line.

After Michael emptied his bladder onto the the ground they walked the short distance through unmown grass to the dappled shade of the drooping trees. Pa was at the wagon helping Ma lift the heavy, sweating jugs of cold water to the ground where everyone could reach them. J.J., Andy, and Charles were hunkered down in the shade of an ancient oak, guzzling water from a tin cup passed from one mouth to the other.

Michael grabbed a cold, sweating jug and raised it to his thirsty lips. He took several large gulps before stopping for air. Handing the jug to Edward he joked, "sweetest spring water in York County. No wonder Rebert Whiskey is the best around."

"This is better than any whiskey ever made," Edward said, laughing. He hoisted the cool earthenware jug to his mouth and took a long draft of the cold water, letting some of it spill down his chin onto his neck and chest. After drinking his fill, he wet his bandanna and wiped dust and bits of grass from his dirty face, before sinking to the ground under a tree.

"Chust a few minutes, yet," Pa ordered. "Take your stones to the blade, once more. Andy, you've an older scythe. Is the edge holding?"

"It's fine, Pa."

"Gute, Gute. Keep an eye on it, already. A dull blade will pull your guts out."

Edward relaxed against the rough bark of the tree. Though tired and dirty he was eager to start again. They had about three more acres to mow; another hour should do it. He turned to Michael slumped in exhaustion beside him. "Someday when I own my own farm I'm gonna have one of those new horse-drawn mowing machines. I hear they can cut five hundred bushels of wheat a day."

Pa overheard, and drew his heavy eyebrows together, fixing Edward with flinty eyes. "New this, new that. No respect do you have for tradition. Rebert men have always harvested by hand." He drew his whetstone from his pocket and began to draw it along the long curving blade. "Time already to finish our day's york. I'll lead and set the pace. A little too fast you vent, Charles. The sun is hot. Don't forget," he added with a rare smile, "you've an old man and a young boy in this group of farmers."

After sharpening their blades one more time, they lined up and waited for Pa's command to start forward. Edward gazed with pride at the field before him. To his right, the newly mown hay lay in perfect rows, each swath having been felled to fall neatly next to the one before it. To his left, the tall grass whispered softly in the faint summer breeze awaiting the cutting blades.

And then they were in motion, once again, six men moving as one down the field, blades flashing in the sun.

SWISH, SWISH, SWISH.

Chapter
-6-

At the annual strawberry festival held by the Ladies' Aid Society of the First Reformed Church of Jefferson Edward eagerly sought out Sally, but she fixed him with a piercing, accusatory look and ignored him. She had turned down his repeated requests to call and he heard she was thick with Amos again. Often at night he dreamed of the conquest that might have been, sometimes with embarrassing results.

Patrick had been by the mill several times and they patched things up, but they carefully avoided talking about the dance. Things weren't quite the same between them and Edward didn't broach the subject of running away. He worried constantly about Ma, watching her carefully and tending to her heavy chores.

He and Andy removed the ruptured kettle from the distillery, but Pa made no effort to replace it. This puzzled him, but he didn't question Pa's reasons. Still it was strange; threshing season wasn't far off, the call for whiskey would be high, and he doubted the two remaining stills would be able to supply the demand.

June had been soft as spring, haying was over, and he ached to be in the open fields with Michael and Charles instead of confined to the distillery. Andy was abed with summer complaint and Edward was working alone, replacing a section of floor, badly charred by the fire, when he looked up to see Patrick lounging against one of the cold fireplaces, holding a tin cup of the morning's whiskey in his hand. Patrick watched him warily for a few minutes before he spoke.

"That's the best I ever tasted. You and Andy are getting to be as good at stilling as your Pa."

Edward grinned proudly and gave an extra hard whack to a hand-forged spike, driving it deep into the new floor. "Don't know about that, but it is good. We ran that batch through three times. I'd say it's about one hundred proof."

"Never did understand that proof business," Patrick said, taking another swallow, whiskey dripping down his curly red beard.

"Pa says the proof number's double the amount of pure alcohol. A pint of whiskey that says one hundred proof is fifty percent water and fifty percent alcohol." Edward rose to his feet and stepped back to review his handiwork.

Patrick took another sip. "Wonder who came up with that reasoning." He smacked his lips. "Wow, this stuff is potent. Bet my red hair is standing straight on edge."

Edward laughed. At times he suspected Patrick had more Irish in him than Scotch. His Scottish ancestors had come to America from Ulster, in Northern Ireland, thus earning them the name Scots-Irish, but a goodly number of them had intermarried with the Irish before emigrating. They were a rugged people of positive convictions, accustomed to asserting their rights and independence. That was Patrick, true as could be. That and his Irish fondness for whiskey. There was a saying about the Scots-Irish Patrick loved to quote: "Brewed in Scotland, bottled in Ireland, and uncorked in America."

"I didn't see you come in. How come you're not working?" Edward asked.

"My saw's down for repair so I thought I'd ride over and pester you awhile." Patrick attempted a crooked smile, but it looked pretty half-hearted. He fingered several heavy keys attached to his belt with a leather thong and stared at the floor. "I kinda need your advice on a little problem I have."

Edward looked at him in astonishment. Since when did

Patrick ask for his advice? It was usually the other way around.

"What I mean is," he went on, jiggling his keys, "a couple days ago I got a note from Inger. You remember Inger, don't you?"

Edward nodded somberly.

"Aye. Well, she wrote that she wanted to talk and asked me to come by on Sunday afternoon when she had time off. I was some surprised because I hadn't seen her since that dance back in April. Anyway, I went over on Sunday and we went for a walk. Soon as we were away from the house she started to cry. Edward, she took on something awful. Said she was in the family way, that it was my baby."

Patrick looked at Edward with anguished eyes. "How do I know 'tis mine?"

Edward didn't know what to say. The short time he'd been with Inger he'd liked her a lot. He'd always blamed Patrick for what happened that night. "You can't deny that you lay with her, Patrick. I don't know a whole lot about these things, but it looked to me like it was her first time. I mean," he stammered, "I saw blood and all."

"But God, Edward, a baby. I'm only eighteen!"

"I guess she wants to get married doesn't she?"

"Aye, but I don't even know Inger, so I sure don't care enough about her to marry her and, furthermore, I don't earn enough to marry anyone. I couldn't support a rabbit."

Edward watched him and said nothing.

"I didn't rape her, not the way you think. She was as caught up in kissing as I was and when it got to a certain point she got scared and wanted to stop. Hell, I'm a red-blooded man and I'd had a lot to drink. She'd let me go so far I couldn't stop what I'd started and I thought she really wanted me, but was just afraid I'd think badly of her. Maybe I was a little forceful, but she didn't put up that much fight. She didn't cry until it was all over. I didn't mean to hurt her, Edward and I'm terrible sorry it happened like it did." Patrick's body was slumped against the fireplace, his face haggard. He was paying dearly for his misdeed, that was clear, and Edward felt his pain. Still . . .

"You know the old saying, when such things happen those that dance have to pay the fiddler."

Patrick grunted. "Well, I'm figuring on packing up and heading west. Want'a come with me?"

Edward laughed in spite of himself. It was supposed to be the other way around. He was supposed to ask Patrick to run away with him. So much for that dream. Somehow, deep within him, he'd always known the West with all its glorious adventure, was not his destiny.

Patrick looked at him in surprise. "What's so funny about that?"

"A coupla months ago I was gonna ask you to do just that. But this changes things, Patrick. Inger can't be left with a little baby, without a father for it. You can't do that to her. I know you better'n that."

"But I can't keep a wife and baby on what little money I make at the saw mill," Patrick argued. "When the streams freeze over, there's no work or pay. And my folks can't keep us; there's still three wee ones at home. They barely make ends meet as it is. And don't forget Inger's an indentured girl. I'd probably have to pay off the Petersons.

"Don't you have any money put by?"

"Nope."

Edward shook his head. He'd always been aware that Patrick's family was much poorer than his, but up until now it had never made much difference. He'd have to help somehow.

"Maybe I could talk to Ma. She needs help in the house with Catherine gone and Henry would probably take you on at the tannery over the winter. Then if you and Inger can't get along together you can split up after the baby's born. At least the baby would have a name."

"Edward, you know good and well if I'm forced to marry

a girl I don't love the marriage doesn't have a chance of working out. Inger's pretty enough, that's what got me into trouble, that and the whiskey, but she's too mild for my taste. When I marry I want a girl with more spirit, more fire. The kind I'd likely find out west. I want to get away from here. Us Scots-Irish have wandering feet—not like you Dutchmen who like to stay put on your land, behind your stone walls." Patrick started to move about, waving his arms, pulling at his hair, as he was apt to do when he was excited. "Maybe I can talk her into getting rid of the baby. She was so hysterical I didn't mention that to her."

"How?"

"There's medicines you can take. And doctor's you can go to."

"I know that, but do you know how to get the medicine or where to find such a doctor?"

"No, but we can find out."

"We? I don't want no part of this. Besides Inger didn't seem to be the kind of girl that'd go for anything like that."

"All she wants is a husband," Patrick said bitterly. "She probably planned the whole thing." He shook his head, his shaggy red hair tumbling about his head.

Edward doubted that. He remembered only too well Inger sobbing in Sally's arms. He started to get angry. That was another thing. He had lost his chance with Sally, Inger had lost her virginity, and his dream of going west seemed lost forever.

"Well you done the deed that made you a father and there's no point in denying it. You think I don't want to go away too? I've been dreaming of it for months, and if you'd a kept your pants buttoned we could'a gone. You've spoiled everything"

Patrick had his hands on his hips, his stocky legs set far apart, the earlier hang-dog look replaced with glowering defiance that roused something in Edward that was close to admiration. Against all reasoning he loved Patrick.

Patrick gradually lowered his eyes to the floor. "I'm still gonna try to find out about a doctor. That would be best for me and Inger." He raised his eyes and gave Edward a pleading look. "We've been friends a long time. I need your help."

Edward sighed, his anger melting away. He found himself returning in memory to a time when he was five and Patrick seven—when his mother took him to his first Easter Egg hunt at Lischey's Church.

The ladies of the church had carefully hidden dozens of eggs around the picnic grounds, all of them dyed with bright colors, but only four with a special golden color that would claim a prize animal cooky cut in the shape of a rabbit from a mold made by the local tinsmith.

Edward ran everywhere, looking under every bush and behind every rock, excited with each discovery of a precious egg. When the church bell signaled the end of the hunt he stood looking at the pretty basket clutched in his hands, filled with brightly colored eggs, but none of them golden.

He looked up to see an older boy, a stranger at the church, watching him. The boy had curly red hair and was wearing patched, but clean overalls. The boy's eggs had been stuffed into a torn pasteboard box and lying right on top were two of the prized golden eggs.

"Hi, I'm Patrick," the redhead said.

"My name's Edward."

With a gentle smile Patrick picked up one of his golden eggs and held it out to him. Edward was amazed. His own five year old heart had not yet learned to share. Still he took the egg with a mumbled thanks and he and Patrick ran to the church to claim their prizes. Later they sat in the churchyard, backs against a giant hickory tree, munching on rabbit cookies sprinkled with red sugar, getting acquainted.

Over the years Patrick had shared more than his golden eggs. He had taught Edward how to win at marbles, taught him how to smoke corn-silk, and had explained the intriguing connection between what the farm animals were doing during mating season and Edward's own mysterious urges.

Shaking himself free of the memory he turned back to Patrick. "I'll see what I can find out," he said, with a rueful smile.

It was several days before Edward found the right opportunity to confide in Andy. Briefly he outlined Patrick's problem.

". . . and what he needs is the name of a doctor he can take Inger to, 'cause he can't afford to get married," Edward finished lamely.

Andy had never taken his eyes off him and now he spat contemptuously. "I reckon there's more to that tale than you're telling me, little brother."

Edward felt the heat creep into his face. "Inger wasn't guilty of any wrong doing," he muttered.

"Then how'd she get pregnant?"

"Patrick was pretty forceful. He was drinking and lost control."

"Bastard!"

"But it's over and done with now, Andy. There's no use laying blame. I thought maybe, you being older an' all, you might'a heard of a doctor that could fix things for them."

Andy hooked a finger under his suspender and looked at him carefully before answering. "Patrick ain't worth a fart in a whirlwind. Pa always said so. It's a dangerous thing you're getting mixed up in. That gal might die. Is your friendship with Patrick worth that risk?"

"He asked for my help," Edward said, softly. "I promised no more than to try and find a name for him."

Andy continued to lecture him and he listened politely although he already knew all the reasons why he shouldn't get mixed up in this mess. In the end Andy promised to ask around. They both hustled back to work and no more was said.

A week later Edward delivered some hides to the tannery and while he was unloading his wagon a seedy looking old man sidled up to him. "I hear you got some gal in the family way and are lookin' fer a doctor," the man said with a leer.

"Not me! My friend," Edward said hastily.

"I heard that before," he laughed, his stinking breath causing Edward to back away. "Happens, I know of such a Doc. It'll cost you, though."

"How much?"

"Two dollars for the name and address. The rest is between you and the Doc."

"How do I know it's a real name and address?"

"Smart young fellow aren't you. Well now, I guess you'll jest have to trust me. Yes-siree, you'll jest have to trust me."

Edward hesitated. Two dollars was a lot of money. Still this was the first positive lead he or Patrick had gotten. "I don't have that much. I'll have to talk to my friend, see if he can come up with some money. Where can I find you?"

"I'll be back tomorrow. Your gal can't wait too long, you know," he said with a wink.

As soon as he could get away from the tannery without rousing Henry's suspicions he rode out to the sawmill where he had to wait an hour for Patrick to finish work. When Edward told him the news Patrick groaned in relief. "I got one dollar. Can you loan me one?"

"If that's all you have how will you pay the doctor?"

"Sell my horse. But first we gotta find out how much he charges, and then I have to talk to Inger."

Edward was already having misgivings. This just wasn't right. Maybe Inger would refuse; he hoped Inger would refuse. "Give me your dollar. I'll see the old man tomorrow and get the name," he said, trying to keep the anger from his voice.

The next day he found an excuse to ride back to Jefferson and found the old man lounging near the front door of the tannery. Darn if Henry wasn't nearby, unloading bark. He seemed surprised to see Edward, again, and watched him walk past the seedy looking fellow lounging against the wall. All Edward needed was for Henry to get wind of this. Henry wouldn't approve—he was an awful lot like Pa.

Edward passed the man with a slight nod and walked into the tannery. Within minutes he felt his presence beside him. Without a word he handed over the two dollars and received a dirty scrap of paper with a name and address printed in childish letters. He stuffed it in his trouser pocket and ran outside to his horse. Henry was still watching.

Edward rode up Hanover Street then turned north on Berlin Street heading toward the Jake Hotel where Patrick was waiting. He kept fingering the slip of paper in his pocket. It was evil information. Maybe he should tear it up; tell Patrick the man hadn't showed up. Patrick would probably marry Inger and the baby would be born safely. Would Patrick really be that unhappy married to Inger? But he said he didn't love her. Edward shook his head; he had promised to help and here he was with the answer in his pocket. What in sam-hill was he to do?

At the hotel he mounted the steps and crossed the wide porch to where Patrick was leaning against the wall. Without a word he handed the note to him. Patrick looked at it quickly then jammed it into his own pocket. "I'm to see Inger tonight," he muttered in a voice so low Edward had to strain to hear.

"Does she know about this?"

"No." Patrick shook his shaggy head. "I'll talk to her tonight."

Edward turned and walked away. It was Patrick's problem now, he'd done what he promised.

* * *

Edward dug his heels into Brandy's flanks, urging him to a gallop. The searing heat fanned Edward's flushed cheeks and he gripped the reins tightly as he and Patrick passed through Porters Sideling on their way to Hanover. He couldn't believe that once again he had given in to Patrick. Yet here he was, astride Pa's horse, riding in search of the doctor instead of going to the church social he was supposed to be attending.

He glanced at Patrick, riding silently beside him, seemingly drawn into himself, his small eyes hooded and worried. Patrick still had not mentioned his plan to Inger. First he wanted to find the doctor and talk to him, find out how much the operation cost. Selling his horse might not be enough. Edward hoped the price would be too high, putting an end to the whole foolish idea.

He clucked to Brandy, increasing their pace. The sooner this ride was over the better. The trip was probably for nothing anyhow. Inger would surely refuse the operation. That Inger might go along with what Patrick was proposing was something he wasn't ready to deal with yet.

They cantered across Codorus Creek at Dubb's Mill. The creek, normally broad and swift-moving, had dried to a mere trickle during the recent dry spell, the dense growth of hickory, walnut, and oak lining its banks motionless and forlorn. Even the nuthatches, usually busily conversing while they flitted from tree to tree, were sluggish and quiet.

Brandy flicked his tail at pesky horse flies and Edward relaxed in the saddle as they passed through a canopy of low hanging branches following the trail through the tiny hamlet of Marburg toward Hanover. Though taking action seemed to have put Patrick in better spirits Edward thought it a temporary poultice; regardless of the outcome of this trip Patrick would have to cope with his conscience. Patrick's major problems—convincing Inger to go along with his plan, or marrying her and coping with his poverty—would remain the same.

The trip took nearly three hours and it was late afternoon before they reached town. Briskly they guided their horses into Hanover's center square and pulled up in front of the bustling Market House.

The Market House served all of Hanover's needs. The town jail was under one end and several pieces of fire equipment were under the other. Five roads radiated from off the Square and Edward looked about in confusion. Barns and stables crowded the dirt streets and wagons swayed in deep ruts as they maneuvered the narrow road. Dogs barked, men shouted and the roadway echoed to the sound of clopping hooves and creaking wheels. He jerked Brandy sharply to the curb to avoid a herd of cattle being driven down the street, headed for a pasture outside of town.

Patrick pointed to the Central Hotel, an imposing three story brick building, on the southwest corner of the square.

"Let's tie up there. The hotel's a good place to ask directions, and I'm dry as a toad out of water."

Edward frowned, but said nothing. Maybe a brandy would stop the nervous flutter in his stomach.

Inside the taproom they perched on high stools and ordered drinks. Trying to appear casual, Patrick questioned the barkeep. "Could you maybe direct us to Doc Fetterhoff's residence. It's said to be off Middle Street."

The barkeep looked at him, through narrowed eyes, before answering. "Go south out'a the square on Baltimore Street till you pass the brewery and McAllister's tavern. First lane past is Middle. Only the Doc's house isn't on the street . . . it's in the lane behind. An' I don't know as how you'd call it a res-e-dence. It's an old weather-beaten shack. You'll see his sign." The barkeep gave the gleaming surface of the bar a vicious swipe with his towel. "An' he ain't much of a doctor!"

Edward took a large gulp of his brandy. It seemed to lodge half-way down his throat and he felt like throwing up. Patrick avoided his eyes, downed his whiskey, and heaved himself to his feet. Without a word, they left the hotel.

It was market day in Hanover and Baltimore Street was alive with street vendors, lurching wagons, and shouting draymen. Nearing Middle Street, Edward reined Brandy to get a better book at the sprawling two story building on the corner. In addition to being a good sized dwelling it housed a tavern and store.

Patrick noticed his stare and pulled himself erect in his saddle. "That's the Richard McAllister place. Aye, and he was a handsome, strapping Irishman like meself. A force to be reckoned with. Ruled with his fists, he did. Laid out this low-lying swamp into a town and called it McAllistertown." A huge grin lit up Patrick's face and he cocked his shaggy head toward Edward, adding, "then some Pennsylvania Dutch Commissioner decided it should be named after Hanover, Germany. The joke is Hanover means "High Banks" . Typical of you dumb Dutchmen!"

"Ach," Edward grunted, raising his eyes to the heavens.

They reached the lane they were looking for and Edward felt his face tighten with despair. A battered sign, nailed to the side of a harness shop, marked Middle Street. Houses were so close together they seemed to lean against one another—ramshackle buildings, not much more than sheds, that had never known a coat of paint. Pigs and chickens picked their way through garbage rotting in the hot sun.

They found the doctor's shingle hanging by one nail on the side of a small weathered building, sporting what looked like a new tar-paper roof.

"Things must be looking up for the good doctor if he can afford a new roof," Patrick said, attempting a smile.

"Well, I don't like the looks of this place. Maybe we should just go home and forget the whole thing. There's got to be another way."

"Come on, friend. We've got this far. Don't quit on me now."

Patrick jumped to the ground and started toward the door.

Reluctantly, Edward followed. Dad-blame it, how had he ever gotten into this?

At Patrick's knock, the door squeaked open and a shadowy figure hurriedly waved them inside.

They entered a gloomy, windowless, room dominated by a long table covered with a gray looking sheet. The doctor, sitting at a desk in the corner, was unshaven and wore a long frock coat, stained and dirty. He peered at them intently through bloodshot eyes.

"How can I help you, boys," he asked in a raspy voice.

Patrick cleared his throat. "I've got a girl who's in the family way. I was told you might be able to help us out of our trouble."

"How far along is she?"

"Seven weeks."

"Do you have any money?"

"Some. How much?"

"Seventy-five Dollars. Payable before the operation."

Patrick gulped. "I'll have to sell my horse. I guess I can raise that much," he said.

"You'll have to sell it fast. The operation can't wait. Can you have the money by next week?"

"Aye, but I'll have to bring the girl on a Sunday. She's a house servant and that's her only day off."

"Next Sunday, one o'clock. You'll be taking her home, so bring a wagon and plenty of blankets. And be sure you have all the money. I don't give credit."

"I understand."

Edward stood motionless, during this exchange, his eyes raking the dirty little room. A long white coat, spotted with blood, hung from a peg on the wall. Something that looked like a surgical tray sat on an unpainted chest, holding a long, evil booking hook and several knives. He nudged Patrick in the arm, trying to indicate the tray. He saw Patrick's eyes follow his and then look quickly away.

"Sunday, then," the doctor said, rising and leading them

to the door. He grasped Edward's arm with claw like fingers, his long fingernails ringed with black grime. "I don't think I have to tell you boys to keep your mouths shut. You'll be in just as much trouble as me, if word of this gets out."

Edward hurried through the door and down the path, heart thumping. He vaulted onto Brandy, and without waiting for Patrick, headed for Baltimore Street.

He glanced over his shoulder at Patrick. "Let's go back to the hotel, we need to talk," Edward shouted.

This time they took a table in a secluded corner of the taproom, sitting silently until the barmaid placed drinks in front of them. Edward stroked his chin, feeling guilt, then desperation, and finally anger. What could he possibly say to dissuade Patrick? He stretched his hand across the table, speaking only with his eyes.

Patrick threw down a double shot of whiskey and wiped his mouth on his sleeve. He looked at Edward and smiled, then reached over and squeezed his arm. "Stop worrying, old boy," he said, in his soft voice. "I could never do that to Inger."

Edward's mouth dropped open. Then, absorbing Patrick's meaning, he smiled back, raising his drink in a salute.

* * *

Patrick, now that he had accepted the inevitability of marriage, regained his Irish good-humor and began to rib Edward unmercifully about his virginity. Edward pretended to take the jokes lightly, but he seethed inside, resenting Patrick's inference that he wasn't quite a man.

Late in September Edward was invited to the wedding of one of his Amish neighbors. Over two hundred guests were treated to a grand feast and Edward was busy heaping his plate, for the third time, when he spied Sally Stremell standing alone at the far end of the table.

Plate in hand, he strolled toward her.

"Hello, Sally," he said, trying to hide the uncertainty in his voice.

Sally smiled fully at him, her eyes bright with welcome. "Why, Edward Rebert. I haven't seen you in a coon's age. Where have you been keeping yourself?"

Edward blinked in surprise. The last few times he saw Sally she ignored him. "It's been a busy summer, what with the distillery and farm work, and all." He hesitated, then added, "I'd have called on you again, but I heard you were practically engaged to Amos."

Sally pulled at her skirt and looked at the ground. "I am, but we had a spat this morning so I came to the wedding alone. Seems we are always disagreeing about one thing or the other." She looked at him coyly. "I'll bet you wouldn't always find reason to fight with me," she said, taking his arm possessively and leading him to a bench away from the crowd.

They sat, talking and laughing, while the afternoon dropped away and shadows moved across the lawn. Sally pressed her plump thigh against his at every opportunity, flirting with him until his heart raced. There was no doubt in his mind that she was interested in him, and he was certainly interested in her.

When he could no longer resist Sally's attention he pulled her to her feet, tucked her hand in his, and strolled toward the darkening orchard behind the house. There on a bed of seckel pear leaves, he left behind the final vestiges of his childhood.

Chapter
-7-

October—smelling of fall—brought welcome rains and the countryside blossomed with color. Sumac and Virginia creeper blazed crimson against the stream banks. Yellow goldenrod and wild blue asters stretched across empty pastures. The top of the maple outside Edward's window wore a cap of golden leaves and Ma's plants turned brown with the first frost.

Saturday afternoons, Edward was required to work at the Jug House a small frame shed sitting in front of the distillery facing the main road. Open only on Saturday, it housed several kegs of aged whiskey and the locals stopped by to fill their jugs and exchange local news.

There had been a steady stream of customers all day and time passed quickly as Edward enjoyed the jokes and banter of his neighbors. He hefted a heavy jug of whiskey into the back of Widow Zeigler's wagon and tipped his cap to her as she paid him fourteen cents for a good gallon measure. The sun was sinking behind the distillery and Widow Zeigler appeared to be the last customer of the day. He flexed his aching shoulders and sank down on the stoop of the small wooden shed.

Pa rode up on Brandy and jumped to the ground, letting the reins fall to the ground. He seemed disturbed.

"I just this minute sat down," Edward muttered. "It's been a busy day. I emptied three barrels, and got a good start on the fourth. We'll need more for next Saturday."

Pa grunted, staring at him intently. "I chust come from the tannery, talking mitt Henry. Henry told me some things I don't care for." Edward blinked, but didn't say anything, and Pa continued. "Mighty disreputable fellow vas seen talking to you a few veeks back. Your Pa vanders vhat about."

Edward's gaze dropped to the ground. Dang that Henry, now he'd have to think of a reasonable lie. He wasn't good at lying, never had been. "I was talking for Patrick," he stammered. "Patrick needed some information and I got it from this fellow, cause Patrick was working."

"Could only be bad from the vay Henry talked of him. Vat kind of news vas it?"

"About . . .ah . . . about a job at the lumber mill, over in Spring Grove," Edward stammered, his face hot, looking at Pa hopefully.

"Gott imm Himmel, such lies! That a man must vork hard all day, and then listen to lies from his son."

It wasn't going to work. He'd have to tell Pa the truth, take whatever trouble came his way. He took a deep breath and started to explain. "Patrick needed the name of a doctor. His girl is in the family way. Patrick didn't do wrong, though. He didn't take her to the doctor. They're going to be married, Pa. The bans have been posted."

"Nothing wrong, yet? He chust got her pregnant. He chust used you to do his dirty work. Patrick is a bad boy, not good for you. He thinks of nothing but sex and drink. Drink, drink, drink!" Pa's lips tightened into a thin line and he scowled at Edward. "You can no longer be friends mitt him. I do not allow it. Tell him your Papa says you must find another friend."

Edward jumped to his feet in disbelief. The hairs on his neck stood on edge and his throat felt dry. "No, Pa. Patrick's doing the right thing by Inger. He could have run away, or taken her to that dirty doctor, but he didn't. I know he's got some rough edges and all, but he's really good, down deep. He's taught me a lot of things, like sharing and being true to our friendship and not being afraid to be myself. I favor him highly and he favors me."

"From his kind you don't need favor. Vork hard, do vhat I say, and be a man if it's favor you're after. You vill not see this boy again."

Edward swayed, dizzy with the urge to smash something, his emotions raw and confused. But he stood mute before Pa. To defy one's parent was a sin—he had been raised to believe that. Rage and despair waged within him. Which was worse: to defy Pa, or be disloyal to his friend? The bottom of his stomach dropped to his boots as he raised his eyes to Pa. "No! I'll not turn from my friend. I'm old enough now to make my own choices."

A vein throbbed in Pa's forehead and his eyes were like blue ice. "Then you vill make your choices somewhere else. Not in my house. Under my roof, you listen to me—fathers are not to be defied! You must learn a lesson. You vill apprentice with Henry at the tannery and live with his family in Jefferson."

The rejection was like being hit below the waist by your best friend. Edward's belly hurt and he couldn't swallow. Pa had denied him the chance to make the break on his own. Still he was being offered an out. He looked straight into Pa's eyes and stood as tall as he could. Tears threatened, but he looked upward and blinked. His voice, not yet grounded in maturity, changed pitch as he croaked out his answer.

"All right Pa, you want me to be a man. I'll be a man. I'll not spend another day making whiskey and I'll not go back on my friend. I'll live with Henry. But don't forget, it was you turned me away!"

* * *

Before the month was out Edward moved his meager

possessions and began his apprenticeship at the tannery.

He faced the future with grim determination. He was cut off from his father, Patrick was getting married, and his dreams of western adventure were not going to happen. Still he looked eagerly ahead. He was out of the distillery and new and exciting things were happening all around him. If his old dream was dead, well then he'd just have to fashion another one.

Prospects were looking better for Patrick. Mrs. Peterson reacted with typical Pennsylvania Dutch charity when she learned of Inger's condition. Knowing the couple's financial plight, she offered to let them stay on until Inger's indenture was satisfied. A double brass bed was moved into Inger's tiny room under the eaves and with October fading, vows were exchanged in the Peterson parlor.

Surprisingly, Edward found living in Jefferson to be fun. At times he missed home, but things at the farm seemed different now—sadder and uncertain. Ma had accepted his leaving with resignation. Her failing health was now visible to everyone. She was so short of breath she could no longer go the stairs and Pa had placed a cot for her in the kitchen next to the stove. The boys talked among themselves, dividing up her heavy work, and Catharine came every week to do the upstairs cleaning. Edward knew his dispute with his father was an added burden on Ma's heart, but he didn't know what to do about it.

When Grandfather Eyster died Ma fell into a deep depression, realizing that the Eyster homestead in Adams County where she grew up would have to be sold to settle his estate.

Pa too, seemed strangely withdrawn and troubled.

* * *

Jonas was in bed only a short time, having fallen into that first light slumber of the night, when an unexpected noise tugged him awake. Soft sobs broke the stillness of the dark room and he reached tentatively over to touch the warm body of Maria. He realized, with a start, that she was trembling in an effort to still her crying.

"Ei, ei, ei. Vhat's troubling you, dear?" He asked gently, now fully awake.

She rolled over and placed her head on his shoulder, her night cap brushing his cheek. Her body relaxed and the sobs quieted when he drew her close, trying to comfort her with his nearness.

"Oh, Jonas," she said, softly, speaking in German where she always felt more comfortable. "I'm not sure why I feel such despair. I've no reason to be unhappy, but sometimes I feel overwhelmed with homesickness for my home-place. I know it's wrong of me, disloyal to you and the children."

"Maria, Maria," he answered, stroking her fine, grey-streaked hair and leaning over to kiss her beloved face, for he did love her, deeply and fully. "It's no sin to long for the place of your birth. Your childhood was happy, filled with love. I understand that." He spoke tenderly, at ease also in his native tongue.

"But . . . .but . . . I came to this home as your bride and I've given birth to all of our babies here. You've worked hard to make this one of the best farms in the country. I know you've been thinking about buying Papa's place to please me and I feel so disloyal to you and the children to have these childish longings for my old home."

Jonas turned her face towards his and very, very, softly brushed her quivering lips with his. "Thirty years of love and ten wonderful children you've given me and I'm not an easy man to live with. If you've a fancy to buy your Papa's place then maybe God plans for us to move to Adams County and tend his land there."

"I couldn't ask such a thing of you! Your father built his first home here, believing it would remain in the Rebert family for generations. Your roots go deep, Jonas"

"Ja, but maybe one of the boys will want to buy this farm. Three hundred acres I no longer need and a smaller house would be easier for you to care for. With the boys getting married I'll soon be forced to take on more hired help and good help is hard to find. They all want to go west for that free government land."

"You still have five boys at home to help with the work."

"My dear woman, J.J. plans to marry his Rebecca soon, Charles talks of nothing but Eliza, and Henry wants Michael, as well as Edward, to join him at the tannery."

At the mention of Edward, Maria's eyes once more filled with tears. "I worry so about your relationship with Edward. And I do miss him terribly. You're so harsh with him, Jonas. He feels you favor his brothers and have no love for him."

"Don't put an apron on him, Maria," Jonas answered, his voice suddenly harsh. "Of course, I love him, but he needs to learn discipline. That's a father's job—to teach his sons discipline."

"But he's not a disobedient boy. He never liked working in the distillery. He truly thought distilling was against the teachings of the church, yet he obeyed you and worked there when you commanded him to."

"Respect for his father comes first. When he's older he can tell what is right and wrong."

"I know you mean well and I know you love all your children the same. But Edward is different in nature than you. He is so very, very, idealistic. He values his friendship with his friend Patrick to a degree even I don't understand. He doesn't have your strength, Jonas."

Jonas lay quietly, searching for an answer. Finally he took Maria's small, work worn, hand in his own rough palm and squeezed it gently. "A perfect world we don't have, Maria and all my boys must learn that at times things like childhood friendships must be set aside in order to obey more basic laws. I can't promise that I'll ever understand

Edward. From his heart he acts, not his head. Chust watching birds or playing with his dog instead of doing a man's work, although Henry says he is serious and learning the tanning trade well. For your sake, more softness will I show toward him when he comes home, but Maria, I want all my boys to be strong; strong like me. I will not coddle them."

"Thank you, Jonas. That's all I ask. And thank you for being so understanding about my foolish tears tonight. I do pine for my beautiful Adams County. I think I could die happy there. But you must pay no mind to my midnight weeping. Tomorrow when the sun comes up, all will be forgotten and I will be my old self."

"Ei,ei,ei. No more talk of dying," he chided her, looking deep into her blue eyes. "I've thought much about this since your Papa died. There's been love in this house, but grief too. Besides," he added with a chuckle, "I think you secretly agree with this Temperance talk Edward gets so riled up about."

"I never said so!"

"Jonas chuckled. Enough talk for tonight. Dawn comes early. Tomorrow I'll talk with my good friend Reverend Geiger and ask for his guidance."

The next evening Jonas saddled Brandy and rode into Jefferson. He tied up in front of St Emanuels Union Church, a two story wooden structure that served both the Reformed and Lutheran congregation in Jefferson. After several sharp raps the parsonage door was flung open by Reverend Geiger.

"Gute Abend, Reverend."

"Good evening to you, dear friend. Come in, come in."

Reverend Geiger led the way into a small, sparsely furnished, sitting room. The room was completely dominated by a heavy oak roll-top desk, its numerous cubby-holes jammed with bits and pieces of paper. Stacks of papers and books covered its entire surface and on top of everything a cat lay sleeping peacefully. Several large bookcases, reaching to the ceiling and filled to overflowing with more books and periodicals, covered another wall. The room smelled of old paper and tobacco smoke, only slightly relieved by a faint breeze coming through one small window.

Reverend Geiger settled his heavy bulk into a large leather chair in front of his desk and motioned Jonas toward a sturdy rocker. Jonas looked at him with a critical eye. Jacob's new wife was feeding him too well. His round face was full, with fat cheeks and heavy jowls. A thick grey beard covered several double chins and he sat with pudgy hands folded over a belly of considerable girth.

"Do you mind if I smoke?" Jacob asked, pulling a pipe from atop the cluttered desk.

"Nein, I'll join you."

"What brings you to my door on this fine evening, Jonas? It's been many a day since we had an opportunity to sit and talk over a pipe of good tobacco."

Jonas sighed, knocking the bowl of his pipe into the palm of his hand. "Can we speak German? English still comes hard for me."

"Of course," Jacob replied slipping easily into their mother tongue.

"It's your council I need, Jacob. Both as a friend and as a Minister of God. I'm thinking of selling my farm. You know that Maria's father died recently and her home-place over near Hanover in Adams County must be sold. It would give her pleasure to return there."

"This is indeed a surprise, old friend." Jacob leaned forward in his chair and looked at Jonas with concern clouding intelligent eyes. "Your sons are third generation Reberts in Codorus valley; your father was a pioneer settler; you helped build this church. There must be some very compelling reason for you to think of such a thing."

Jonas didn't answer immediately. He drew deeply on the

clay pipe and watched the sweet smelling smoke drift slowly toward the open window. "Ei, many reasons," he said quietly. "First, there is Maria. She has borne me eleven children and the last one came upside down, very hard on Maria, and as you know the baby died. She knew it had to be her last baby and she took his death very hard. When the baby died, he took part of Maria with him. Her laughter used to ring through every room—now the house is like an empty barn."

"You must love her very dearly."

"She is my life," Jonas answered simply.

Jacob stroked his full grey beard thoughtfully. "Then it is your hope that taking her back to her childhood home would be like a tonic for her? Bring back her laughter?"

"Ja, Ja, that's it," Jonas responded eagerly. "She talks with such fondness of the Conewago Valley and worries about her Mama who is now alone. Then too, the Eyster farm has only one hundred fifty acres, easier to care for now that most of my boys are moving to town and going into trade."

"I hear you sold the tannery to Henry."

"Ja, he is good with business. Edward is apprenticing for him and it is good for the boy." He puffed deeply on his pipe. "Truth be, that is another problem. Edward I don't understand, Jacob. He isn't like my other sons. They are serious minded, loyal to our traditions. They don't question a father's authority. Edward is restless; his head is always in the clouds."

Reverend Geiger smiled, knocking the ash of his cold pipe on the palm of his hand. "And a foe of yours when it came to operating the distillery, I believe."

A faint shadow crossed Jonas's face and he replied with tight lips. "That's my other reason for thinking of selling out. Tell me, Jacob, do you believe operating the distillery is such a sin?"

Jacob sat silently, watching Jonas intently while forming

his answer. "This is shaky ground we are traversing, Jonas. We've been friends a long time, but I suspect we hold vastly different views on this very complex subject. I believe that men, because of their inherent sinful nature, have taken what was once an acceptable custom and abused it to the point where it is harmful, both to themselves and society. That abuse, or overindulgence, is surely a sin. But your question is much harder to answer. Making available to the abusers the means to abuse may not be a sin, Jonas, but I do believe it is wrong."

"Some call distilling the second oldest profession," Jonas offered.

Jacob smiled. "I've heard it said that the Mesopotamians were brewing beer over six thousand years before Christ. I admit the scriptures are full of stories about the use of spirits, even telling of Noah making wine after the flood and drinking himself into a delightful stupor. But Jonas, while there is plenty of evidence that wine was on every table in biblical days, man's demand for more potent brews has increased. Now we distill hard whiskey for which many have no tolerance and become addicted. War helped create bad social patterns which the church is uncomfortable with. I have tried to preach a doctrine of temperance, but many preachers are talking total abstinence."

"Trouble all started when Adam and Eve ate those blasted fermented apples," Jonas grumbled.

Jacob laughed heartily, slapping his thigh while his double chins quivered.

Silence settled around them while they relit their pipes and sat smoking.

Jonas pondered what Jacob had just said. Finally he took his pipe from between his teeth and pulled himself forward in his rocker, looking steadily into Jacob's eyes. "I didn't rebuild after the fire. Distilling's made me a rich man, but it isn't as profitable as it once was. The pot stills are old fashioned; I'll convert to the new column stills if I stay in business. But the truth is, I've been half afraid the fire was God's judgment. I must think about what you've said."

"You're a good man, Jonas Rebert. If you'll put all your trust in God, He will give you far better answers than I'm able to. Now enough of this serious talk for awhile. I hear my wife in the kitchen rattling some dishes around. Join us for a piece of shoofly pie and a glass of cold cider. She's a mighty fine cook, as you can well see," he said, with a chuckle, patting his bulging stomach and linking Jonas's arm in his.

Part 2

Jefferson,
York County, Pennsylvania

1840 - 1848

Chapter

-8-

Edward took his heavy woolen jacket from the peg by the back door of the tannery and pulled it on quickly. His wrists extended a good inch from the sleeves. The jacket was a hand-me-down from Henry, but at twenty Edward was a good two inches taller than his brother. He'd have to get his sister-in-law, Elizabeth, to make him a new jacket before winter set in.

He liked living in Jefferson with Henry and his family. Pa had surprised everyone by buying Grandfather Eyster's farm—the old Bear-Garden tract—over near Hanover, in Adams County. J.J., Michael and John moved with Ma and Pa, but Edward stayed on at the tannery. He no longer saw Sally—she had married Amos after all—but there were lots of girls in Jefferson and he was never at a loss for a partner to one of the church socials.

It was only mid-October but already there had been several light frosts and just yesterday the rain barrel had a thin pane of ice. Geese, honking their way south, were low in the sky, telling of a hard winter ahead.

Duke was waiting by the door, tail in happy motion, eyes bright with anticipation of an outing to which he had not yet been invited. Now four years old, he had grown into a magnificent animal, alert, confident and intelligent. A snowy white ruff extended from the back of his head, down his deep chest and forepaws. He had a tan underbelly, white paws, and the distinctive tan collie face tapering to a black nose and tan and black silky ears.

Insofar as it was possible for a dog to convey his devotion, Duke let it be known again and again, that he was a one man dog. Where Edward sat, Duke sat. Where Edward walked, Duke walked. Where Edward rode, Duke trotted beside him. They were inseparable and the best of friends.

"O.K. boy, you can come along," Edward said, rubbing Dukes's heavy chest. "We'll probably be at the blacksmith shop for a good while but I imagine you'll find plenty of friends to run with." Duke licked Edward's hand in gratitude.

They walked into the cold October morning. Henry had already hitched the horse and Edward piled broken tanning tools into a wooded box near the rear of the wagon. He climbed onto the rough seat and Duke leaped up to take his place beside him.

Gently Edward eased the wagon through the narrow lane running behind the tannery and onto Hanover Street. It was about five miles from Jefferson to Spring Forge where George Hoke operated his blacksmith shop. There was a perfectly good smithy right here in Jefferson, but J.J. would be marrying Rebecca soon and the Hokes were like family.

A cold wind pulled at Edward's jacket, reddening his cheeks and ruffling Duke's coat. Patches of white frost still covered the ground and a mist hung above the distant mountains where long, gliding skeins of Canada geese were outlined against the sky. Shocks of dun colored corn stalks, stacked like wigwams, stretched across empty fields.

"I wonder," he mused aloud, "if I'll see little Katie this trip?" Duke looked up and cocked his head to one side, as though listening intently. Edward continued, "Guess I shouldn't call her little, she must be close to fifteen now. Wonder how she feels about her sister leaving the Mennonite church to marry? J.J. says the Bishop at Garber's Mennonite Fellowship gave them his approval. I don't think the Hokes are too strict; the women dress plain, but the girls go to barn dances and socials."

He clucked to his horse and turned onto a heavily rutted farm road, still thinking about the Hokes. People in his church called the Mennonites *sect* people and some thought them peculiar, but he admired them. In fact he was just a little envious of their serenity.

As he understood it, the Mennonites, followers of Menno Simons, emigrated from the mountains of Switzerland to the German Palatinate, and from there to Holland, England and America. They separated from the established church over the practice of baptism, rejecting infant baptism in favor of baptism when they became adults. Other Swiss settlers followed the stricter leadership of Jacob Ammen and became known as Amish. Both sects were called Plain People, but the Amish were much plainer—more severe in their dress—and in their religious views.

We all interpret God's Word a little differently, he thought pensively. I guess as long as God is the Master in our lives that's all that really counts.

It was mid-morning when he reached the Hoke farm and tied his horse behind a small shed, out of the biting wind. Duke bounded out of the wagon with a joyful bark, eagerly racing off to join several farm dogs playing in the barn.

Edward hefted the heavy box of tools to his shoulder and carried it to the blacksmith shop, dumping it on the dirt floor beside a pile of old horseshoes, broken buggy wheels, and iron rims. His gaze swept the crowded shop, missing nothing.

A sooty forge occupied most of the space, its coals glowing warmly as Mr. Hoke's youngest boy pumped air from a large overhead bellows, coaxing the charcoal to life. A horse, being shod, tossed his head and nickered when the hot shoe met his hoof. Several farmers, seated on overturned nail kegs, engaged in a heated discussion about the forthcoming 1840 election. The warm air was pungent with the smell of hot iron and the earthy smell of droppings from the nervous horse. Edward took a deep breath, savoring it all. It was a man's world, masculine, warm, and comfortable.

"Mornin' Mr. Hoke," he said. "Henry sent over a few tools needing repair."

"Guten Morgen, Edward," George Hoke replied, while continuing to pound a hot horseshoe on the iron anvil. Hot sparks from the glowing metal flew into the air and fell on the heavy leather apron reaching from his neck to his boots. He was a large man, not particularly tall, but massive across the shoulders, with heavy, muscular arms. His square, clean shaven face was ruddy from years in front of the hot forge. "I'm shoeing this mare for John Dubbs and then I have a wagon wheel to mend for Asa. Sit a spell and catch up on the news."

"I'm always glad for a chance to talk some," Edward said, sauntering toward the conversing men. "Morning Mr Dubbs . . . Mr Emig . . . Peter."

They grunted and nodded, barely interrupting their stream of talk.

Edward settled himself on a nail keg while the men continued their animated conversation. He'd been looking forward to the political talk he knew would be a part of this visit. Since joining Henry at the tannery three years ago he spent all his spare time reading and studying whatever newspapers he could get his hands on. He did not intend to work for Henry, or any man, the rest of his life. Over the past year he had dedicated himself to improving his knowledge, his manners, his dress, and his speech. If he was going to make something of himself he needed to become more worldly, more aware of public affairs and politics. This was a good place to test his newly acquired knowledge.

Each man seemed to be trying to outdo the other when it came to talking; old Asa's voice thin and quivery, John Dubbs, slow and forceful, Peter's young and impatient, and

George Hokes's' deep and Germanic. When there was a sudden lull, Edward edged himself into the conversation.

"Will you be going to the Whig Convention in Harrisburg next month, Mr. Dubbs?"

Dubbs, a portly, white haired, retired school master, now a county commissioner in York County, assumed his best political posture, his deep sonorous voice carrying to all corners of the shop. "Yes, and I'll be supporting General William Henry Harrison for President. He's the only man certain to be popular enough to trounce that tyrant, Martin Van Buren."

This brought a barrage of comments.

"Van Buren's for the laboring man. Wants a law says a man needn't work more'n ten hours a day."

"Try tellin' that to a cow."

"Hangin's too good for that Dutchman."

"Damn die President, damn die Kanggress."

"He and that damn fool Jackson single-handedly wrecked the Bank of the United States. Do you hear me, the Bank of the U-nited States," Asa said, waving his cane.

"Clay's got the nomination all sewed up, Harrison hasn't a chance," Edward said.

John Dubbs spread his stocky legs and waved a finger. "Clay doesn't have a chance. Harrison's a war hero, an Indian fighter; he won the Battle of Tippecanoe, Americans like war heroes."

"Ei, but how's he feel about owning slaves? Now that's a question everyone oughta be askin'," Asa shouted.

"He's from Virginny, aint he?" young Peter asked.

Asa crossed knobby hands on his cane and stomped it on the floor. "I hear he's a farmer, just like us. Not one of those fatass Washington politicians."

"Sure came a long way just by killing Indians."

"Ei,ei,ei, but that's the only good thing he done."

"Killed old Chief Tecumseh. Downright murder it were," Asa said.

"How can killing in a battle be called murder?" Edward asked, looking at him in surprise.

Asa clutched his cane with knobby hands and splashed the floor with tobacco juice. "No man's ever the same after he's done a killin', battle or no. I was at Saratoga, during the Revolution. Maybe you boys heard of that battle; over in New York State, it was. One of the biggest battles of the war. Well, there I was, young and scared. There'd been gunfire all day and nothing but confusion. Folks were running back and forth and nobody seemed to know where the enemy was. Only way you could tell one from another was the color of their coats, blue for us and red for them. Shooting and smoke all over the place. Confusing as all get out it was.

Comin' on towards dusk, I set myself down in a clearing close by a tree. I was just sittin' there when I heard somebody running through the woods. I took up my musket and cocked the hammer. It was loaded, I hadn't ever fired it.

A boy came out of the woods, running. He stopped when he saw me an' he wasn't more than a stones throw away. A little fellow, didn't look more'n fifteen,, with a red coat, covered with dust. But it was red, all right. I put the musket to my shoulder and fired.

He was close and I heard the ball hit. He went down in a heap.

I grabbed my musket and went over to him. I was young too, remember, and this was the first Redcoat I'd ever seen, close up. Thing is, he wasn't dead. His head was throwed back and his shirt pulled open in front. He had a face like a baby's, with cheeks too young to sport more than a little peach fuzz, an' jet black hair. He kept looking at me, not mad, just surprised that this had happened to him. He tried to talk and I pulled my canteen out and poured some water on his lips but he couldn't swallow. And then he died.

It wasn't like I thought war would be. This wasn't like killing in battle. It was just the two of us. It was murder, plain and simple.

I was sick then—puked my guts out. An' I never forgot him. When you do a killing you never forget."

Asa stopped talking and the room was quiet, each man pondering his words. Edward's eyes stung with repressed tears.

Peter Stambaugh bravely broke the heavy silence. "Well, Van Buren has kept us out of war, that's one good thing. He settled that terrible squabble between Maine and Great Britain and reached an understanding with Mexico over the Texas boundaries without a shot being fired."

"You may have to reckon with the south, someday," Dubbs said .

Edward stroked his chin, organizing his thoughts. He wanted to sound knowledgeable and well spoken, especially in front of Councilman Dubbs. Finally he spoke. "Tension between the North and South does worry me. There's so much hatred on both sides, real bitterness. We all share the same language, the same history, the same Constitution, yet one would think we were two separate countries."

"Yes, my boy, the same Constitution. The Constitution that says all men are created equal. Slavery is in defiance of the very law of the land." Dubbs face had turned a fiery red. "For that reason I believe Harrison is the only Whig candidate that can win. The Abolitionists will never support Clay; he's too middle of the road. Like it or not, this country, and the party are divided. Very divided."

Edward got up and brushed straw from his trousers. Time to leave. Tempers always flared when men discussed issues of slavery or states rights. He wasn't ready, yet, to debate those complex issues.

He stepped outside and looked around, the crisp air welcome after the warm, smoky interior of the blacksmith shop. To the west of the Hoke farm smoky-blue haze lay softly on the Pigeon Hills. The forest burned with the colors of fall—maples, a rich honey gold or scarlet; oaks, wine-red;

and hemlocks and junipers, black-green.

Edward started toward the Hoke farmhouse, wondering if Katie would be there, smiling as he considered it. What was it about this child that intrigued him so?

Morning frost still coated muddy places along the path, but he walked cautiously, careful not to stain his trousers. The Hoke homestead, built of pale grey Pennsylvania fieldstone, was an enlargement of the original log cabin built by Kasper Hoke, Katie's grandfather, in the early 1700's. Edward chuckled. George Hoke certainly needed more than a log cabin to house his brood of eleven children.

Edward entered the house by way of the kitchen door, his nose at once assaulted by the yeasty smell of baking bread. The kitchen was humming with activity. A large wooden table squeaked in protest as Mrs. Hoke vigorously kneaded heavy dough while Rebecca and Magdalena filled heavy baking trays with molasses cookies which Katie was brushing with egg yolk.

Mrs. Hoke looked up from the pastry she was rolling and smiled sweetly at him while tossing a handful of flour on the mound of sticky dough. "What a nice surprise, already What brings you to our door, Edward?"

"I brought some tools to the forge. Thought I'd drop by and say hello to you and the girls while I wait for your Mister to fix them."

"I'm always glad to see one of the Reberts. Mercy, Edward, I do think you've grown several inches since I saw you last."

"I'm a full five feet, ten inches when I stand good and straight."

"Ei, and I see you're growing a fine beard."

"Henry encouraged me. Says it makes me look more manly for work in the tannery." Edward self-consciously stroked the close-cropped tawny beard covering the deep cleft in his chin.

He didn't know if it made him more of a man but it

certainly made an easier job for his straight razor.

"My, those buns do smell good," he said, sniffing the air.

"Did your nose lead you to my kitchen, already?"

"That and my hungry belly."

Mrs. Hoke laughed, her double chin shaking. She was famous for her potato buns, her rotund figure evidence of her skills. Barely five feet tall, she had an open placid face, with rosy cheeks and clear grey eyes. Her brown hair was pulled back in a tight bun and she wore a small, round, white net cap on the back of her head. A dark blue dress brushed the tops of her high black shoes. The plain cut of her dress bespoke the Mennonite faith. It was the shawl-styled cape worn by most older Mennonite women, made with an extra piece of cloth over the shoulder, fastened at the waistline, but open at the sides. The cape was intended to conceal the chest, but Mrs. Hoke's ample bosom defied disguise.

She continued kneading the dough, smiling at Edward warmly. "We stand on York Market tomorrow and the girls are making soft molasses cookies to sell in addition to my potato buns. You came at a good time, already. A batch of cookies is just about to come from the oven."

Edward grinned in delight. The kitchen, scrubbed until it shone, was cozy and inviting, warm with smells of yeast and flour that set his stomach growling. The three girls giggled, pretending not to notice him. Dark haired, Magdalena, was the oldest and showed signs of following in her mother's robust footsteps. Rebecca was just the opposite, slender as a reed, with thick blond hair, tightly braided and wrapped around her head. And then there was Katie, blushing furiously as her sisters nudged and whispered to her.

Edward looked in amusement at a flustered Katie. She's certainly not a child anymore, he thought, feeling a queer lump in his throat. Not beautiful, but very, very, appealing. A smattering of freckles still dusted a cute upturned nose, smudged with flour, and her auburn hair, pulled back from an impish face, was secured with a snippet of yarn. A few tendrils of fly-a-way hair escaped their fastening and she reached up to brush them back, smudging her face with more flour.

Katie took a tray from the oven and, ignoring her sisters, came toward him carrying the warm cookies. "Did you bring Duke along? I heard the dogs barking a while back and thought they must be greeting a friend," she said, offering him the tray.

"Ei, and he was happy to run with them. If you don't mind I'll take an extra cookie along for him. He'll be disappointed if he smells molasses on me and I don't have a treat for him." Edward stuffed a cookie into the pocket of his jacket.

"Take a good handful for yourself." She motioned to a nearby chair, adding, "why don't you take your jacket off and sit for a spell. Some of Mama's buns will be out of the oven soon and you can have a sample of them too."

"That sounds mighty inviting," he said, suddenly eager to spend more time talking to her. He settled himself on the chair, searching for something to say to keep Katie beside him.

"Do you stand market, tomorrow, with your Mamma and sisters?"

"Oh, yes. I always go. I love market days—they're ever so much fun. We have a new stall this year. It's next to the funnel cake man and he attracts lots of people. You must come with us some Friday."

"Would you put him behind a counter, then, selling potato buns?" Rebecca called gaily from across the kitchen.

"I'd probably eat more then I'd sell," Edward said, with a chuckle. He sobered, remembering the few times he'd been to market. "I've helped Pa take corn to market, but he was never one to linger and visit the stalls."

Katie rushed on with enthusiasm. "They have everything

you can imagine for sale. Jams and jellies, plump chickens and smoked sausage, cheeses of all kinds, cakes and pies, pretzels and homemade potato chips. And everyone is in such a happy mood. Oh, Edward, you'd laugh at the women with their fancy hairdos and rouged lips, hanging on to children begging for a sugar cookie while they argue with the butcher for the meatiest ham hock or the leanest cut of meat."

She paused to draw breath and Edward laughed at the picture she painted. "It does sound like fun. I'd like to go with you sometime—especially since you're next to the funnel cake man."

He couldn't take his eyes off Katie's animated face as she continued her tale of market. Despite himself he felt his eyes move down her young body where young breasts pushed against the fabric of her dress. He flushed, looking quickly away. She's too young, he reminded himself, and I shouldn't be looking at her that way.

Mrs. Hoke approached with a plate of warm buns. "Pull your chair up to the table, son. The buns are best hot and spread with molasses. And you, young lady, had best get back to helping your sisters."

Glad for the interruption, Edward seated himself at the big oak table covered with flowered oilcloth and looked around the bustling kitchen. Deep windows held tins of rising bread covered with linen cloths. Edward ate slowly, gazing through the window to the yard beyond, where ducks were following one another around the barn, single file, as ducks do. He swung his gaze back to the work tables, covered with flour, where Rebecca still cut rounds of cookie dough with a glass jar. He could feel the warmth and love in the room, clearly the heart of this happy home. Contentedly he finished off several buns and a few more of the cookies with a mug of cold, sweet, milk Katie placed before him.

Rebecca wiped her hands on her apron and directed a smile at him. "J.J. is coming to the corn husking over at the

Myers farm on Saturday," she said. "We'll all be there. Why don't you come along, Edward?"

Katie peeked at him from beneath lowered lashes. "Maybe you'll be lucky and find the red ear," she said blushing prettily. "Then you can kiss your favorite girl."

With a start he realized Katie was flirting with him. Her brown eyes had turned almost black and for a moment they held his before she dropped them in confusion. A spark flared in him, immediate and intense.

There was no doubt in his mind what he would be doing Saturday evening. And he'd make sure he had an ear of red corn tucked away in his pocket.

He rose and recovered his jacket from the back of the chair. "Thanks for the buns, Mrs. Hoke. I'd better get back down to the forge and see if my tools are ready." He looked at Katie, who was watching him intently. "And I'll see you Saturday evening," he said softly.

After Edward left the kitchen Katie resumed her work, stirring the stiff batter needed for the crumb cakes they would make next. She was unusually quiet, her face serious and thoughtful .

Rebecca watched her for several moments before speaking. "Why so solemn, Katie?"

"Oh, Rebecca, I'm not yet fifteen. He's so handsome, he'll be married long before he notices that I'm a girl."

"Unless I'm mistaken, little one, he noticed today that you are very much a girl. I saw that look in his bright blue eyes when he looked at you."

Katie blushed furiously at the knowing look in Rebecca's eyes and began stirring the batter with such vigor the bowl fairly bounced on the old wooden table.

An hour later, after securing the wooden box with the newly repaired tools in the back of his wagon, Edward gave a sharp whistle for Duke. The dog came bounding toward him, his strong muscled frame seeming to float above the ground. With tongue lolling and eyes shining, he leaped up to the wagon seat and collapsed with a deep sigh.

They started back to Jefferson and Duke stretched out on the seat, resting his head wearily on Edward's knee.

"Well, you look like you had a busy day, my friend. Did you find yourself a girlfriend?" he asked, gently stroking the silken ears. Duke whined and closed his eyes in sublime contentment, his tail beating a heavy thump, thump, thump, on the wooden seat.

"Humm, I take that as a yes." Then, thinking of the vibrant, laughing Katie Hoke, Edward mumbled softly, "Well, she's a little young yet, and she is Mennonite, but maybe, just maybe, I found me a girl too!"

Chapter
-9-

Edward thumbed through the almanac, until he came to October 18, 1840. There would be a full moon tonight and hopefully, Katie would be allowed to ride home from the husking with him. "Ja, Gute," he mumbled, smiling at his use of Pa's favorite expression. Would he never lose his "dutchiness?"

He placed the dog-eared almanac back on the shelf and left the tannery by a side door. He couldn't remember a more glorious fall afternoon. The air had a winelike crispness and he felt almost drunk with its sweetness striding along tree-lined Hanover Street toward Henry's house, where he had a small room beneath the eves of the garret. Lemon and gold maple leaves had been raked into a neat pile beside the road and playfully he aimed his foot at the center and kicked, scattering them in all directions. Duke ran beside him, delighting in this mischief, eager to join in the fun.

Edward whistled a few bars of Turkey In The Straw' as he strolled along. He felt quite pleased with himself, he'd struck a hard deal for the rent of a fine rig from Thoman's Livery. And he had a new black suit, with a matching vest, hanging in his room. Not homemade this time, but fashioned by Henry Deagen, the tailor. Now if he could just cajole Elizabeth into letting him take his Saturday bath in her kitchen, earlier than usual, everything would work out fine.

He stopped to admire a new house under construction, a fine brick being built for the Hahns. Jefferson had over twenty houses now, two churches and a school. Duke, racing ahead, barked impatiently and Edward grinned broadly. "Wait up, now," he called. "I want to gather a few of these shellbark hickory nuts for Elizabeth." He hunted among ocher leaves for nuts spilled from the tall hickory and jammed a handful into his pocket. They would please Elizabeth.

An hour later he sat partially submerged in hot water in the large wooden laundry tub. Elizabeth had given him a cake of her special lye soap, lightly scented with rose-water, which she made only for bathing. She used only clean, sweet smelling grease, no rancid lard, and a minimum of lye. Vigorously he rubbed the cake across his hairy chest. He splashed hot water onto his shoulders with cupped hands, feeling his muscles relax as the water slowly slid down his back.

"Umn, that feels good," he murmured, sliding the slippery soap across his flat belly and onto his thighs. His long legs were bent almost double in the small tub and gingerly he extended one leg into the air, working the soapy lather down as far as he could reach.

He washed his hair in the rapidly cooling water, then reached for a huck towel, drawing its fresh abrasiveness across his skin. Clean linens, carefully folded, were piled on a chair next to the tub and he dressed quickly. He pulled on the trim black trousers and tucked in a shirt of bleached linen, starched so stiff he was afraid he would crackle when he moved. Finally, he snapped new suspenders into place, pulled on the black boots he had spent hours rubbing to a fine luster with bear grease, and snugged a jacket over his shoulders.

He strolled over to a small mirror Elizabeth kept hanging on the back of the kitchen door and examined himself. The suit was admirably tailored and he ran his hands slowly over the rich material. He did look fine. He gave himself a final admiring glance and with an airy confidence called Elizabeth back into the kitchen.

Elizabeth hurried in, carrying Michael in her arms, and stopped, looking at him intently, admiration plain on her face. "Why Edward, you look downright handsome. You'll have all the girls in a dither when they see you in that new black suit. It looks fine with your fair hair and makes your eyes blue as sapphires. Katie should be properly smitten when she sees you."

Edward flushed with pride and unconsciously pushed out his chest and fingered his beard. "I best. . .better. . . be going," he said. Jauntily he strode to the back door. "It's quite a ways to the Myers' farm and if Katie is allowed to ride home with me it'll be quite late when I get back tonight, long after you're in bed, I imagine. I'll take the horse and buggy back first thing in the morning so don't wait breakfast for me."

"Have a good time, Edward, and give Katie our love."

Bright bands of crimson and grey streaked the twilight sky as Edward turned the frisky horse into the Myers' farm lane. The barnyard was already full of buggies so he pulled around back and tied up next to the wagon shed. A corn husking was usually the first big social get-together after a busy summer and everyone looked forward to it. The large bank barn would be filled with neighbors from all over the valley. He adjusted his broad brimmed black hat and hurried in.

At least seven hundred bushels of unhusked corn had been dumped in the center of the threshing floor and the noisy group of corn huskers were seated on rough benches encircling the huge pile of corn. He spotted Katie, standing along the wall beside J.J. and Rebecca, watching the door with eager eyes.

He stood there staring. He saw a slender young girl of medium height—no longer child, not yet woman—with luminous dark eyes and gleaming auburn hair parted cleanly in the middle and drawn in soft waves back from her face into a neat bun. Katie was lovely in a dove grey dress with a slightly flared skirt and a snug fitting bodice that more than hinted at her small round breasts. Black stockings and a pair of high-topped black shoes peeped from beneath the skirt she kept patting nervously.

He swallowed a lump in his throat and walked toward her. He wondered if she had any idea of the effect she had on him.

"Hello, Katie. You look awfully pretty tonight." Certainly an inadequate greeting, but it was all he was capable of at the moment. He felt more like a schoolboy then a grown-up twenty year old.

"Thank you," she said, blushing at the intensity of the blue eyes staring at her.

Rebecca laughed, watching their flushed faces. "J.J. and I will join the Brodbecks. Why don't you two sit over there with your young friends?"

Edward led Katie to a bench, where she sat down demurely, folding her small hands in her lap, watching him from lowered eyes. But Katie Hoke couldn't stay serious for long and soon her shyness fled and she joined the huskers, laughing gaily, eagerly pulling dried husks from the corn and throwing the golden ears across her shoulders into the bins behind them.

Edward fingered the rough ear of corn resting in his pocket, the red ear that would earn him a kiss. During the long, fun filled, evening there wasn't a moment when he wasn't aware of Katie's presence beside him.

Midway through the evening a break was called and everyone crowded around a long table, filled with sandwiches made from the meat of one of Mr. Myers' fattened lambs, ginger cookies, cakes, and coffee. Everyone scrambled to find a seat on one of the long planks resting on wooden crates along the wall. It was crowded and when

Edward settled into place beside Katie he found his right thigh pressing against the softness of her left leg.

Edward closed his eyes. Was she as aware of him as he was of her?

He raised his arm to take a bite of cake and felt his elbow brush her breast. He had an immediate reaction. He was afraid to look at her, afraid to move. He would humiliate both of them if he couldn't get control of himself.

Katie had fallen silent and he turned slightly to glance at her. Her eyes were on her plate, the dark lashes thick and curling. Her fingers toyed with her fork.

"You're not eating," he chided her gently.

She looked at him and smiled. Her soft brown eyes revealed a warmth and tenderness that stunned him.

"I'm not very hungry. Besides, this Angel Food isn't near as good as Mama makes."

A vision of the rotund Mrs. Hoke flashed through his mind and he chuckled. "I'm afraid if I spent much time around your Mamma's cooking I'd be round as a barrel. I'm surprised you stay so slim," he said, his eyes sweeping her slender body.

Katie's face turned a rosy pink and she dropped her gaze. "Here, take my cake. Mama says growing boys need lots of sugar to make them strong. But then, I guess you think yourself a man now, not a boy."

And he hoped he could show her how much of a man he was before this evening was over. He reminded himself to take it slow. Katie was still an innocent child, a Mennonite child, barely fifteen.

Patrick would tell him he was crazy to fall for her.

Before he could answer her last remark Katie reached for his hand and started to rise. "Come, everyone is going back to the husking circle." She laughed gaily, her brown eyes twinkling. "Maybe some lucky boy will come up with a kissing ear."

They resumed husking and he placed his hand on the red

ear still hidden in his pocket. He felt a tingle of excitement. This was not going to be a quick peck on the lips. Katie was going to know she had been kissed.

When no one was looking in his direction he withdrew the ear of corn and waved it in the air.

"Look what I found."

"Bet we know the lucky girl," someone shouted.

Katie's face was scarlet and she kept her eyes on the floor.

Edward took her arm and raised her to her feet. Amid hoots and hollers he led her to the back of the barn where deep shadows hid them from view.

Gently he placed his hand on her chin and raised her face to his. He had thought of nothing but this moment since seeing Katie from the doorway. He lowered his lips to hers, brushing her mouth lightly, soft as a whisper in the night. He pulled back, looking deep into her eyes. She smiled slowly. Her lips, softly pink and full, were parted and this time he gathered her into his arms, kissing her deeply and fully.

For a delicious moment he felt the whole length of her body against his as she moved close in his embrace, returning his kiss, not with a child's shy response, but a woman's ardent promise.

"Geb acht! Sell is genunk," a German farmer shouted, breaking the spell.

Maybe he thinks that is enough, Edward thought, but I plan on more of this before the evening is over.

"I'll take you home after the dance?"

"Yes," she whispered.

Edward led Katie back to the circle of jeering friends and the rest of the evening passed in a blur.

Katie's thoughts were in a wild turmoil. Her response to Edward had been immediate and natural. It never occurred to her not to answer him, not to give herself to the embrace she had so long ached for.

But she well understood the problems ahead. She was Mennonite; Edward was German Reformed. Religious differences had destroyed many a love, many nations and people for that matter. And her faith was her; she was her faith.

It didn't take much to convince J.J. and Rebecca to let her ride home in Edward's carriage. She guessed that they, too, welcomed the chance to be alone.

Edward followed J.J.'s carriage at a circumspect distance, the stillness of the night broken by the soothing clip-clop of horses hooves and the jingle of harness bells. The night air was sharp and caught at Katie's throat. Edward tucked a lap robe over both of them, ensuring that she would be snuggled beside him. The horse trotted slowly along the dirt road, the countryside bathed in light from a hunter's moon of pumpkin yellow. With his left hand casually holding the reins he folded her tiny hand into his right palm and she felt at once the exquisite thrill of flesh touching flesh.

He stroked her fingers with his thumb. "Your hands are so soft and fragile, like Duke's velvety ears when he was a puppy."

"And yours are strong and comforting," she said snuggling a little closer under the warm robe.

They fell into easy conversation. "Do you think J.J. and Rebecca will marry soon?" he asked.

"I believe they will. Becky talks of nothing else. She says the only thing holding them back is J.J.'s uncertainty about staying on the farm with your father. J.J. would like his own place, but Becky says that will take years and she doesn't want to wait."

"Religion isn't a problem, then?"

"Becky says she will marry in your church and Papa has given his blessing. There really isn't that much difference in our beliefs, you know."

Edward was silent and she felt a twinge of uneasiness.

He cleared his throat and turned to look at her. "I can think of a lot of differences, especially the Mennonite refusal to fight for their country. I've often thought about heading west and becoming a soldier. A wife of mine would have to accept that."

She moved away, distressed by the anger stirring within her. "It's Becky and J.J. we are talking about and they have resolved their differences. It has nothing to do with your ambitions."

Katie watched him tug at the lap robe. He gave a nervous laugh. "I admit I know very little about you or your faith, Katie. For one thing I've never understood why the older Mennonites dress differently than the rest of us."

Surprised and dismayed by the question, she said, "After we marry and join the church, many elect to dress plain."

"I guessed as much," Edward said with a wry laugh. "What I don't understand is why they must be so plain and drab."

She looked at his handsome face in the soft moonlight, a deep frown deepening the loveable cleft in his chin, and tried to still the pain rising inside her. Why did he ask questions like that? Questions that only exposed the differences between them. How could she form an answer that didn't sound pompous? "When we were little Papa explained it this way, and it's always given me comfort. Papa said God created all things. He gave birds and butterflies all the glorious colors of the rainbow, He made the sky many shades of blue, tinged the grass green and splashed flowers with bright color. Berries go from green to ripe red, and leaves go from yellow-green in the spring to summer dark-green, and then in the fall into a display of unbelievable color. But only man was created in God's own image. It's unnecessary for man to seek to beautify himself, his beauty lies within. Only for things of the earth does beauty lie without."

Edward sighed deeply and squeezed her hand in understanding. "You are beautiful, you know, when you talk of such. Your face shows such joy and inner peace. I envy that. You seem to have a very close relationship with your Papa."

"He's the center of my world," she said, simply. "A closeness with my Pa is one part of life's experience I've missed."

"How so?"

"Pa wields absolute rule over our house and family. He believes he should set the course for each of us to follow and that his choice is the only right one. My brothers don't seem to mind, but I do. I want to please Pa, but I know I can never live up to his expectations."

Katie felt his despair as though it were a pulsing presence in the carriage with her. Did she have the strength of faith to help him carry his burdens? She squeezed his hand. "Have you told your father how you feel?"

"Only in anger and for that I'm sorry. I want desperately to feel his arm on my shoulder and hear him say he understands. I want to tell him I know he is only trying to help me, that I love him for caring. But he doesn't invite displays of affection, Katie."

"He's wrong, though, in trying to mold you in his image. Earthly man hasn't the right to do that." Katie watched him closely. "I'm sure it's the love he has for you that makes him act as he does."

"German people seem cold, at times, severe. Mennonites have no trouble showing affection, yet you're German too."

"I think it's more a matter of our beliefs. We're really a very simple people, our goal in life is simplicity and love. We believe strongly about expressing our love for one-another."

Edward smiled ruefully. "I've worked hard for Pa's approval, always competing against my brothers for his good opinion and craving his attention. Pa is awfully stingy with his praise."

"Don't you crave his love as well?"

"Sure, and I guess maybe he does have regard for me. He just doesn't ever show feeling. I've never seen him hold my mother, or kiss her for that matter."

"Doesn't she show her love for you?"

"Yes, but she knows Pa doesn't want her to be soft with us boys. He wants us to be strong and independent, like him." He grinned wryly. "When I marry and have children I want to be a different kind of father. I want to hold my sons in my arms and let them know they're loved. A person needs to feel love." Edward chuckled. "Now, how in the world did we get on such a serious subject? I sound like a preacher."

She laughed and they rode on in friendly silence. Edward began talking again, telling her of his dream to someday have a large farm and raise trotting horses. He told her of his efforts to learn good English and rid himself of all traces of the hated Pennsylvania Dutch dialect. She felt her admiration for him growing.

He turned to look at her. "I don't want to be backwards, tied always to the Old Country way of doing things. Why, Katie, every day Americans invent something folks never even thought of before." He chuckled. "New opportunities are flying by my head so fast I just want to holler "Whoa" and reach out and grab one for myself."

Edward's boyish laugh touched her in some innate part of her being. When his gaze moved over her, she felt a rush of warmth. She drew away, suddenly needing to feel some space between them.

Far too soon they approached the Hoke farm and Edward guided the buggy up the lane toward the barn. J.J.'s carriage was already there, parked in the shadows of the tool shed.

"Whoa there," Edward called softly gentling the large black to a halt. He turned to Katie. "St. Emanuel's is having a box social next Saturday. Would you go with me?," he

asked shyly, his face shimmering in the moon-glow."
"I'll have to ask Poppa, but I think it will be all right."
Far away a dog barked and in the barn a cow lowed. The
great handle of the Big Dipper had swung away up in the
northern sky and frosty stars seemed to have come down till
they were almost touching her. Muted night sounds of bull
frogs and cicadas enfolded them and Edward moved to tuck
the rug tightly around her.
"Chilly?" he asked.
Katie shook her head. A curl escaped from her cap and
fell across her forehead .
She knew he was going to kiss her.
He leaned toward her and their lips touched, gently and
searchingly. The kiss was soft at first, but when she felt the
passionate tenderness of his lips and his arms she knew deep
in her subconscious that it was right.
He released her suddenly, squirming in his seat, dropping
his hat onto his lap.
The horse nickered softly, pawing the ground, and deep
in the woods an owl hooted. With a self-conscious laugh
Edward pulled her close and began stroking her hair.
She reached up and drew her finger over the cleft in his
chin, smiling into the blue eyes she was falling in love with.
They sat quietly, the farm pale in the light of the moon.
"You must think me awfully forward, to kiss you so,"
she said, a slight tremble in her voice.
"You forward . . . never, Katie. I'm the one who is being
forward, giving you more than a hasty peck on the lips. I
can't seem to get enough of you."
"Nor I, you."
With a groan he crushed her to his chest, and kissed her
again.
"I guess you know how I feel about you," Edward
whispered in a husky voice. "I think I've loved you since
that night I talked to you at the Peterson barn dance."
"And I always remember that you were afraid to dance

with me," she said, with a merry giggle. You were so grown up and handsome. Oh, Edward, why do I have to be so young. Every time someone mentions your name I'm afraid they will tell me you're getting married."

"It'll be several years yet before I have the where-with-all to even think of getting married. And by that time, Katie Hoke, you just might have grown a little more."

The moon reappeared from behind a dark cloud and Edward waved his hat high. "Mr. Moon, meet my new girl, Katie Hoke," he called, softly. Katie giggled and he gathered her in his arms once more and kissed her tenderly.

Katie finally pulled away and sank back against the seat. His blue eyes seemed to embrace her. "I do care for you Edward. Too much."

"Enough to think of marrying me some day?"

"But you're of the World's people, Edward, and I'm a member of meeting. I can't marry out of the meeting."

"J.J. and Rebecca are solving that problem."

"Rebecca has never been close to the church, like I have. Maybe, if. . ."

Katie jumped as the kitchen door was flung open and flickering lamplight illuminated her father standing on the front porch.

"Catharine . . . Rebecca, is that you? Get in this house at once," he bellowed.

With a quick "good-night", she jumped to the ground and ran lightly up the path to the house.

Chapter

-10-

Katie, scattering corn for the flock of squawking chickens, shivered in the frigid morning air. The noisy cackle of hens and roosters blended with the sounds of other early morning chores. From the forge came the ring of Poppa's anvil and from behind the barn the thunck of George's axe as he worked to replenish the woodpile.

She quickly threw the remaining grain to the ducks and hurried down the worn path that led from the barn to the blacksmith shop. If she hurried she could talk to Poppa before the shop filled with customers.

Poppa was fashioning a hot horseshoe on the anvil and flashed her a look of surprise when he saw her approach.

"What do you want, child?"

Katie tried to keep the excitement from her voice. "Edward Rebert has asked me to the box social at St. Emanuel's on Saturday."

Poppa frowned and moved to the bellows over the forge. He gave it a few sharp pumps and held the horseshoe over the glowing embers before he turned to answer her. "I don't think it's a good idea, dear"

Katie felt her mouth drop open and her eyes widened in disbelief. "But Poppa, it's a church social."

"A social at the Reformed church, not our meeting house. And with a boy not of your faith and five years older than you. And a boy who defied his father for a friend who is getting quite a reputation for his drinking escapades."

"But you've known Edward all his life."

"That doesn't make him an acceptable suitor for my daughter." Katie blinked her eyes, aware of threatening tears, completely surprised by Poppa's unexpected refusal. "You allow Rebecca to keep company with J.J. I don't . . . I don't understand the difference."

Poppa laid the horseshoe aside and led her by the elbow to a nearby bench where he pulled her down beside him. She turned to look at him and watched his stern face soften with sympathy. "Katie you are different than your sister. Rebecca is more worldly . . . always has been . . . and I'm not surprised by her willingness to marry outside our faith. I've given her my blessing because for Rebecca it is right. I do not think it would be right for you. Your faith is too much a part of you. I have seen it since you were a tiny child. The plain life is right for you. Marriage to a Mennonite farmer and . . . ."

"Poppa, I'm not asking permission to marry Edward. Only to go to a social with him," she cried in exasperation.

"One leads to the other. You are looking at heartache, my child."

Katie lowered her gaze to the floor and bit her trembling lip. Only moments ago she had been so happy, so sure of Poppa's approval. It would do no good to argue. Besides, children did not argue with a parent's authority and she had already said more than she should have.

Poppa reached over and squeezed her shoulders. "You are still a child and it is my duty to direct your life in the direction I feel best for you. Trust me. Promise you will wait until you are sixteen before you make such a choice."

"Yes, Poppa."

"Then for today the answer must be no. Now run up to the house and help your mother." He jumped to his feet and patted her head before striding back to the glowing forge.

Katie could hide her emotions no longer. She ran out the door tears streaming down her cheeks.

For weeks she moped about the house and for once her sisters, apparently sensing her misery, did not tease her. Deep in her heart she knew Poppa was right. Unbidden memories of her conversation with Edward came back to taunt her. The way he stuck his chest out when he confided his thoughts of soldiering in the West, his loyalty to Patrick who he laughingly called a reluctant bridegroom, and his seeming contentment to live in town instead of on the farm she had always dreamed of.

But his image haunted her. What her mind told her, her heart rejected. No girl could fail to notice how handsome he was, with his lean hips and his shoulders that were disproportionately broad. She remembered seeing him once with his shirt sleeves rolled to the elbows, baring muscular brown forearms and strong capable hands. Surely any girl would jump at the chance to marry him.

* * *

The December Sunday dawned clear and cold, with a light fall of snow covering the ground. After a hearty breakfast of scrapple and fried potatoes the Hoke family piled into the carriage for the brief ride to Garber's Meeting House.

The service was simple, a message about strength. "Don't trust in your own strength," the bishop counseled. "None of us is strong in him or herself. It's the Lord who upholds us." It was as plain as that.

After dinner, when the dishes were washed and put away, the family members drifted off to their own pursuits. Mamma's hands were busy with her knitting needles and Poppa napped in his rocker by the fire.

Katie felt the need for a walk in the cold outdoors so she slipped into her warmest cloak, pulled on a black bonnet, and set off for the back woodlot. She passed hemlock, spruce and cedar, powdered in white, etched against the bleak grey sky. Her boots crunched in the snow and frozen leaves and she bent her head in the brisk wind, lost in thought.

Suddenly she heard the sound of a thudding hoofbeat and stopped to stare at the approaching horse and rider. It was Edward! Her beloved Edward—wearing a black lambs wool jacket, his blond head bared, the familiar crease in his chin deepened by a smile.

"If I want to talk to you, I guess I must hunt you down," he said pulling the horse to a stop. "I come this way every chance I get, but this is the first time I've seen you."

"I don't usually walk alone," she stammered.

"Then this is my lucky day."

Katie's heart thumped and her throat was so dry she could hardly speak. I won't let myself feel this way! she thought frantically. I won't let my heart pound and make me half sick. She looked bleakly at him. "We can't see each other, Edward. You know Poppa has forbidden it."

He slid from his horse and tossed the reins over a nearby sapling. "Katie, I had to see you. I can't get you off my mind. I think of you all day and dream of you all night. You're the only girl I want."

Katie's heart began to hammer, her eyes moistened, and she lifted her gaze to his and then quickly away. Her chin began to quiver and she shivered as she fought to control herself.

"You're cold," he said softly. "Let me hold you . . . just for a minute, Leibchen." He pulled her into his arms. "Oh, Katie, dearest. I can't help myself. I love you."

Despite her resolve she felt her knees grow weak and she lowered her head to his chest, crushing the brim of her bonnet against the rough fabric of his jacket.

As his arms tightened around her she jerked herself from his embrace. "No! Don't say that to me. We're different, don't you see?"

"You're the one who said there isn't that much difference

in our beliefs. Don't you remember that night in the carriage?"

Remember? She had thought of little else since that night. "I'm sorry, Edward. I promised Poppa I'd wait 'till I was sixteen to make a decision. He knows how important my faith is to me."

Edward looked at the ground, his eyes dark with pain. He looked uncertain and oddly vulnerable. "I love you enough to wait." His lips pulled into a smile. "I think I've been waiting since I watched you at that long ago tent revival, when you interrupted your prayer to swat a pesky fly."

Katie bowed her head. Hope, and faith, that her Christ would show them the way to bridge their differences swept over her and a sob caught in her throat. Edward reached out and brushed his thumb along her cheek then lowered his lips to hers in a kiss as light as a butterfly.

With a little whimper she moved into his embrace and surrendered herself to the moment. She felt the beat of his heart as it thudded against her chest, felt the hard muscles of the arms encircling her, drew into herself the strong male scent of him. She thought she would drown in the emotions that flooded her as his lips laid claim to hers.

She drew back and looked into his eyes, more deeply blue than she remembered, and full of love.

"I'll be sixteen next summer, free of my promise to Poppa and better able to make my own decisions," she said with a small smile.

He placed his hand on her shoulder and returned her smile. "I'll be waiting, little one. There's no mountain we can't climb if we take it one step at a time." He leaned over and kissed the tip of her nose then turned and walked over to his horse.

"I'll keep in touch, Katie." He swung into the saddle, then wheeled around and rode away.

Katie stood motionless, her hands out, palms up, looking into the heavens.

* * *

Winter turned into summer, and then into fall again, and suddenly it was Christmas.

Katie celebrated her sixteenth birthday and Mr. Hoke gave Edward reluctant permission to pay court to her. At first they were so glad to be together they made no mention of the questions facing them. They spent every moment they could together, holding hands, whispering endearments to each other, looking into each others eyes. Edward ached with the agony of loving her.

He received his journeyman papers from Henry, but was restless and vaguely unhappy. He wanted so much and it seemed to be so slow in coming. He was desperately in love with Katie, but she was young and innocent and he had to admit to a strong sex drive. It was hard waiting for her.

The difference in their faith became more apparent. He taught Sunday School at St. Emanuels and was active in their youth program. Katie elected to wear the small round Mennonite cap of transparent white net, supposed to subdue vanity by hiding her beautiful auburn hair, but which only added to her soft loveliness. The cap perched on the back of her head with its strings hanging loose around her shining face gave her a look of sweetness that tore at his heart.

Two months before Christmas, George Hoke suffered a massive stroke and within days was laid to rest at Garber Mennonite Church near the tiny village of Menges Mills. Katie was still a minor and the court appointed Andrew Hershey, Magdalene's husband, her legal guardian. Katie would inherit a tidy sum from her father's estate, but that would have to wait until her twenty-first birthday. She made it plain to Edward that she considered it her duty to stay with her mother while the younger children were still at home, and Edward stared at the empty years stretching ahead of him with misgiving.

Then, as Christmas grew near, it became increasingly clear that his mother was desperately ill. A severe cold, early in the fall, had left her worn and thin, with a hacking cough that racked her frail body and strained her weak heart.

Everyone gathered at the Rebert farm for the holidays determined to put on a cheerful front. Toddlers ran everywhere, and the beds in every room were filled with babies, some crying, some asleep. The women decorated a huge tree in the front parlor, hung pine garlands from every mantel and tried to outdo each other with baked pastries of every description—strudel, fruit cake, sugar cookies, sand tarts, molasses cookies and ginger snaps. Laughter rang loud and crumbs littered the floor.

Edward asked Katie to join him Christmas eve and they joined the family singing Christmas carols. He kissed her under the mistletoe, but their love and laughter were tinged with sorrow as Katie grieved for the loss she had just suffered and he for the one he feared was soon to come.

On the winds of a bitterly cold day in January, J.J. rode into the tannery with a message that Ma wanted to see him. Edward quickly threw aside the hide he was skinning and rode out to the farm, filled with foreboding.

He found Ma in bed, propped up with several large feather pillows, smiling brightly, wearing a fresh night-dress, her grey hair neatly combed and gathered into a tight bun at the back of her head. She gave him a wan smile. "I'm sorry if I took you away from important work, but I do feel better today and I realize I've been putting off something that is quite important to me. There was simply too much noise and confusion at Christmas to talk about it."

Edward grinned. "I'm glad for the excuse. I would much rather visit with you than work, any day."

She patted the bed beside her thin body. "Sit here beside me. Hold my hand."

Edward settled himself and took her hand in his own,

pressing it against his cheek. It's so cold, he thought in alarm. Cold and thin. Edward took a deep breath and winked at her. "You always smell so good. Ever since I was little I remember you smelling of lavender."

"It's always been your Pa's favorite scent. I keep dried flowers for crushing each year." She sighed deeply. "Edward, I called you here today because I want you to have something." Her faded blue eyes looked beyond him and came to rest on the beautiful wooden chest that sat at the foot of her bed.

"I want you to have your grandfather's chest, Edward. When he came to America it carried everything he owned in this world. It was his only link with his homeland and his parents. It represents family, Edward . . . family and tradition. German tradition."

"But why me, Ma? Why not Henry who's the oldest?"

"Because you're the most like your grandfather. Oh, I don't mean just in looks, son. I see in you the same compassion and tenderness he had. When I watch you look at your Katie I see the same open love he showed his Catharine till the day he died. He never stopped being her lover and he never tried to hide his feelings for her. Why, his last will and testament was three pages long, telling of all that should be done for her after his death.

You and Katie will work out your differences and marry someday. She's the proper girl for you, Edward. Put this chest at the foot of your marriage bed, as Johann and Catharine did, and as Jonas and I did. And someday, son, pass it to your children. It is a symbol of your heritage."

Edward moved quietly to the chest and ran his hand across the smooth surface, feeling the subtle texture and grain of the golden pine beneath his fingers. It was fairly small, only three feet in length and stood on squat round feet. A painted thistle-finch, called a *distelfink*, adorned the front panel of the chest, its once vivid colors softened and faded by time, like one of the old daguerreotypes in the family bible. The sides of the chest were beautifully fitted with mortise and tenon and a gleaming brass lock held an elegant hand wrought key.

Sunlight, streaming through the glass window, set sun motes dancing across the lid of the chest and it felt warm to his touch, like a woman's silken skin. He passed his hand over it, caressing it.

"I'll cherish it always, Ma. And I know Katie will too." The room was quiet and in the hall the clock struck eleven. He felt the sting of tears against his eyelids as he held his mother's frail hand and looked into her sweet face. She had taught him everything that was good in his life—A love of nature and the land—the need for one person to love another. All he would ever know of loving was possible because she had shown him the way.

Ma smiled weakly. "And now I'm getting tired, son. Help me to lie down if you will. I think I want to take a short nap."

Edward eased her grey head gently against the snowy white pillows. "I love you dearly, Ma, and I thank you for the chest. I've always admired the beautiful workmanship, but it'll have far deeper meaning for me now." He tucked the white counterpane around her shoulders and kissed her sunken cheek. "Rest well."

One week later, on a cold snowy night, Jonas rode into Jefferson to bring his sons the news of their mother's death.

* * *

Snowy white Dogwood and May-pink Judas trees crowded each side of the narrow road as Edward drove Katie into Jefferson to do some shopping. It had been raining off and on for days, but this morning dawned clear and he and Katie were in high spirits as Duke sprawled across their feet on the floor of the crowded, bumping carriage.

Edward tied up in front of Kraft & Spangler's on the northwest corner of the square and Katie laughingly pulled him into the store's marvelous interior. The walls and floor were crammed with jars, boxes, and barrels; kerosene, coffee beans, cheeses, and pickles; barrels of flour, apples, molasses, potatoes, sugar, and salt. Domestics of every description spilled from counters: yard goods of calico, challis, flannel and silk, and sewing notions. And on a long table along the wall, red clay earthenware, pots and pans.

Katie clapped her hands in delight. "Mother wants some of Dr. Townsend's Sarsaparilla Wonder and a jar of McAllister's Ointment. And, Edward, look at this pretty calico. And I must have some of this penny candy!"

"Whoa there, girl," Edward said, with a broad grin. This sounds like girl-shopping to me. I noticed Patrick's horse in front of the Jefferson Inn. I think I'll join him for some man talk while you shop. Will an hour do?"

Katie frowned. She usually tried to hide her distaste for Patrick, but Edward was well aware of her disapproval.

"If you feel you must," she said. She stuck her chin out. "Bring the wagon to the back door in about an hour and I'll be waiting for you."

Duke was waiting, on the porch, under an old wooden table laden with willow baskets and he jumped up when he saw Edward emerge, sending baskets flying. Edward knelt to pick them up while Duke dispensed a flow of affection by licking him generously on the face.

"At least I know YOU still approve of me," Edward said with a laugh, stroking the silken ears. Duke's tail lashed ecstatically.

With the dog trotting at his side he started up Berlin Street for the tavern. The dirt-packed road was deeply rutted from passing freight vans and farm wagons and the air sang with the snap of the driver's whips and squeaking wagon wheels. Jefferson was thriving, an important crossroads since they built the new east-west road to Hanover that intersected with the Patapsco Road and now served the York and Baltimore markets.

He found Patrick, sitting alone at a small table, concentrating on a newspaper open in front of him. Patrick looked up when Edward approached and looked at him owlishly. "Gad, I wish they wouldn't use such fancy words when they write these papers. They forget there are those of us who didn't get very far in sehool."

Edward pulled a chair to the table and settled himself, while Duke plopped down at his feet. "The news must be important, though, or that Irish face of yours wouldn't be all screwed up and serious looking."

"Darn, if I don't believe those arrogant Southerners aren't tryin' to bring Texas into the Union as a slave state. That's the whole trouble. They aren't content to keep that filthy slavery, a sin against mankind, in the cotton states. They want to spread it to all the new territories."

"The thing is," Edward said thoughtfully, "from everything I read I don't think slaveholders in the south regard themselves as sinners. They think that they're good for the blacks, shielding them from crime and poverty, while protecting their own economic growth and supplying the world with cotton."

"'Tis a foolish thing you're sayin'. Don't you believe that the soul of a nigger is just as valuable as that of a white man? You with all your saintly ideals? How can it ever be right to own another man?"

"It isn't," Edward admitted. "And I think the spread of slavery should be stopped. States coming into the Union west of the Mississippi should be free. But, I can see the argument of those in the south who resent the interference of northerners in their way of life. A lot of southerners think we in the north are just as sinful for letting women and children work in sweat-shops for hardly any pay."

"They do get paid, though. An' they're free to come and

go."

"Yes, but low wage labor isn't much better than slave labor. Those factory bosses are a lot like slaveowners; they tell you what hours you must work and how much they will pay you. Employees live in constant fear of them. I'm just saying there are evils in both systems."

"Aye, but at least in the free states a man can better himself if he works hard enough. Slaves have no hope of ever doing that."

"I'm not defending slavery, Patrick. I'm just trying to turn the coin over and see both sides."

"Well God Almighty, I think 'tis too much education you're gettin'. What kind'a newspapers you reading?"

Edward laughed. "Every kind I can get hold of. I don't have much else to do with myself, alone every night."

"And hasn't that wee gal agreed to marry you yet?"

"I don't have enough saved yet, and Katie feels she should stay with her mother until her little brother is older. Besides, we still have some differences to settle. Among other things, I want my children to be raised Reformed and baptized when they are little."

"Mennonites don't believe in fighting in wars, either, do they?"

"No, that's another problem. If I was to be called up some time I'd want to defend my country."

"There's going to be a war with Mexico, mark my words. The York Militia is being formed for that very reason." Patrick's soft voice dropped so low Edward had to strain to hear him. "I've half a mind to join up."

Edward looked thoughtfully at his friend. Gone were the laughing, impish eyes with their hint of recklessness that had once been so attractive. Patrick's face was deeply lined, his eyes sunken and haggard. His beard was unkept and his mane of red hair more disorganized than ever. His heavy fingers trembled slightly as they clutched his mug of ale.

His marriage isn't working, Edward thought, with a start.

Patrick is very unhappy. I should have seen that sooner.
Friendship asks for more.

"How are your little boys?" he asked, tugging absently at
his chin, aware of the inadequacy of his words.

"Fine, growing like wild weeds. 'Fraid they're a real
handful for Inger, with tempers to match their red hair." He
ran his hand through his own springy red curls and gave
Edward a forced smile. "Inger's expecting again, got me
shut off. I'm thinkin' of going over to York to pay a visit to
a place I know. You must be hurtin' yourself, waiting so
long for Katie. Want to come along?"

Edward fidgeted. The idea wasn't too far fetched. He'd
been having quite a time keeping his urges under control.

"Did you ever get a dose?"

"Nah, but you gotta be mighty careful—or lucky."

"How did you take care of yourself?"

"Washed it off with good strong whiskey and prayed a
lot."

Before Edward could ask more questions, the barmaid
appeared with more cold ale. While Patrick was kidding her,
they were joined by several friends and the conversation
turned to sulky races and spring fairs.

It was time to pick Katie up and Edward left the group of
laughing men reluctantly, his eyes giving Patrick a silent
message of promise.

A brief rain had fallen while he was in the tavern and he
ran toward the square, jumping over several large puddles.
A triumphant Katie was waiting for him on the front porch
of the emporium. "I bought ever so much," she said. "Mr.
Spangler put everything together in the back. He says we
can pick it up later, if we want."

Edward smiled at her glowing face. She never stayed out
of sorts for long. Katie showed such excitement for life—it
spilled over, making him feel young, eager to laugh with
her.

"Good, I want to walk over to Hanover Street. There's an

empty lot there that I've had my eye on."

He took her hand to traverse the square, dodging mud being splattered from the passing wheels of a gaily painted Conestoga wagon. Katie held her long skirts high and Edward got a rare glimpse of her slender ankles. He caught his breath, looking eagerly.

Hand in hand they strolled down Hanover Street, past the alley leading to the tannery, pausing at the Sauble home to sniff air sweet with flowering crabapple and admire beds of tulips and Dutch Iris. Pink and white peonies bent to the ground with moisture from the recent rain. The Sauble cottage was close to the street, and behind sparkling clean windows, rows of colorful spring flowers sat on deep window sills in practical tin cans.

Katie gave a small sigh and Edward looked at her with raised eyebrows. Was that a wistful sigh?

Near the end of the street he stopped her in front of a large empty building lot, bathed in filtered sunlight and dappled with shadows from three grand elm trees.

Edward had worked late many nights drawing plans for the house he wanted to build; a two story structure with long porches running the length the of house, one above the other, the porches shaded by stately elms. He dreamed of the wife and children that would fill its rooms with laughter. Always in his dream the wife was Katie.

She was gazing at the empty lot, her face reflecting the knowledge of his dreams. She was so beautiful and serene, his heart thumped against his chest and the sudden longing that swept over him was so intense he felt choked with pain.

"Katie . . . .

"Yes."

"You've never really said you would marry me." He watched her eyes drop, her fingers toy with a crease in her long skirt. "You know how much I love you," he insisted, suddenly anxious.

"And I love you. I really do."

"But . . . you're still not saying you will marry me. Why?"

She looked up at him, her brown eyes searching his. "You and I are not alike. You would expect me to leave my faith, wouldn't you, Edward? To join your church and raise our children Reformed. I don't know if I can promise that."

Edward felt a tightness in his chest. This was the one question they had never faced, head on, until now. "I think we could compromise," he answered, a slight quiver in his voice. "I would be willing to be married in your home by your Bishop, but I would want to remain a member of the Reformed Church. You could still attend Mennonite meeting if you wanted."

Katie's eyes blazed with anger. "That's mighty big of you, Edward Rebert. And what about our children?"

"I'd like them baptized in my church as infants."

He saw Katie flinch and added quickly, "maybe just the boys—the girls could follow in your faith."

"Never! A family cannot be sliced into pieces like a pie. A family must worship together."

"Is there no compromise then?"

"Not if it's only to be compromise on my part."

Silence like fog enveloped them. Edward kicked the ground with the toe of his boot. "The children could be baptized twice—once when babies, and then again as adults," he said hopefully.

Katie looked at him sadly. "That might be done. I've always hoped you might feel driven to join the Mennonite faith, but I guess that isn't going to happen. I do believe, though, that our churches, Mennonite and Reformed, are brethren in Christ. Maybe that's all that really matters." She gave him a tremulous smile. "I love you, Edward. I'd be willing to attend your church and have our children—all our children—baptized there."

"Ei. That's good then. There is no problem."

"And what about my feelings about non-resistance? I

worry, Edward, when I see you talking to Patrick. He's so full of vigor and patriotism. You've always followed his lead and should there be a war he'd be the first to go."

"But Katie, if Pennsylvania went to war would you expect me to stay home and tend the cows? People would say I am a coward!" He looked at her anxiously.

Katie's lips tightened and a deep furrow appeared between dark eyes that stared into his. "Yes, I would ask that of you. We are often misunderstood and ridiculed for our belief. You must understand that the Mennonite stand on non-resistance is an opposition to war rather than to the American cause. It's the very center of our faith, Edward. The Bible says that Christians are to love their enemies. You can't ask me to change the very core of my religion. To take human life is to forsake Christ, and waging war is a violation of Christian love. It's our way of life. I'll join your church so we can worship together, but I'll always be Mennonite in my heart."

Edward cut his eyes from hers and looked out at the horizon. She was right, of course. That inner light that shone from her eyes and softened her voice was what he loved most about her. He could never change the heart of Katie—nor would he want to. But refusing to fight if war ever broke out and Pennsylvania was threatened; that was a lot to promise. Or was it? His mind drifted back to the time he'd sat in the blacksmith shop and listened to old Asa Emig tell of killing the young Red-coat. Murder, Asa'd called it and the story had touched Edward's heart.

Would he ever be able to look into the eyes of another frightened boy and pull a trigger? Just because politicians couldn't settle their differences without sending young men into battle to prove who was the strongest. The Amish and Mennonites were right—killing was never the proper solution to men's arguments.

Edward had been silent a long time and he glanced sideways at Katie, quietly watching him. He reached over and pulled her to him. "If you'll promise to marry me, Catharine Hoke, I make you a vow that I'll always honor your Mennonite belief in nonresistance. I don't believe I could ever kill in anger. And Katie, I don't ever want you to stop being the person you are."

Katie's eyes locked with his and her face, clouded with worry only a moment before, softened and broke into a hesitant smile.

"A solemn vow, Edward?"

"Yes."

She raised up on her toes and kissed him on the chin. "Then I will be honored to marry you."

He felt breathless with relief and it was all he could do to keep from grabbing her and swinging her in the air.

"When?"

Katie looked away. "Momma still needs me. It . . . it won't be for long. Can you wait just a little longer?"

Wait! He had been waiting an eternity already! "Young lady, patience has never been one of my virtues," he said, fighting to keep the anger from his voice.

Katie bit her lip and said nothing.

"I will settle on this lot and build our house over the summer. I hope by fall your Momma will feel free to let us post our bans. I love you too much to wait much longer."

"And I do love you. I love you with all my heart and soul. "Build our house, dearest."

Edward smiled with relief. Surely his vow would never be tested. And Katie had agreed to marry him. And there on Hanover Street, for all to see, he kissed her long and hard.

Chapter

-11-

Early summer rains delayed the accustomed routines of plowing and planting. Jonas despaired of ever getting the north field, formerly used only for pasture, cleared of stumps and plowed for winter wheat. He and the boys finished the morning chores, anxiously watching black clouds gather overhead, bespeaking another day of rain.

Andy shook his head dejectedly. "Sure looks like this day is lost. Guess I'll take that load of bark to Henry today. I'm glad I was able to get at least half of the plowing done yesterday."

"Becky has been wanting to visit her Mama and pick up some medicine from the doctor," J.J. added, "so if you don't care, Pa, I'll take her into Jefferson."

"Go ahead, boys. Your old Pa can take care of himself," Jonas said, gruffly.

The boys no sooner left for town when the rain clouds moved off to the east and the fickle sun began shining brightly. Jonas looked at the sky and smiled. Might as well finish Andy's plowing while this weather lasts, he thought to himself, walking briskly to the stables.

He'd have to use the new riding plow J.J. was trying out. He hated all these new fangled inventions, but his old plow was at the blacksmith shop for repair. Jonas muttered angrily under his breath about young people and their new ideas as he walked to the stable area for his two powerfully muscled Belgian sorrels, Pearl and Belle.

Belle pranced nervously, snorting and shaking her head.

She was the daughter of Pearl, young and inexperienced, but a beautiful, intelligent animal that with proper training would be a valuable asset to the team.

He decided to harness the older horse first, placing Pearl's leather collar around her neck while he talked softly, sliding a practiced hand between the horse's neck and the collar, snuggling it gently until it was just right.

"Guess we have our day's work cut out for us, girl," he said, hoisting a heavy harness from a stout peg on the wall and carrying it to the patient animal. He seated the hames to Pearl's collar, then attached the breast chains.

After he finished harnessing Pearl he approached Belle who was impatiently pawing the ground. He calmed the nervous animal, speaking quietly to her, showing her the collar before starting to dress her for the plow. He ran his hand over Belle's quivering belly as he fastened the belly band, speaking reassuringly in her ear.

The harnessing complete, he attached check lines and led the horses from the barn to the waiting plow. The experienced Pearl stepped over the tongue and patiently waited while Jonas attached her breast chains to the neck yoke, then snapped trace chains to both singletree and doubletree. He repeated the procedure with Belle and they were ready.

Jonas took hold of Pearl's bridle and gave the horse an affectionate slap on the rump. "Darned if I like this new fangled piece of machinery these young fellows foisted on us but we'll show 'em we aren't to old to learn, won't we Pearl?"

He rode the plow to the edge of the field where Andy had stopped plowing yesterday and Pearl knowingly stepped into her expected position. He would use the older horse in the furrow and Belle could walk on the unbroken ground next to it.

Jonas positioned the plow next to the last furrow and climbed down to the ground to glare fiercely at the two levers confronting him. The lever on the left was used to raise and lower the plow into the ground and the one on the right regulated the depth of the furrow. "Always need to complicate a simple thing," he grumbled to the animals. He climbed onto the high metal seat directly over the wheels in front of the gleaming plow and with a grunt threw the heavy control lever forward, plunging the metal plow-share into the soft ground behind him.

"Git up, Git up," he called clicking his tongue and urging the horses forward. He held the reins gently to protect the soft mouths of the horses. Young Belle was doing just fine although she gave him a little trouble when he had to turn the team at the end of the furrow. She'll learn, he thought grimly, just like her old master.

The sun was at its zenith now and Jonas began to perspire freely. He glanced over his shoulder, watching the rich brown soil curling from the plow-share, savoring the sight and smell of the damp, newly turned, earth. It was quiet and peaceful in the fields, the only sounds that of squeaking harness, the occasional rattle of chains, and the plodding feet of the horses. The plow-share cut through the rich ground and he heard the cracking of an occasional stone against the moldboard. Birds chattered in excitement, pulling fat worms and insects from the open furrows.

By mid-morning Jonas had gained confidence and was more comfortable with the new plow. He felt his muscles relax as he neared the end of the field. Several more rounds and he would be finished. Sweat was running into his eyes and freeing one hand from the reins, he reached back to pull a handkerchief from the pocket of his work pants.

Just then the plow-share caught on the edge of a submerged rock, stopping it dead in the earth with a tremendous jerk. Jonas flew forward, catapulted from the unprotected seat. He landed on the singletree and became entangled in the traces. The excitable Belle reared in terror. She lunged forward, her powerful muscles yanking the plow-share free of the rock, breaking the singletree and dragging it and Jonas forward.

Desperately Jonas tried to free himself from the traces and avoid hoofs and plow as he was dragged along. The frightened Belle continued to lunge forward and pulled the usual docile Pearl with her. The plow careened over his body and the rounded point of the heavy plow-share struck his leg, puncturing his left thigh, just as he was thrown free.

In horror he looked at the thick stream of red blood spurting from his leg. With each pulsebeat the rich soil beneath him turned red and Jonas knew that the big artery in his groin had been punctured. He placed both hands over the huge gash to try to stem the flow, but he knew it was hopeless. He was terrified and screamed to the empty sky, knowing in his heart no one would hear him. Tears cut a furrow in his weathered face as he lowered his head in prayer. He began to grow weak and a bone chilling cold settled over his prostrate form.

In despair, clutching the gaping wound with his right hand to stem the flow of blood pumping out onto the warm soil beneath him, he raised his other hand toward heaven and in a voice suddenly strong he shouted, "Father into your hand I commit my spirit!" Then merciful blackness swept over him.

The horses stood quietly now, the only noise the chattering birds and the hum of insects.

* * *

Temperatures soared to over one hundred degrees in. Adams County that day and nightfall brought slight relief after a day shrouded in hazy, shimmering heat and humidity. Edward thrashed on his narrow cot, his bare chest covered with a film of perspiration. He had just fallen into a light, fitful sleep when a shout and a loud pounding on the door jolted him awake.

"Edward, Edward open up. It's me, Andrew" Recognizing the urgency in Andy's voice, Edward stumbled to the door, clad only in his underdrawers, and fumbled with the heavy lock before yanking open the door. Andy's foam-sweated horse, sides heaving and head hanging low, told of their hurried journey through the hot night. Andy staggered into the room, his sweaty, dishevelled hair framing a tear streaked face.

"Andy, what's wrong?" Edward stammered, a sudden knot of dread swelling up in his chest. "Is something wrong at the farm?"

Andy stared at Edward, tears once more streaking his dirty face. "It's Pa," he blurted with a sob. "He's dead! I found him this evening when I returned from Jefferson. It was just awful, Edward. The plow cut his leg and he bled to death."

All vestiges of sleep vanished as Edward gaped in disbelief. "No! No! Oh, God no! How . . . how . . . what happened?"

Andy fought to bring his quivering voice under control. "Well, you know how bull-headed he is. When it didn't rain he must have decided to finish the north field himself with that new riding plow J.J. has been trying out. He wasn't used to it at all. Besides, he had Belle hitched and you know she ain't used to plowing. I guess the plow hit a rock and threw him. Just about cut his leg off. J.J. and I were both in town and neither of us got back until near supper time. The horses were standing by the barn, with the plow hanging behind them, so we went looking for Pa. Found him in the field."

"Have you told any of the others, yet," Edward asked, sobs choking his voice.

"No, I came for you first. If you'll rouse Henry I'll ride out to Jacob's and then go tell Catharine. Maybe Moses can go for the rest of the boys. I want to get back soon as I can. J.J. and Becky are all alone. I . . . I laid Pa on the kitchen table and cleaned him off some."

Edward's mind was in a turmoil. He was already pulling on his trousers and struggling for calm. Had Pa been drinking? Sudden anger collided with his grief. They were all concerned over Pa's increased reliance on whiskey to ease his grief since Ma's death only six month before. Duke whined softly and burrowed his nose into the palm of Edward's hand, sensing his distress. Edward knelt beside him, grabbing the dog's head in his arms and let his tears fall on the silken hair. With a deep shudder he rose and turned to Andy. "Go, then. I'll tell Henry first off and then get Rev. Sechler. We'll see you at the farm, soon as we can."

As Andy made a hasty retreat Edward grabbed a light cotton shirt from the wooden chest holding his few belongings, pushed his hand through sweat-darkened hair, and ran from the room into the night.

Pa lay on the kitchen table, covered by a clean sheet Becky had mercifully placed over him. She was standing in the corner crying softly in J.J.'s arms.

"I'll help bathe him if you want," Becky said, through trembling lips. Edward looked at her slim body, bulging in the late months of pregnancy, and took a deep breath. "Thanks Becky, but it's not a fit job for you in your condition, it might mark the baby. J.J., take her to the parlor and make her lie down. Stay with her. I'll clean Pa up, before the rest see him bloodied like this. Everyone'll be here soon. Keep them in the parlor 'til I'm finished."

He waited until J. J. led Becky out of the kitchen before pulling the sheet away to look at the still face. The room was stifling hot and smelled of blood.

Sightless eyes stared up at him and with a gasp he dropped the sheet back into place. He had not expected the eyes to be open! Edward's entire body shook with the horror of what he was about to do. But he had to do it. He owed this much to Pa. It was the kind of thing Pa would have expected him to do.

With trembling fingers he removed the sheet and folded it carefully, placing it on a chair beside the table. Before proceeding, he closed the faded, blue eyes, then took the hands, fingers bent with arthrtis and callused by years of labor in the fields, and folded them across the still chest. First, he had to remove Pa's clothing. Edward drew a long, sharp knife from a drawer and carefully began cutting away the blood-stiff overalls.

After removing Pa's clothing he covered him once more with the sheet and wrapped the ruined clothing into a tight bundle, placing it in the kindling box next to the fireplace to be burned later.

Becky had thoughtfully heated water and put out soap, towels, and fresh sheets, so he filled a granite basin with warm water and carried it and the fresh linens to the kitchen table.

He rolled Pa's rigid body over onto his belly and wadded a small piece of cloth into his rectum, then returned him to his back and dipped a clean piece of linen into the basin, wringing it out carefully before he began to wipe the face. Tenderly he moved the cloth over the broad forehead, around the surprisingly small nose and then into the deep life-lines creasing Pa's cheeks and mouth. Edward's tears dripped onto Pa's aged face and he gave a loud sob, stopping his ministrations until he could gain control of himself.

Next he washed Pa's hair, matted with mud and traces of blood, then his chest and lower body. He realized he had never seen his father's privates before and he hesitated, feeling a shameful sense of intrusion.

Lastly he bathed the lacerated leg, the basin turning red from congealed blood. He emptied the dirty water into the yard and refilled it with clean water before completing his task. Satisfied at last, he went to the wash stand and got Pa's straight razor. He applied soap to the stubble on his father's face and gently moved the razor over his jaw and cheeks. Finally he combed his hair and covered him once more with a clean sheet. They would have to find two silver dollars to place on Pa's eyes, as that was the custom. When Catherine arrived she could pick the burial clothes from the wardrobe upstairs and dress him.

Vaguely he had been aware of the sound of horses and carriages in the barnyard and now he heard voices in the parlor. Hastily he emptied the basin, put the soiled washing cloths next to the bundle of clothing and opened the kitchen door to the family.

Edward moved through the next day as though frozen. He felt incapable of emotion, knowing he should cry, but feeling oddly suspended, like he was watching events from some place outside his own body.

The suddenness of Pa's death was the hard part. Why had he hitched a plow he was unfamiliar with to a horse high-strung and untrained? Harder to accept was the knowledge that he may have lain in that field for hours, calling for help, alone and slowly bleeding to death.

Because of the heat the funeral was held within two days. One by one the family entered the parlor, where Pa lay in his simple pine coffin, to say their private goodbys. Edward held back, feeling a need to be last. When it was his turn he took Katie's hand and entered the darkened parlor, cloyingly sweet with the smell of death and fading flowers.

Standing before the coffin, he prayed that tears would come to loosen the terrible knot in his chest. But he stared dry-eyed at the face of this parent he had loved and resented with such youthful passion.

He felt a tug of Katie's hand and looked down at her. She reached up and placed both hands on his cheeks, her brown eyes awash with sympathy.

"Leave it go, Edward," she whispered. "All that anger harbored for so long. Cut loose all those years wasted in hostility, all that self-blame. Let love heal the wounds."

With a cry he flung his arms around her and sobs racked his body. When his tears were finally spent, he knelt on the floor beside the still body, filled with pain and regret. Regret that he had not had the chance to tell Pa that, despite the wall of misunderstanding that had always separated them, he loved him. Such simple words. Why had he never spoken them? And why had Pa never said them to him?

He rose and placed his hand atop Pa's marble-cold hands, folded across the still chest. "I'm sorry Pa," he choked, in goodby. "Only God knows how sorry I am."

As he left the room he felt that he had not only said goodby to his father, but to the last of his youth; that this release of sorrow had swept him into manhood.

Chapter
-12-

"Now what am I bid for this sturdy wash bench?" the auctioneer called, hefting the little bench to his beefy shoulder. "Will someone give me a bid of fifty cents to get us started? Fifty cents, fifty cents, fifty cents. . ."

The sale had been under way since early morning and Edward slouched against a stanchion in a dark corner of the barn watching strangers paw through his parents personal possessions. He just couldn't understand Pa not making a will—necessitating this agonizing public sale.

Farmers milled around the barnyard examining tools and livestock while the women waited patiently in the shade for the sale of household items. Children raced everywhere, sending chickens squawking, dogs barking, and cats into hiding.

The auctioneer moved into the barnyard and within fifteen minutes the three milch cows, Primrose, Daisy, and Rosebud had new owners. The horses went next, Pearl and Belle staying together as a pair.

Whispers of appreciation hummed through the crowd when Brandy, Pa's beautiful bay was led into the barnyard. Edward's heart started to race; he had to have Brandy. He fingered the roll of bills in his pocket. If only he had enough!.

Brandy was led in a wide circle, then halted to stand in profile for all to admire. The horse stood proudly, his reddish-brown coat glistening like copper under the golden October sun, his ears pricked in interest, his tail high.

Edward chuckled. Brandy was handsome and he knew it.

The auctioneer looked intently at the hushed crowd. "Now, folks, we've an animal of tremendous value here. All of you have had an opportunity to examine this fine horse and study his credentials. I think we should start the bidding at one hundred dollars. He's worth every penny of that. Do I hear anyone at one hundred dollars?"

Edward took a deep swallow and looked at the ground. Surely he wouldn't have to go that high. J.J., standing at his side, whispered, "don't start the bidding. You don't want to seem too interested." Edward stroked his beard and tried to look unconcerned.

He jumped when he heard the auctioneer acknowledge an opening bid of fifty dollars. It came from Henry. Ei,yi,yi, he was in for it now. His own brother would be bidding against him!

Doc Hambaugh joined the bidding and the auctioneer was calling for fifty-five. Henry nodded his head and Edward felt a moments panic. He didn't want to lose Brandy, brother or no. He raised his hand. The bidding kept rising until it was up to seventy-five dollars. J.J. nudged him and leaned close to his ear. "Don't hesitate now or they'll think you're ready to drop out."

Edward felt like a fist was pounding his chest, but he held himself ram-rod stiff and raised his hand sharply. Doc Hambaugh dropped out at sixty-five dollars so it was between him and Henry now. They studiously avoided looking at one another.

"Seventy-nine," Henry bellowed.

"Seventy-nine, seventy-nine I'm bid," the auctioneer cried in glee, clearly enjoying the family rivalry. He looked straight at Edward. "Will anyone go eighty? Just look at this beautiful animal, he's worth far more than eighty dollars."

Edward had exactly seventy-nine dollars and fifty cents in his pocket. Brandy nickered softly. Edward raised his hand. "Seventy-nine, fifty."

Henry fixed Edward with a baleful glare and turned on his heel. "He's finished," J.J. muttered softly.

The auctioneer saw Henry's departure and wasted no time. He banged his gavel on the old wooden table. "Then SOLD to Mr. Edward Rebert for seventy-nine dollars and fifty cents."

Edward's heart was still racing as he led Brandy from the sale ring. Gently, he drew the horse's forelock out from under the browband, parted it and smoothed it out. "Gotta look smart, fella, before I show you off to my girl."

He led the prancing horse to the hitching rail at the side of the house and tied him securely, slapping Brandy affectionately on the withers. "We're going to be great friends, you and I, and someday, you handsome fellow, your sons and daughters may be racing all over York County"

Brandy nuzzled Edward's shoulder, his intelligent brown eyes looking at Edward with interest. Edward rubbed the velvety muzzle and leaned his face against the sleek neck.

This day, sad in so many ways, was the beginning of his long buried dream.

The morning wore on; the auctioneer cleared the barn and moved to the contents of the house. Edward couldn't bear to watch; these were Ma's treasures.

And then it was all over. A life-time, sold in bits and pieces.

Evening wrapped the farm in its soft folds, as Edward and Katie sadly crossed the yard one last time. The noisy crowd was gone, the grass trampled flat, the small food stand barren of its goodies. The barn and house were empty. *Empty*, Edward thought swallowing painfully, *as my life will be empty without a mother or father.*

* * *

It was a race now to see who would marry first—Edward

or his younger brother William. William was working at the tannery with Edward and could talk of nothing but his "Lucy Ann." *Of course,* Edward thought with chagrin, *he probably talked of little but his* "Katie."

Each day blended into the next and soon winter had its heavy grip on the Codorus valley. The tannery, Jefferson's largest industry, bustled with activity. Pa's estate was finally settled and Edward had a nice sum of money in the bank. With Pa's death, and the farm to dispose of, Edward's work on his own new house had been delayed and he had stopped pushing Katie to set a date. He worked hard, surprising Henry, and also himself with his steadfastness. Henry was a demanding employer—much like Pa in his ways, stern and frugal to a fault.

But Edward felt frustrated. He suspected he had made a mistake in choosing to work in the tannery, but he drifted along, unable to think of a better alternative. His hands were stained with the yellow tannic acid and his clothes and hair smelled of its stringent odor. He seemed doomed to work at vile smelling jobs.

Early in May Katie celebrated another birthday and Edward decided the time had come to put an end to their waiting. He gathered a large bunch of wild daisies and rode out to the Hoke farm.

He suggested a stroll to the barn to get away from the family and with barely suppressed giggles they climbed nimbly up the old wooden ladder to the loft and snuggled in the hay-mow.

He pulled Katie into his arms kissing her sweet eyelids, then her soft neck, and finally her warm tender lips. Each time they met he found it harder and harder to honor her innocence. They had been waiting so long and he was a man now, not an inexperienced boy.

With a shudder he pushed her away and lay miserably staring up at the ceiling. Katie bit her trembling lip and sat up, pulling her rumpled dress into hasty order. She sat quietly, with her hands clasped tightly in her lap, while a small tear found its way down her cheek.

Dismayed, Edward raised himself from the hay and carefully took her soft face into his work-roughed hands. With the utmost tenderness he brushed the tear from her cheek with his thumb and tilted her head back to search the voice in her eyes.

"Leibchen, you must name a date soon," he said gently. "I find it harder and harder to control myself when we're together like this." Seeing the look on her face, he added quickly, "it isn't only desire that makes me say that. I love you so much. . . so terribly, terribly much. I want to share a home and family with you, Katie."

Katie raised her eyes and looked directly into his. The love he saw mirrored there almost staggered him.

She let her breath out slowly. "My heart is quiet now, Edward. I believe God means us to be together. Mama doesn't need me so much now and she said only yesterday that I must get on with my own life."

He gathered her into his arms once more and this time he kissed her with subdued passion. "I take that as a promise, then. We'll go up to your house and start making wedding plans right now." A mischievous grin spread across his face. "That is, after my girl removes the straw from her hair and the smudge of dirt from her cheek."

"Oh Edward, you do fuss me sometimes," she said blushing.

After Mrs. Hoke and Katie had exhausted the subject of weddings and wedding feasts, Katie's brother, George, joined them and they sat comfortably around the large kitchen table talking seriously of the growing political unrest in the nation.

"Mark my words, there's going to be a war in this country over slavery," Edward said gravely. "The north and south hate each other. They can't agree on anything. Just yesterday I read in the Gettysburg Compiler that nine fugitive slaves were helped by northerners through Oswego on their way to Canada. They were only part of a group of over seventy men who escaped from their owners in Maryland. The south claims that runaway slaves are property and must be returned when they're found. And, George, they're furious with people in the north who refuse to do so."

"I'm always surprised at how well read you are, Edward," Mrs. Hoke commented.

"Well there isn't much for a young fellow to do in a small town in the evenings while he's waiting to get married, so I read a lot," Edward replied with a twinkle in his eye.

"You got more schooling than I did," George said wryly.

"Not much, but I find the newspapers are a good way to learn. I bought a dictionary at a public sale and I look up the words I don't know."

"I admit I don't read the newspapers much, but it certainly doesn't sit right with me for black people to be held in bondage against their will."

Edward nodded in agreement. "Still it's a complex problem, George. The South developed it's entire economy around the need for slave labor. They don't have small family farms like ours. They have huge cotton plantations that cover hundreds and hundreds of acres. Mind, this doesn't make me a southern sympathizer, but I do see their problem."

"Haven't some of the blacks in the South been allowed to buy their way free?" George asked.

"Yes, and that seems to satisfy some northerners. The real fight that's brewing though, George, is over new states . . .like California and New Mexico . . . being admitted to the Union as free-soil."

"What does free-soil mean, Edward?" Katie questioned.

"It means that slavery is prohibited before that state can be admitted to the Union. The south wants people to have the freedom to choose for themselves once they're a state and have the vote." Edward frowned and drummed his fingers on the table.

"I'm certainly opposed to the institution of slavery and the spreading of it, but I do agree the issue should be decided by vote within the state, not by federal intervention. Furthermore, the newspapers say the South is just plain jealous of the North because they're so far ahead economically, with low-paid labor in their factories. That's why southern politicians want to extend slavery into the new states."

"Well," Mrs. Hoke sighed, "it's too much for an old lady like me to understand. I hope you're wrong, though when you think of war." Her eyes locked with Edward's. "You wouldn't be tempted to be a soldier, would you?"

"Nein. I made Katie a vow."

"And true to his word a Dutchman always is. Now I think you have a long ride back to Jefferson and it will be dark before long."

Edward chuckled. "Well put, Mama Hoke. And I want to have a few minutes to kiss my promised bride goodnight."

* * *

Edward sat on the steps of Jacob Spangler's store talking with Patrick, his lungs still stinging from the hot fumes of the tanning vats. Patrick had a free evening, an unexpected rarity, and they had been exchanging news for the past hour.

"Edward, the only remedy for a hot day like this 'tis a little libation at the local tavern. I know, I know . . . you don't drink. But surely one small glass of ale won't send you to purgatory and it will surely clear your lungs of that vile stuff you inhale all day."

"I'm sorely tempted," Edward admitted.

"Then let's ride out the Patapsco to Ziegler's. The ride will cool us off and his ale is always cold."

They mounted their horses and within an hour had pulled

up in front of the popular tavern. Packhorses and wagons crowded the hitching posts and Edward was forced to tie Brandy to a nearby fence rail. The inn, built of grey fieldstone, looked warm and inviting in the ruddy afterglow of sunset. It was large enough to board only a few travelers, but its massive combination kitchen-taproom was a beehive of activity, and he and Patrick entered its cool, dark interior laughing with pleasure.

The room was noisy and reeked of stale beer, sweat, and greasy food. The interior walls of plaster were whitewashed and rose to a high raftered ceiling and an enormous walk-in fireplace dominated one wall of the taproom. Numerous trammels, chains, and hooks hung from an iron crane supporting a heavy black pot, bubbling with a stew that made Edward's mouth water. Sawbuck tables, set with pewter plates, tin tankards, and wooden handled knives and forks, lined the west wall so as to leave room in the center for the milling customers.

A free lunch of tempting roast beef, pig's knuckles, sauerkraut, ham, cheese, and pickled eggs was set up at the end of the bar and they loaded up plates before taking a table across the entry from the tavern kitchen.

Patrick sauntered back to the bar where a white aproned barkeep was dispensing drinks. "Two bottles of ale for me and my friend and make sure they are plenty cold," he ordered in a hearty voice.

He carried the drinks to the table and set them down with a loud thump. Drawing the cork, he poured the stout beer into a pewter mug, and took a long drink.

Edward smiled and followed suit, smacking his lips at the heavy malty taste. He liked this room, with its masculine odors of sawdust, and cigars and he had to admit he'd been missing Patrick's company.

"It does cool one off," Edward admitted as he took another gulp of the cold beer.

"Wine to gladden the heart of man," Patrick grinned as he

tipped his cold mug to Edward's. "Psalm 104:5 I believe."

Edward grinned back. "Isaiah denounced drunkards saying, "they err in vision, they stumble in judgement."

"Noah carried onto his ark 'beer, oil and wine.' After the flood first thing old Noah did was plant a vineyard and make wine. Why, the bible is full of references to drink."

"And just as many references to the evil of over-indulgence." Edward answered, with a chuckle.

"Aye, but friend, I can't see all this fuss about Temperance. 'Tis just a bunch of silly women and stiff-necked preachers getting their feathers ruffled. I hear tell Maine is trying to pass a prohibition law. Imagine what'll happen when all those sailors coming into port find they can't buy a drink in the whole blamed state. They'll riot; 'tis a fact."

"Things might get interesting if they elect General Zachary Taylor president," Edward said. "He's a "tee-total" temperance man."

Patrick slapped his knee. "Now that'll be some President, let me tell you. Another war hero like "Old Tippecanoe" only they call General Taylor "Old Rough and Ready". 'Tis said that during the Mexican war he slept in the sand like his men and never wore a proper uniform. The story is that he rode around the battle front wearing a battered straw hat and a blue-checked gingham coat, chewing and spitting, and getting into the thick of every fight. Now ain't he a fittin' candidate for President of our country?"

Several bottles, and much more laughter and discussion later, Edward looked at Patrick in bleary-eyed admiration. "Guess we've worked out the probems . . . problems . . . of the whole dern country," Edward said, his voice slightly slurred.

"And I think, for a temperance man, you're dronk."

"Never was pure temperance. My brother, Charlie, now, he's pure temperance. He don't touch, taste, nor handle the stuff."

"He moved over East Berlin way didn't he?"

"Ya, he landed with both feet on the ground. Married money, bought himself a prosperous grain mill, and now he's building a fancy brick house."

"Do I hear a little envy there, old friend?" Patrick asked with raised eyebrows.

"Nein. . .well maybe a little," Edward admitted. Patrick always could see right through him. "Do you ever wonder what our lives might be like if we'd gone west when we had the chance?"

Patrick grasped a sweating bottle of ale and poured it into his empty mug. "I think of it all the time. 'Twas wrong what I did to Inger, but marrying her when I didn't love her was worse. In a way I guess I ruined both our lives. The only thing makes life worthwhile is our two boys. 'Tis great kids they are." Suddenly sober he fixed Edward with a penetrating look. "How about you and Katie? Seems like you've had a lot of issues to settle."

"I've never doubted my love for Katie. It's just that she was much younger than I. And then there was this business about not soldiering. I made a vow to her, an' all, and I'm half-way sure she's right, but I really don't know if I could just stand by if war came."

"Whatever happened between you and Sally? You were pretty thick with her for awhile."

Edward felt his face grow red and he took a deep gulp of ale before he answered. "Ya, but she was more right for Amos. They have two little ones now. I liked Sally and she satisfied a need, but I never planned on marrying her. I never made her any promises. Of course, if anything had happened I would've done the right thing. . .like you did."

"That was a dangerous game you were playing. Guess I got caught and you didn't. You and Katie have set the date for next month, haven't you?"

"An' none to soon, I wanna tell you."

"You never saw me about that little trip to Yorktown."

"I managed." Edward rose unsteadily to his feet. He felt a momentary pang of guilt at his inebriated condition, remembering his youthful zeal for total abstinence. "I think we better get more of those eats before they're all gone—and then get home."

Patrick just grinned a cockeyed Irish grin.

Chapter
-13-

After spending a restless night in the Hoke's unfamiliar spare room Edward crossed to the window to look out on frost-white fields. Was that a lamp glowing in a window on the far side of the house? Was Katie lying awake, apprehensive and anxious, as he was. This, after all, would be her last night in her childhood bedroom.

Taunt with an inner tension, his indigo eyes troubled and uncertain, he felt the need for time alone.

Duke, who had been forbidden access to Edward's bedroom, was curled into a tight ball against the kitchen door. He jumped up, planting his big paws on Edward's chest, his tail lashing, his rear-end swaying back and forth.

"You're all confused about this turn of events, aren't you old friend?" Edward ruffled Duke's ears and they touched noses. "Come along, I'll explain things to you . . . and myself while I'm at it."

They found a rock in the south pasture, not as large as Edward's thinking rock back in Codorus, but large enough to afford a good seat. Duke flopped on the wet grass beside him, tongue lolling and mouth panting with pleasure.

"It's like this, Duke," Edward said softly once he had regained his breath. "I've known I wanted to marry Katie Hoke since the corn husking almost six years ago. Only I had to wait for her to finish growing and I had to get some money ahead, and we had a few problems to settle about our church. I love her desperately and . . . well . . . I made her a vow that I wouldn't soldier if our country got in a war . . . a vow I'm not sure I should have made. But I was impatient, Duke. And now that the day has finally come, I'm scared. Taking on a wife and raising a family is a lot of responsibility. A man has to think real seriously about that."

Duke cocked his head and gazed at Edward, listening to every word, his right ear twitching in concentration.

"What worries me most is whether I'm man enough to be a good husband and father. And, I guess, whether I could keep my vow."

Edward turned his head to the distant Pigeon Hills, gazing across fields of faded brown cornstalks, somber against the vivid hue of coloring trees and let his mind grow calm and quiet.

Canada geese trumpeted overhead, their long return flight to the warm South underway; every wedge of wild geese either a family, or a neighborhood of families, led by some strong old gander. The spring journey of the geese is a honeymoon trip; in the fall it's a family excursion. They spend the summer raising their young and teaching them how to fly so they can travel together as a family during the southern flight and on until the next spring. Next to the need of mate and offspring is the need for this flight, a need of the spirit. Edward watched and pondered. What meaning, and what mystery, that wedge of flying geese represented.

He jumped to his feet and started to run. There would be many autumns to come and go and he would teach his children to spread their wings and fly. He called to Duke. "Come boy, we've got a wedding to go to."

The ceremony itself, conducted by a local Protestant minister, was a simple one, attended only by family members. But now the house and yard teemed with over a hundred wedding guests feasting on platters of roast, the traditional Pennsylvania wedding dish of stuffing and chicken. In addition to the roast there were peas and carrots, dried corn, baked beans, seven sweets and seven sours, and more cakes and pies than Edward could name.

The dinner was finally over and some of the guests showed signs of leaving. Edward noticed a group of laughing boys, standing near the door, looking furtively in their direction. Several girls joined the boys and from the giggles and nudges he could guess what they were planning. Only last week he himself, had been a willing participant when they shivareed Michael and Lucy Ann. It was an expected tradition.

"Katie, honey, I think we are in for a serenade of bells tonight," he said, nodding towards the group of young people moving toward the front door.

Katie frowned and a worried look crept into her brown eyes. "But you told everyone we were going to Lancaster on our honeymoon, didn't you? No one knew we were going to your new house in Jefferson."

"Well, Rebecca knew different, and she probably told J.J. who never could keep a secret." Edward chuckled. "Best thing is to act like we don't suspect anything and pretend we are getting ready to leave on a trip. After the guests are gone we'll take the buggy into town, sneak down the alley behind the house and go in the back door. And Leibchen" he added, smiling at the serious look on her face, "it's our home now, no longer just my new house!"

Edward, sure that a shivaree was afoot, convinced Katie to wait up for the bellers. She seemed only too willing to put off the unknown experience awaiting her and they sat together on the side of the bed growing increasingly quiet and uncomfortable.

"Maybe I was wrong, honey, and they aren't coming," Edward finally stammered. "I'm awfully sleepy. I think we should go to bed."

Katie giggled nervously. "Turn down the lamp then and turn your back, please, Edward, while I put on my nightgown and get under the covers."

They had been in bed for scant minutes when a shotgun

blasted into the silent night sky. An unimaginable din followed. Horns tooted, spoons banged on dish pans, bells rang and everyone in the yard below shouted at the top of their voices.

Edward and Katie ran to the window. In the light of the moon Patrick, supporting a double barrelled shotgun on his shoulder, stood on a woodbox and shouted orders to a group of excited youngsters, a few older men and women, and twenty or thirty laughing young people. They carried anything capable of making noise—pots and pans, horns, cowbells, and sleigh bells. A big dinner bell suspended from a stout pole sat on the shoulders of two young farm boys. J.J. and William had rigged up a "pig fiddle" by stretching wires across a trough used for scalding pigs. The bow, a piece of two by four covered with rosin, produced an earsplitting screech.

Dogs for miles around barked and howled as they gleefully joined in the ruckus. Any barnyard animal able to make a noise did so. The din went on and on.

In the darkened room Edward began to laugh. "Our friends are surely giving us a good welcome. We might as well show ourselves, like they want, or they'll keep this up all night."

Edward relit the lamp, looking apprehensively at Katie. She was grinning at him.

They padded downstairs, in bare feet, and opened the front door. Edward was resplendent in a new linen nightshirt and Katie had hastily wrapped a small blanket around herself. Both grinned sheepishly at the crowd.

"Kiss your pretty little bride," someone shouted. Edward put a protective arm around Katie's waist and planted a chaste kiss on her cheek. "You can do better than that," another voice called from the darkness. Soon numerous ribald suggestions were being shouted at them and Edward tightened his arm around Katie when he noticed tears appear in her eyes. A nerve twitched in his eyelid and his jaw tightened. Things had gone far enough, tradition had been served, and he began to get angry.

Patrick apparently saw Katie's distress and Edward's mounting anger because he waved the crowd to silence and walked up to the open door and extended his hand. "Your friends and neighbors congratulate you both and wish you much happiness."

"Thank you," Edward said, shaking his hand solemnly. "Now, if you'll wait just a minute I'll bring out a treat for everyone."

He led Katie inside and gathered up two boxes of hard candy and a box of cigars, the traditional compensation for enthusiastic bellers, which he had made certain he had on hand. He distributed the treat to everyone and they bade each other a happy and satisfied goodnight.

* * *

It was quiet now, the crowd long since dispersed, and Edward lay beside Katie in the big double bed. A full moon shone through the narrow window throwing an oblong shaft of light on the wooden floor. Edward could hear her soft breathing, but they lay motionless on their backs, not speaking and not touching.

I wonder how much she knows about love making and how babies are conceived? he mused. Slowly he moved his arm sideways until he found her hand. "Are you sleepy?" he asked in a tentative voice.

"Not really. Just a little nervous," she whispered softly.

Edward looked at her with understanding and squeezed her hand. He was still amazed that this wonderful girl chose him to be her husband and lover. He caressed her arm gently for a few minutes, then turned sideways to cup her full, warm body. Katie turned to face him and his hands encircled her slender waist drawing her close.

"Katie, Katie . . . I've waited so long for this moment."

"I know, my dearest. And you've been so patient and gentle with me. I love you so much, I hurt from it." As she spoke an urgency rose in her voice and she let out her breath slowly. "Is it loose of me to admit I want to posses every ounce of you?"

"Loose! Of course not. I hope . . . I pray . . . you feel the same desire I do."

Katie sighed, deep and long, as she pulled closer. "Then kiss me, Edward. Kiss me as a man kisses a woman."

Gently he moved Katie onto her back. He bowed his head and moved over her, braced himself on his elbows, looking down at her face awash in the soft moonlight. Her thick auburn hair, loosened from its pins, spilled across the white pillow and he could see her eyes looking into his with adoration and trust.

"Teach me, Edward," she whispered. "I don't know what to do."

"Did your mother tell you what to expect?"

"My sisters did."

"I'll try not to hurt you, Katie," he murmured tenderly. "Just relax and let me help you."

And then instinct took over and they joined together as God had intended they do, in the age old ritual of love and procreation. Together they soared, traveling slowly to the summit of the mountain, giving freely to each other their wondrous gifts of love.

Katie, finally and forever, was truly his wife.

Chapter
-14-

The bright red sleigh glided across the glistening snow with a soft hiss and small puffs of steam from Brandy's nostrils floated in the cold air like wisps of white fog.

"Heavens, Edward, you'll crush me if you pile on one more lap robe," Katie said, laughing at his attempts to protect her from the cold. "Sitting next to you is like being next to a warm stove on a cold winter day."

Katie looked at Edward's strong hands holding the reins, at his rugged profile and the quietness of his expression. He had been so excited and gratified when she announced she was going to have a baby. She ran a hand over her belly, still flat, of course. It was only two months, but already she could sense the child's presence. She flushed, happy and proud.

"Your mama seemed real pleased at our news," Edward said, stroking the tawny beard he had allowed to grow heavy since his wedding day.

Katie didn't like his beard. Edward had a boyish face and a deep cleft that didn't show under all that disgusting hair. But Edward thought his beard looked manly. Funny how he always seemed to be striving for maturity. She suspected it had a lot to do with his feelings of inadequacy with his father.

"I guess Mamma wasn't too surprised. After all, it's a woman's place to have babies; Mamma had eleven. Oh, but I do feel such awe, like I'm the most special person in the world."

Edward chuckled and reached over to run his hand across her cheek and into the wisps of hair escaping her cap.

"Stop it now," she giggled. "You'll get my hair all stroubly."

He laughed and pulled her close. "I love you, Mrs. Rebert. You're the most special person in the world to me. I know what you mean, though. I'm filled with wonder every time I look at you. I can't believe that my seed could grow into a human being in your body. I know men aren't supposed to talk of such things, but I keep wanting to put my hand on your belly to see if I can feel his presence yet."

"Please, not now. It's too cold." Katie giggled. "He! What if it's a she?"

"That's fine with me," Edward said, sheepishly. His nose was red from the wind and tiny flecks of ice lay on his beard. He snuggled closer. "I just realized we haven't talked of names yet. I'm partial to Alexander, if it's a boy. It has a ring of nobility about it."

"It reminds me of warriors . . . soldiers."

"There were a number of great kings named Alexander. Alexander the Great wasn't only a warrior, he was a great leader."

Katie narrowed her eyes and pressed her hands tightly together. "Still, I don't like anything that reminds me of war. Seems everywhere we go, men talk of a confrontation with the south. I don't know as how I want to raise a boy in these times."

"It'll never come to war. The politicians will find some solution to the slavery issue before a son of ours is old enough to be caught up in this dispute between north and south."

"Still, a little girl would be nice. Sarah has always been my favorite name. It means *Princess*."

"Alexander or Sarah, it will be," Edward said with authority, pulling the reins to turn Brandy onto Lescheys Church Road and home. Contentedly Katie pushed closer to him. Bright sunlight sparkled on the pristine snow as Brandy pranced along, tail high and harness bells jingling merrily.

Snow clung to the corners of the window and piled up on the outside sill, but the kitchen was cozy and smelled delightful.

Katie had been up since daylight baking cookies and the smell of molasses and ginger wafted on the warm air. For once it didn't make her sick at her stomach. After several terrible bouts with morning sickness she had called on Becky for help. Becky gave her a vile smelling herbal tea that helped calm the queasiness in her stomach and once that unpleasantness was conquered she relaxed and enjoyed the changes in her body.

She sank into a rocking chair beside the window and looked out at the softly falling snow. The last batch of cookies was in the brick oven built against an outside wall, next to the fireplace. Edward had been so clever and thoughtful, designing the fireplace so she wouldn't have to go to the outside summer kitchen to do her baking. She placed her hands on her stomach and gave a deep sigh of contentment. But then, Edward was thoughtful in everything he did.

It was only a week until Christmas and she had to admit she was feeling twinges of homesickness. This would be her first Christmas away from her family and Menges Valley. Her eyes roved over the walls of her cozy kitchen and her heart lurched in memory.

Memory—not only of Mama baking great batches of potato buns and Christmas cookies in the old farm kitchen—but of her sisters and the love and laughter they had shared growing up. She remembered snuggling close to Becky and Magdalene in a warm feather tick, whispering and wondering about the wondrous gifts that would await them on Christmas morning.

They had all shared the same bed until they were well into their teens. Then Magdalene became so plump she took up more than her share and was moved to a narrow cot of her own. Katie remembered all the whispered secrets and giggles as each sister awaited her wedding day in that room, Magdalene to Andrew, Becky to J.J., and finally she to Edward.

A slow smile spread over her face thinking of them. She had been so frightened on the evening before her marriage to Edward. Her two sisters had come upstairs to squat on the bed beside her—Magdalene on one side, Becky on the other—and talked to her about the duties of being a wife.

Magdalene, always the sensible one, solemnly spoke of the hard, demanding role of a wife. Katie would no longer be free and unburdened by responsibility. She would be confined to her home, accountable to a large brood of children, saddled with endless sewing, mending, cooking and cleaning. It was up to her to bring joy into that existence and make it a rewarding one.

Becky, on the other hand, spoke with glowing eyes of the pleasure of sharing life with one you loved; of companionship and laughter.

"And what of the marriage act itself!" Katie had asked with a nervous giggle, propped against the pillows, hugging her knees to her chest.

"The first time hurts like sin. Afterwards it's quite pleasurable," Becky admitted, her fair face turning pink.

Katie laughed aloud, remembering. And pleasurable it was. When Edward kissed and caressed her she felt an alarming response in her body that she was certain was quite unladylike. She flushed thinking of her undeniable pleasure in love making. She was as willing as Edward to experiment with ways that gave them pleasure. Edward teased her that she had a profound earthy streak, but it seemed so right to her. It was, after all, God's gift—this act of procreation.

She rose and moved to the oven. The molasses cookies

were a golden brown and she carried the hot tray to the big round table in the kitchen's center where she carefully removed each one, placing them on a heavy board to cool.

She wondered if Edward liked plain sugar cookies. She still had time to make a batch before he came home for lunch. She pulled an empty bowl towards her and as she began seperating egg whites her mind drifted. As familiarity with her husband grew so did vague apprehension. She was uncomfortably aware of Edward's need to prove his manhood, a result no doubt of years of domination by his strong willed father and Patrick's forceful personality. If the Union broke up and war came would Edward follow Patrick into battle? Edward was such a sensitive person—she just couldn't see him as a warrior. Still the worry was always there, in the corner of her mind.

Each day she learned something new about Edward's quirks and habits. He hated to do things on the spur of the moment, always planning his days well in advance. He was punctual to a fault, insisting all the house clocks be set ten minutes ahead. He liked to be clean and tidy, to put things away, to push the chairs beneath the table in a straight and orderly fashion, to fold his newspaper so all the edges were even.

Edward stoutly maintained he wanted to rid himself of his *Dutchiness* but despite himself he was a traditionalist, prideful of the accomplishments of the Pennsylvania Dutch.

Christmas was to be a compromise between her customs and his. Coming from a "plain" home she was not accustomed to the uniquely Pennsylvania Dutch custom brought from the Rhineland of adorning the parlor with a stately Christmas tree. Last week she had accompanied Edward to his former home where he secured permission from Mr. Renol to cut a tall pointed juniper from the fence row on the rocky hill behind the farm.

Now she could detect the scent of pine coming from the parlor mixing with the appetizing aromas of the kitchen. *Oh, she thought, humming to herself as she stirred fresh batter in the heavy bowl, I can't wait for Christmas to get here.*

On Christmas eve Katie gaily attached apples and animal shaped cookies, covered with red sugar, to the tree while Edward draped long chains of popcorn and cranberries over its fragrant branches. Carefully they tied tiny wax candles to the end of each branch and Edward climbed on a chair to proudly place an ancient wax angel on the very top of the tree.

But it was the "yard" under the tree where Edward outdid himself. Small, grey, pointed rocks were placed against the wall, representing mountains, with mounds of green moss for fields. Tiny, gaily painted, wooden houses and barns were placed carefully among the rocks and fields and carved ducks and a black swan swam on a miniature pond made from a piece of broken mirror. Lastly he fixed the nativity scene with small German figurines he had discovered, wrapped in cotton, in Grandfather Johann's pine chest. Katie had molded clay into sheep, painstakingly covering the little animals with bits of wool, inserting wooden matchsticks for legs, and daubing a spot of red vermillion on the tips of their heads to represent noses and these Edward stood beside the wooden manger.

Edward sat back on his haunches after placing the last little figure in the "yard" and beamed with pleasure. "Next Christmas will be even better. We'll have the little one with us and I'll be able to dress up as Kris Kringle," he said.

"Just so you don't dress up as the Belsnickel. I think that is a terrible custom. Imagine carrying a bag of switches and scaring little ones on such a happy occasion."

Edward laughed. "I always got a wrap on the knuckles, or my behind, from the Belsnickle. Pa always made sure we got a visit from both the Belsnickle and Kris Kringle."

Katie tucked several strands of hair into her cap and got up from the floor. "One of the customs we followed at home was to wait up on Christmas eve to see the Christmas cactus bloom. It always blooms on Christmas eve you know."

Edward stood and brushed his trousers free of pine needles. Casually he walked into the kitchen where he removed his heavy jacket from the door and slipped it over his broad shoulders.

"Where in the world are you going at this hour?" Katie asked in surprise.

Edward grinned sheepishly. "Ach, woman, there are two customs your husband devoutly believes in and that you must learn. One is to eat lots of sauerkraut on New Years day for health and wealth during the coming year and the other is to make sure of a bountiful crop of fruit by singing a special little ditty to our fruit trees. Now put on your coat and mittens and come with me."

After stopping at the stable for a bundle of old straw he marched her to a small orchard behind the house, then paused in front of a young apple tree and tied the straw securely around its trunk. She doubled over with laughter when Edward stepped back, and with a perfectly straight face, chanted an old Pennsylvania Dutch ditty:

On this night Christ was born
You have not yet frozen
I wrap you with rags;
Now hang thick with fruit.

Laughing and holding hands they returned to the house and Edward built a roaring fire in the parlor fireplace. With a secretive smile Katie spread a heavy quilt on the floor next to the fragrant tree and pulled Edward down beside her.

Christmas week was clear and cold, the ground covered with over ten inches of snow. Katie urged Edward to take her for a long leisurely sleigh ride into the Pigeon Hills. She was happy beyond belief, strong and able, bursting with good health and convinced she was made to bear babies, lots of babies. She glanced at Edward, at the lean, handsome profile, the eyes blue as the chicory sky. He saw her look and reached down to kiss the tip of her nose. They sped through the brilliant countryside, the snow sparkling like tiny diamonds in the reflected sunlight.

"Go past Grissinger's farm pond, Edward. I'd like to see the skaters."

"I've a better idea. Why don't we go home and get our skates and come back to the pond for the afternoon. The tannery is still closed and chores can wait for one day," Edward said with a boyish grin.

"Oh, sweetheart, that would be such fun. I haven't been skating at all this year. I'll need just a few minutes to get our skates down from the attic." She clutched his arm in excitement. "Oh, hurry, please. I can't wait."

When Edward pulled up to the front gate Katie jumped

nimbly to the ground. Edward hustled off to the stable to feed the chickens and put out extra oats for Dolly, boots screeching on the snow. Within the half hour they were on their way to the pond, sleigh bells jingling merrily, Brandy whinnying in delight, his sharp hoofs crunching on the crusted snow.

The millpond was thronged with laughing, swirling skaters. Boys and girls held hands gliding across the frozen ice, their breath a white mist before red cheeks and redder noses. Skates screeched as boys played crack-the-whip, showing off before their girls. Displaced ducks squawked in confusion as they slid across the frozen pond and little girls screamed in excitement.

Katie was sitting on a tree stump while Edward laced her skates when she looked up and saw Patrick approaching with his youngest boy, three year old Jamie. She felt an uncharacteristic twinge of jealousy at the look of pure delight on Edward's face when he jumped up to greet his friend. She often wondered about the friendship between Edward and Patrick. They were opposites in so many ways. Watching them laughing together, Edward's golden head bent close to Patrick's red curls, she pondered the mystery. I guess, she thought, they are friends because, for all their differences, they are both gentle, caring men, with a feeling of real concern for each other.

"What takes you away from the sawmill on a workday?" Edward was asking Patrick.

"Streams are frozen over so the mill closed down. Thought it time young Jamie, here, learned to stand on a pair of skates." He patted the little boy on the head with affection. Jamie looked hardly old enough to walk, let alone skate. A heavy muffler was wrapped around his neck and a woolen cap, much too big for him, practically hid his face. Only a bright button of a nose and lively blue eyes poked from the cap's depths.

"Where's Inger?" Katie asked Patrick, suppressing an irresistible urge to hug the adorable youngster.

"She's expecting again and feeling poorly. 'Tis obvious you're feeling mighty fit, though, if you've come to skate," he said with a big grin. "When's the baby due?"

"July. . . and believe me today I'll make certain Edward never lets go of my hand."

Patrick poked Edward affectionately on the arm. "See you take good care of that pretty lass, then." With that he lifted little Jamie in his arms and carefully placed him on the ice.

Later in the afternoon, hands and feet numb with the cold, they joined a group of friends warming themselves before a fire glowing in a big metal drum. Wood smoke scented the crisp air as the men talked with excitement about the gold rush to California, and the girls giggled over the latest fashions featured in "Home Journal".

That evening Edward pulled a chair before the hearth and lit his pipe. Katie sat in her rocker with a bowl of ice cold winesaps in her lap. She pared her apple and cut it into thin wedges, but Edward munched his apple whole, juice dribbling onto his beard.

Edward took a big bite and looked at her thoughtfully. "Patrick seems to be making the best of an unhappy marriage. I often worry about pushing him to marry Inger when she got pregnant. It's not the life he wanted. Still, he's crazy about those two boys of his and he's a good father."

"But Inger is a very bitter person, Edward. Her years as

an indentured servant to the Petersons were hard ones. Her marriage was forced on her, she's had two babies, and no man's love in her life. And Patrick barely makes ends meet. That shack they live in is disgraceful."

"Well part of that's her fault. There's no disgrace in being poor, but there is in being slovenly. Despite the fact she was trained to be a house servant Inger is a terrible housekeeper." He grinned deeply. "Not like my adorable little wife who scrubs every thing till its near wore out." Edward reached down and pushed several bricks close to the red coals. "When these are good and warm we better wrap them up and head for bed. The almanac calls for a blizzard and from the looks of that sky tonight I'd say we're in for it!"

All day Sunday dense grey clouds drifted across January skies and the moisture-laden air hovered just below freezing. Edward scurried to prepare for the storm, hauling extra fodder to the barn and putting out extra corn for the chickens.

Katie woke on Monday morning to see snow piled deep on her window sills, the windowpanes frosted with lacy, fernlike patterns. She burrowed deeper into the feather-bed, cupping Edward's warm body, reluctant to rise and use the ice cold chamber pot. But nature's demands were strong, and shivering in the frigid room she rose, wincing as her bare feet hit the cold floor, and settled her warm behind on the shockingly cold surface. Finished, she walked over to the window and laid the warm palm of her hand against its frosted surface to melt a space in which to look out. Snow was drifted high in the yard, still falling in a frenzy so thick she couldn't see the stable a hundred yards distant, and the wind was wailing in the chimney. She hurried to the bed where Edward still slept and shook him roughly. "Wake up, sleepy head. Your farmer's almanac was right, as usual. It's a blizzard, already."

All day long the snow fell and hip-high drifts piled up, changing fence posts and bushes into shadowy mounds. The wind whistled and gusts blew the smoke down the chimney, burning their eyes and giving the house a sharp, woodsy smell.

The next morning it took several tea kettles of boiling water to prime the pump by the kitchen door so she could draw fresh water to make coffee. As fast as Edward shoveled a path to the barn it blew shut and he finally gave up and struggled to the kitchen, his face burning with cold, snow frozen to his eyebrows and beard. Katie hung his snow-crusted coat behind the stove and before long the aroma of wet wool filled the kitchen, blending with that of wood smoke and boiled coffee.

The kitchen stayed dark, dimly lit by a small oil lamp casting dull shadows on the far wall. The wind wailed and Katie tried to ignore the fact that their doors were blocked by foot-high drifts encircling the house. She was three months pregnant and vaguely afraid. They went to bed early and Edward held her close in his big arms until she fell into a fitful sleep.

On the third day of the storm they arose to an unbelievable quiet. The storm was finished. Carefully Edward raised the window, pushing the heavy snow away with his bare hands. Side by side they stuck their heads out the window and took deep gulps of the clean, cold air. Unmarred snow mantled the countryside, and brilliant sun glittered on huge icicles hanging from the eaves. Edward put his arms around Katie and drew her close.

"Oh Edward, chust listen," she whispered.

In the snow covered yard below several tiny titmice,
clinging to the twigs of a bare dogwood, sang joyfully to the
new day.

* * *

Katie and her neighbor, Anna, sat opposite each other at
the large quilting frame which filled half of Katie's kitchen.
Anna was short and stout and the gauzy Mennonite cap with
its narrow black strings gave her round face an aspect of
saintliness. Her dress was of soft grey chambray made with
a full skirt that stopped just short of her shiny black shoes
and a white neckerchief whose ends crossed under her belt.
Anna was a member of a small sect called the Piker
Mennonites, not because they were stingy, but because they
lived along the pike outside Jefferson.

Katie needed no quilts; in Edward's chest at the foot of
their bed and in her painted dower chest in the attic were
dozens of quilts. Her favorite had thousands of tiny half-
inch squares sewed together in intricate circles with sprays
of flowers and graceful birds. This quilt, a log cabin design,
would be auctioned for the alms house in Hanover. Anna
kept up a running commentary as her fingers worked
quickly, the quilting a marvel of neatness. Katie despaired of
ever being as tidy with her stitches.

They were discussing the wedding of Amos Stolfuz and
Leah Good and Anna's eyes grew wide as she told of the
wedding feast supplied to over two hundred guests—Amish,
Mennonnite and a few English neighbors.

". . . the platters they vas piled high with chicken. Zis high, and no backs or vings."

"Edward said Patrick spiked the cider and old Mr. Stolfus was vivid," Katie commented.

"Such a red von, that Patrick!" Anna's lips puckered like she had tasted spoiled milk. "Such a vaste of good cider. It gifs drunkenness."

"I wish Edward would find a new friend," Katie said reaching up to tuck a stray lock beneath the white cap perched on the back of her head.

"You chust tell him so."

"Edward's fiercely loyal to Patrick and takes no criticism of him. In fact he doesn't take censure of any kind well, especially from me." Katie stabbed her needle into the muslin backing, pricking her finger in the process and a small drop of blood stained the fabric. With an oath she ran to the water pitcher and soaked a rag in cold water. As she sponged the spot she thought of what she had just said. She was fiercely independent and determined to be an equal partner in their marriage, a trait her mother assured her was common to Mennonite women, but she noticed that somehow Edward automatically assumed a dominant role. She tightened her jaw. That would do for now, until he got used to having a marriage partner. Later . . . .

The winter passed quickly as Katie worked to turn her precious little house into a home. She painted gay Dutch designs on everything in the kitchen that would take a paint brush and made colorful curtains for the windows. "Chust for nice" she told Edward, laughing gaily as she plodded around, her belly swelling with child. With the approach of spring every window sill in the house sported jars and crocks filled with some kind of growing green plant waiting to be planted in the garden. She dreamed of planting dahlias along the garden path, wine red ones, like Rebecca's that won a blue ribbon at the York fair. On March 13th, right on schedule with the Almanac, she planted her peas and stick onions and as spring turned to summer, flowers in tall grey crocks adorned every room—tulips, jonquils, lilacs and sprays of dogwood.

Edward happily indulged her with the latest household items. Her hooked rug in the parlor was replaced by a new carpet, heavily flowered in bright colors. Candles were replaced by kerosene lights, and they bought a melodeon on which she learned to play Edward's favorite hymn "Shall We Gather at the River?" and her favorites, the new songs of Stephen Foster.

Still Katie clung to her thrifty Mennonite upbringing. Colorful feed bags found in the barn provided fabric for quilts and cord string used to tie the bags were crocheted into exquisite lace tablecloths. The unworn sections of old winter coats were converted into hooked rugs, remnants of yarn into Christmas gifts.

The old pine dower chest, standing at the foot of their bed, held dozens of daintily sewn baby garments and Edward built a beautiful cradle from carefully selected walnut saved from Grandfather Johann's farm.

Katie's confinement was drawing ever closer. July was a busy month, the garden and orchard overflowing with produce. Apples were ripe and raspberries hung heavy on the bushes. The days were hot and shutters were closed early in the morning to keep the heat out. Haze blotted out the nearby Pigeon Hills.

On a hot Wednesday, in mid-July, Katie bustled about the house with unusual energy. She spent the morning churning, humming softly in tune to the slap and gurgle of the dasher as it moved up and down.

That night she woke in a wet nightgown to find the bed soaked with water. Within hours her labor pains began in earnest and Edward, beside himself with excitement, donned his trousers and ran to summon the midwife.

The house seemed unnaturally quiet, the only sound that of the ticking mantle clock and the occasional creak of a floorboard made by the robust midwife, Mrs. Newcomer, moving about. Dusk was beginning to darken the windows; Katie had been in labor all day.

Suddenly a strong spasm clutched her body, stronger than all the others, and she screamed. The mid-wife rushed to her side, urging her to push, frantic with activity as she drew katie's leg into the birthing position. Katie felt herself slipping into grayness, and fought to stay alert. "Please, God," she prayed . . .

And then, with a final mighty push, it was all over and Mrs. Newcomer, her toothless mouth open in a wide smile, was spanking a tiny infant on its bottom. "A girl," she said, laying the squalling infant on Katie's chest.

Katie heard Edward pound up the stairwell and push open the bedroom door. Mrs. Newcomer padded over to him with an understanding smile. "Give us another ten minutes, son, and then you can come in to greet your new family."

While Katie donned a fresh gown, Mrs. Newcomer replaced the bloody sheet with a clean one, and cleaned the baby, wrapping her in soft linen and placing the precious bundle in Katie's arms. Only then did the midwife call Edward, lurking in the hallway.

Softly he approached the bed, his blue eyes wide in amazement, at the sight of Katie and his child. "Come closer, Edward, and meet your new daughter," she said giving him a weary, but radiant smile.

He stood speechlessly, watching while the tiny rosebud mouth sucked instinctively at Katie's full breast.

Mrs. Newcomer moved efficiently to Katie's side and removed the infant. "I think her father should put her in her new cradle," she said placing the soft warm bundle in his arms, "and let the new mother take a well earned nap."

Edward held the baby awkwardly, gazing down into the small red face, puckered in protest at being removed from its dinner. The little arms waved excitedly and as Edward placed his hand on her tiny fist the baby clenched his finger and held on tightly. Emotion clouded his eyes as he looked in awestruck wonder at the tiny hand. "Look at those perfect little fingers," he said, drawing a forefinger gently across the small fist.

Tears formed in Katie's eyes, as they always did whenever her emotions were deeply stirred. She watched him place the baby tenderly in her cradle. "Is her name to be Sarah Jane, then?" she asked sleepily.

"She looks like a *Princess* to me," he answered, grinning broadly.

Chapter
-15-

Heat shimmered and the temperature rose to one hundred degrees during the hottest, driest August in Jefferson's history. Edward was restless, complaining of the heat and unbearable stench of the tannery. Once again, he talked of buying a farm and hauled out his old plans for a breeding stable.

The talk unsettled Katie. She wanted to encourage him—it was his dream, after all—yet she had grown to love this precious little house with its neat garden and sunny flowers. She had taken such care with her flowers, starting rose bushes from slips taken from home, fertilizing them with fish heads and bone meal. She wanted to watch them grow, she wanted to stay in one place. Edward's restlessness worried her.

The only times Edward seemed to be totally at peace with himself were the evening hours when he sat on the shaded front porch holding Sarah in his arms. He adored the baby and could seemingly sit for hours rocking her and stroking her fine blond hair.

Sarah Jane was a sweet tempered baby and seldom cried, but Katie worried that she seemed listless and did not gain weight. Of course, the heat was making them all lethargic, but Katie felt a gnawing concern.

The hot spell finally broke in mid-September and Katie woke one morning full of vigor and enthusiasm. Today was Sarah's birthday; she was exactly two months old. It was a wonderful, cloudless, fall day and Katie sat on the side porch with her morning coffee watching the scarlet gum leaves falling in the quickening breeze.

She fed and changed Sarah then gave her an apple schnitz tied in a bag to suck on. "Now you be a good little girl and go back to sleep. This is a grand wash day, Mamma is going to do all our bedding."

Sarah, however, did not cooperate with Katie's wash day. She was fussy all morning, spitting up milk and crying fitfully. It was lunchtime before Katie could get the last sheet hung on the line and when the baby finally fell asleep Katie decided to take advantage of the cool day and put up some elderberries.

She mixed the wine-red berries with several scoops of sugar and placed them in a deep kettle over a slow fire in the fireplace. It would take several hours for them to boil down into a concentrate she could store in stone crocks for winter and meanwhile she washed and readied a few jars for jelly, then prepared an elderberry pie for supper.

Duke lay beside the cradle guarding the baby with singleminded devotion. The old dog, crippled with arthritis, no longer accompanied Edward to the tannery, electing instead to stay home and help Katie watch the infant.

Katie was placing the filled jars on the window sill to cool when she felt the cold nose of Duke poking her arm. He whined softly and looked anxiously at the cradle in the corner. She rubbed his grizzled muzzle affectionately. "Are you worried about our little Sarah Jane too, old fellow?" she asked, moving to pick up the whimpering infant.

A sudden loud slam of the screen door announced Edward's arrival from work. He strode quickly across the kitchen to Katie, giving her a hasty kiss before eagerly scooping his little girl into his arms. Sarah seemed to look right at him, with eyes as startling blue as his own, and waved her little fists in excitement.

"I do believe that little one has captured her father's heart," Katie said, feeling a small tug of jealousy.

Edward hugged the sweet smelling bundle, nuzzling her soft cheek. "I'm not ashamed to admit that I can't wait to get home to hold her again."

"She's been fussy all day. Does she seem warm to you, or am I just being an overanxious mother?"

"She feels fine to me. I'll take her out to the porch while you get supper. She just wants her Papa to hold her and spoil her a little."

"Spoil her is right! Mind you keep the blanket over her head. It's a mite breezy today." She hid a smile, watching him tenderly brush his lips across the light fuzz covering Sarah's head before tucking the blanket around her face.

Edward tended the baby while Katie cleaned up the dishes and folded the clothes from the line. Fortunately he didn't think that caring for an infant was woman's work, like most of his men friends did. In fact, he seemed to look forward to the human contact of handling the baby. Katie suspected he was still grasping for the affection denied him by his father. Edward needed children of his own, to love and hold, and as she watched him with little Sarah, she vowed that his arms would never be empty. A family would calm his restlessness, she assured herself.

As night approached so did a violent thunderstorm, lashing the small house with driving rain, flattening the garden, and sending the cow hurrying to the shelter of the barn. Thunder crashed and lightning stabbed the black sky. Edward secured the shutters and Katie closed the curtains to cut out the fury of the storm.

The storm seemed to frighten Sarah and she screamed in terror, soothed only when Edward took her from Katie and walked back and forth across the creaking bedroom floor, rocking her in his arms. She finally fell into an exhausted sleep and he laid her gently in her cradle and climbed into bed.

Katie slid in beside him with sigh of relief. "Umn . . . I love the sweet smell of fresh sheets and the sound of rain on the roof. And I'm glad the summer heat is finally over so I can lie close to you again," she said, pulling her finger down his chest.

"So am I, little one. So am I." He tightened his arm around her and drew her even closer. She could feel his interest poking her in the belly and despite her tiredness desire flooded her body. Slowly she came alive under his seeking fingers. Edward was a tender lover, aware of the special places she loved to be touched, holding himself back until she felt release, then exploding into her with vigor. Her response was as violent as the storm raging beyond the bedroom window.

* * *

"Edward, please wake up. Something is wrong with Sarah Jane!"

He jerked upright, shaking his head to clear it of sleep, and looked at her in bewilderment.

"When I picked her up for her usual feeding she felt hot to my touch. Edward, she's burning up with fever."

Edward yanked the nightshirt over his head and grabbed his trousers. He was dressed in seconds. "I'll be back soon as I can," he said running out the door. Within minutes Katie heard the front door slam as Edward raced into the driving rain.

Frantic with worry she knelt beside the cradle. Sarah appeared to be sleeping, but bright dots of red colored each cheek and she did not respond to Katie's touch. Katie's mind raced. Maybe she should have sent Edward for a powwow doctor instead of a regular doctor. She believed in powwowing, the power of the mind to cure. The practice was common in the Pennsylvania Dutch country. But for it to work it needed faith from the patient. Sarah was only an infant.

What was the herb used for fever? Katie had numerous dried herbs hanging from the rafters in the attic—slippery elm, tansy, beebalm, ginseng, wild cherry bark—among others. Oh, God, she prayed, help me remember: what do I use for fever? Dogwood berries! That was it, her Momma used a tea made from dogwood berries when the babies ran a fever.

Katie was spooning the warm tea into Sarah's little mouth when Edward pounded up the steps and burst into the room. He was alone, dripping wet, splattered from head to foot with thick clayey mud.

"Where's Doctor Klinefelter?" she cried.

"I couldn't get Doctor Klinefelter. Doctor Brinkman will

be along in just a few minutes." He dropped to the floor beside her and placed his hand on the baby's forehead then looked at Katie with stricken eyes. "She's worse isn't she?"

Katie just nodded. "Hold her mouth open while I spoon more of this into her."

"What is it?"

"A tonic made from ripe dogwood berries. It's to lower fever. We don't know Doctor Brinkman, why him, Edward?"

Edward sobbed in frustration. "You wouldn't believe it. When I got to the Klinefelter's house, Mrs. Klinefelter answered the door and told me the good Doctor was at the Jefferson Inn. She said he was in need of a little relaxation. He was relaxed all right. When I found him he was slumped over a table, unconscious with drink." Edward pounded his fist on his knee. "Damn the man! Damn the whiskey!"

"Sh, sh. . . you did find another doctor, then?"

"Ei. The innkeeper, George Snodgrass, saw my distress, and suggested the new doctor in town. I'd completely forgotten about young Doc Brinkman over on Berlin Street. Brandy and I highballed it over there and thank heavens there was an oil lamp still burning in the doctor's upstairs window. I pounded on his door and he answered in his nightshirt. He promised to come as soon as he could dress."

Edward jumped to his feet. "I hear his carriage below. Bring Sarah to the kitchen and I'll let him in."

The good doctor worked all night, trying everything he had at his disposal to bring little Sarah's fever down, but by morning Katie could sense his hopelessness, could feel her baby slipping away.

She held the quiet baby in her arms, rocking her gently,

trying to flood the little girl with her love. Edward leaned close to stroke Sarah's golden hair and wrap a soft curl around his finger. He kissed the top of her tiny head and whispered, "Mama and Papa love you, little Sarah—and God loves you." As though Sarah heard her father she opened her eyes and looked into his face. She seemed to sigh and smile. Katie thought she would die with anguish watching them.

The rain stopped and morning came. She and Edward were in the parlor, kneeling in prayer, begging God to let them keep their child, when she looked up to see Doc Brinkman in the doorway.

"No," she cried. "No!" The doctor walked over to them and laid his gentle hand on Edward's shoulder. And she knew.

* * *

Over the next year Edward struggled desperately with his faith. He told Katie he felt God was punishing him for something. He couldn't understand or accept the blows he felt had been unfairly dealt, and Katie searched frantically for words to help him. Even the news that she was expecting again didn't seem to ease his gloom, in fact it seemed to make matters worse.

Katie was not one to sorrow over facts she couldn't change. And despite her anguish over the loss of her baby her faith gave her an acceptance of death, an acceptance she knew Edward resented.

Duke, also, seemed to give up after the baby's death. As fall turned into winter he seldom left his rug by the fire. One day, early in December, he failed to return to the kitchen door after she had let him out to relieve himself. She called and called, but he did not appear. Concerned, she donned her cloak and went looking for him. As she crossed the side lawn she saw a dark mound lying motionless in the snow.

Katie ran to the heap of fur crying Duke's name, but she knew before she reached him that he was dead.

He was too heavy to carry so she took off her cloak and wrapped it around him. For some reason she felt the need to keep him safe and warm against the blowing snow.

She ran back to the house and waited in dread for Edward to come home. How would she ever tell him of another death? He loved Duke so much. She began to cry.

Minutes later she heard Edward's footsteps in the hall and he strode into the kitchen with a cheery hello. He took one look at the tears in her eyes and his face turned pale. With seemingly uncanny premonition his glance flew to Duke's empty rug.

"I'm so sorry, Edward. Duke's dead."

Edward collapsed into a chair and stared at her. Then he took a deep breath and croaked in a voice distorted with grief, "Where is he?"

"Outside. He must have collapsed as he was running across the yard. I couldn't move him so I covered him with my cloak. I found him just minutes ago."

"I'll go see to him. He'll have to be buried. It'll be hard digging; the ground is frozen."

"How about in the barn? That would be easier."

Edward nodded his head and toyed with his cap as though reluctant to go outside and face the awful truth.

"I'll go with you," Katie said, moving to his side.

Edward picked up Duke's rug and together they went outside and trudged through the snow to the lifeless dog. Edward picked him up, wrapped him in the warm rug, and carried him to the barn. After digging a shallow grave in the earthen floor of the barn Edward sat down on the floor and cradled Duke in his arms. He lifted the long lean face to his, to touch noses with him one last time. Tears dripped on the wet fur.

Katie felt her knees grow weak at the torment in Edward's eyes and she sank to the ground beside him. He grasped her hand and with the other hand stroked Duke's silken ears as he said his farewell in a voice ragged with grief.

* * *

Katie woke just as dawn was streaking the windowpanes with rose light, to find Edward pacing the floor of their bedroom, his face dark with anger. When he saw she was awake, he pounded his fist on the bedpost and fixed her with a wild look. "Enough. I've had enough of death and your calm acceptance of fate. Enough!"

"Let's go down to the kitchen, Edward. I'll make some coffee and we'll talk."

In the kitchen Katie added a few chunks of dry wood to the glowing coals in the fireplace, stepped up the fire with a bellows, and pulled the crane holding the kettle over the fire. She added a generous amount of coffee to the already warm water and moved to the cupboard to fetch left-over shoofly pie for dunking. Edward sat quietly until the coffee boiled and she placed a steaming mug in front of him.

Absently he ran his fingers through his beard and looked at her apologetically. "How can I put my thoughts and fears into words you'll understand?" He glanced away from her and stared at the small fire flickering in the fireplace. The light shinning on his face showed fine lines of pain around eyes and mouth. Then in a halting voice he continued, "I guess I'm afraid. I was happy when you told me you were in the family way, but now I'm afraid. Afraid you or the new baby will be taken from me. I've lost so much I love over the past few years . . . my parents, your father, my daughter, even my dog. I'm angry too . . . angry at a God who allows so much misery. My faith no longer sustains me." His eyes, dark with pain, looked at her. "I don't know what's wrong with me, Katie. I don't know if I could handle another death."

Katie thought she knew what was wrong with him. It was, simply and starkly, an awareness of his own vulnerability. An awareness each man must confront on his own terms.

"Edward, dear, I know you grieve for Sarah Jane; I grieve too. But my sorrow is different from yours and I know this, too. There are different ways of feeling sorrow. Often during the day, when I'm most busy, a feeling of sadness will pass over my spirit like a mysterious cloud. A sound, or a smell, will come drifting across my memory, reminding me of Sarah. But, dear, it's a fleeting sorrow, like a cloud suddenly dimming the sunshine on a bright day. But Edward, there's only a minute of gloom and the memories are richer when it's gone."

Edward dropped his head into his hands. "I think the thing I would like most to change in my life is to feel your inner serenity. He raised his head and searched her eyes, the emotions seething inside him showing on his face. "But my arms are empty, this house is empty. My little girl lies alone in that cold box, with no one to hold her. I see nothing but that pine box. The tiny sheaf of wheat on its lid is seared into my mind."

Katie rose and walked to him, raising his fingers to her mouth, kissing them softly. "Don't you also see her soft golden curls, her toothless little smile of joy when she saw you at the end of the day? Remember that, Edward, not the pine box. I wish I could bear this for you, could give you answers that would comfort you. But I can't. Only God can do that. God has a reason, Edward for all things good and bad, but his reasons are unknowable. There is purpose in everything that touches our life and death is a part of his natural order. You'll find your answers, I know you will."

A wishful smile appeared at the corner of Edward's mouth. "Guess I've been feeling mighty sorry for myself," he said. Like I'm the only one who has lost someone dear to them."

"Edward, you always looked at life with joy in your heart. That's why I fell in love with you." Katie smiled at him tenderly. "What we need is a new slate to write on."

Edward sat somberly for a minute and then a light seemed to creep into his blue eyes and he grabbed her hand, squeezing it tightly. "That's it, honey. A new slate! God has already given us the start of a new life, a new baby. Let's take it a step further. You have your inheritance from your father and I have mine. I'm restless working for wages. It robs a man of his independence and his liberty. Farmers now, they depend on no man for a living. Why don't we look for a farm, or a business, somewhere else. I've always felt close to the soil and I'm more than willing to work hard. Charles has settled in East Berlin and J.J. and Becky are close to Hanover. We'll get away from all the sadness here in Jefferson."

Katie's heart sank. Give up her home! This wasn't the answer she'd been looking for. Still, she hadn't seen such eagerness on Edward's face for months. "We would have to sell this sweet house," she murmured taking a big sip of cold coffee.

"Sure, but we'll get an even sweeter one." Edward jumped up waving his hands in excitement. "And I'll buy you one of those ten-plate kitchen stoves you've been wanting. And I might even shave my beard off, like you've been pestering me to do. Just think Katie—a new baby, a new house, and what will look like a new husband."

Katie didn't know what did it—the promise of a clean shaven Edward or a stove—but suddenly she was as excited as he. Her Mama always used to say, "When the Lord closes one door, he opens another."

Part 3

Littlestown,
Adams County, Pennsylvania

1853

Chapter
-16-

Edward held Brandy's reins lightly in his gloved hand as he rode out of Jefferson toward Hanover on a bright February morning in the new year 1853.

Last week Charles had stopped by to tell him of a farm and sawmill that might be for sale between Hanover and Littlestown, some ten miles from Jefferson. Several years had passed since the night he and Katie had agreed to search for a new home and he had looked at many farms, but none seemed just right. This one, though, sounded mighty promising.

Brandy pranced in the cold, brisk air like a young colt. As they rode through the bustling village of Hanover Edward was impressed by the new construction under way. There should be lots of work for an enterprising sawmill. He turned Brandy south on Frederick Street and headed toward Littlestown. The road was patched with ice; recent snow still lay in drifts on either side. He liked the gentle dip and swell of the land; flatter, more open than the farms around Jefferson. Winter barren fields ascended sloping hills until they halted at the base of smoky mountains just visible in the distance. A comfortable land, Edward thought. Like Ma's lap when he was little.

The Hanover-Littlestown Pike was busy this morning

with heavily laden wagons rattling their way to and from the Baltimore markets. Invigorated by the cold and with mounting enthusiasm he urged Brandy forward. They crossed Conewago Creek, Brandy's hoofs ringing loudly on the icy wooden bridge. He noticed a small sign with crudely painted letters pointing down a narrow lane to Kitzmiller's Mill. So this was where old Martin Kitzmiller lived, he thought, chuckling to himself, recalling the story of the famous murder trial.

The murder of Dudley Digges and the subsequent trial of Kitzmiller's son had resulted in the long over due formation of the Mason-Dixon Line. In the early 1700's, John Digges, an enterprising Irishman from Maryland, obtained from Lord Baltimore a grant of ten thousand acres on the "Little Conewago". Digges believed the land was in Maryland, but William Penn considered it to be part of Pennsylvania, which he believed extended all the way to the Chesapeake Bay. The boundaries were vague and uncertain. As a result the land in question was claimed by both John Digges and William Penn.

Over the years Digges sold parcels of the disputed land to numerous settlers, as did the Penns. Some landowners paid their taxes to Maryland, some to Pennsylvania and some not at all. For years the bickering continued until finally it came to a head on the farm of a feisty German farmer, Martin Kitzmiller. During a heated argument one of the Kitzmiller boys accidentally shot and killed John Digges' son, Dudley. Dudley was trying to collect purchase money for the land from Kitzmiller who refused to acknowledge the Diggs' ownership of it, believing the land belonged to William Penn. The courts acquitted young Kitzmiller with a verdict of justifiable homicide and soon afterwards the boundary dispute was settled once and for all by the marking of the Mason-Dixon line, about two miles south of Littlestown, establishing an official border between Pennsylvania and Maryland.

Edward continued up a slight grade until the road leveled out again, looking for the landmark he had been told to watch for. Suddenly he saw it. Christ Church, sitting serenely on the crest of a small hill, its dark red brick warmed by the winter sun, its white bell tower proudly outlined against the cloudless sky; lovely in its simplicity.

He slowed Brandy to a walk and turned onto a narrow lane, unable to tear his gaze away from the little church. White grave markers clustered near the protection of the red church like baby chicks under the skirts of a mother hen. Breasting the hill he paused and looked again, his breath catching in his throat. Why was his heart beating so fast? It was only a church. Yet it exerted a pull he could not explain. He had the oddest feeling that he had come home.

Just beyond the church he forded a small creek and turned up the short lane lined with ancient buttonwoods leading to Jacob Sell's farm and sawmill. Here and there a stand of dark hemlock showed black, etched against the pale sky, and beyond the stone boundary walls corn stubble poked through melting snow.

"Gidup Brandy, ole boy. This here's Jacob Sell's farm, the sawmill we've come to look over." Brandy responded smartly and with ears erect and tail high he pranced up the lane.

Edward could hear the unmistakable sound of a saw so he headed directly for the mill. Three men, taking advantage of an abundance of water from the late February thaw, were busy maneuvering a huge hickory log into the teeth of a water powered up-and-down saw. He tethered Brandy to a nearby sapling and approached a small grey haired man who seemed to be barking orders in rapid German to a slow moving youth.

"Name's Edward Rebert," he said cheerfully extending his hand.

"Jacob Sell," the little man responded. He was slight and wiry, with a strong grip, and a wary look in watery blue eyes. "Your brother, Charles, told me of yuh. From over Jefferson way I hear."

"Ja, I was born and raised in North Codorus. My wife and I live in Jefferson now, with our little girl, Annie. Guess Charles told you I'm looking around for a farm."

"Ei, veil, I don't know if I vant to sell." He picked up a newly sawn pine plank and ran his hand over it carefully, the light glinting from his wire-rimmed spectacles. "It's pretty busy ve are chust now and springs comin' on fast. That's our best time, you know, vhen the creeks run full."

Edward smiled. Charles said Jacob was in ill health and eager to sell, but he would allow the little Dutchman the dignity of the dicker. Up-and-down saws were gradually giving way to circular saws and much of the equipment appeared to be in need of repair, but if he could buy at the right price and make a few improvements the mill should turn a good profit. The possibilities were limitless. With a determined effort, he kept his face impassive. Let Mr. Sell believe he was driving a hard bargain.

"I've been thinking of moving my family to Adams County," Edward said, quietly. "I've looked at a few farms, here and there, but haven't given much thought to a sawmill. My trade is tanning."

"No reason you couldn't set up a tannery right behind the sawmill. It'd give you a ready supply of bark. Get someone else to run the saw for you."

"Worth a thought, I guess," Edward shouted above the thudding racket as one of the men started a new log into the teeth of the saw. "How much land do you have here?"

"Over one hundred ninety five acres. All good limestone land," Mr. Sell answered, leading Edward away from the mill platform and toward a quieter spot. "Most in corn and wheat, with about fifty acres still in prime wood."

"What kind of trees?"

"Oak," he said. "And shagbark-hickory. Some honey locust."

"About the size farm I'm looking for. Tell you what, why don't you show me around while I'm here. Just in case the property does go up for sale, that is." Darn it, he wasn't very good at this game of dickering. "Then if you do decide to sell you can get back to me with your price."

Several hours later he and Mr. Sell returned to the sawmill where they parted with a firm handshake. Edward knew this was the property he wanted. He would be back.

Katie settled into the comfortable cushioned carriage seat beside Edward, while three year old Annie, insisting that she wanted to ride backwards, perched on the seat opposite. Linus, their driver, slowed the team of spirited horses and Katie looked out the window.

"Edward, look!" Katie leaned forward to peer out the window on the right side of the carriage, her eyes fixed on the handsome brick church sitting on a slight rise beside a grove of trees.

"What, Mamma? What do you see?" Annie asked edging forward on the edge of her seat to look out the window in the direction her mother was peering.

"That lovely church! That inviting church sitting there as though it wanted to reach out and gather you into its arms."

"I had the same feeling when I first saw it," Edward commented, half laughing. "That's Christ Church, and our farm, if we buy it, is just behind."

Linus deftly reined the team into the narrow lane that led from Christ Church straight to the brick farm house nestled among stately elm trees.

A silence descended on Edward and Katie as each looked at the house that might someday be their home. The new baby in her belly quickened and Katie rubbed her stomach softly. She sucked in her breath and murmured, "the house looks so warm and comfortable."

"From the porch you can see Christ Church," Edward answered with a smile, reaching to squeeze Katie's hand.

"Look at that pond behind the house, like a mirror reflecting the trees and house," Katie said. "What a wonderful place for Annie to learn to ice-skate."

In one graceful leap, Edward was on the ground, reaching up to help Katie from the carriage.

"What do you think, Katie?" Edward asked his voice wavering as he tried to read the look in her eyes.

"I . . . Oh, Edward . . . I'm overwhelmed. The house is so much larger than I imagined. So lovely. Look how those trees frame it; the house will be shaded and cool all summer." She stood motionless, her hands clasped, her heart thudding.

Mrs. Sell appeared on the porch, wiping her hands on a tidy apron, her lips creased in a wide smile.

"Welcome, Mrs. Rebert, to what I hope will be your new home," the chubby little lady called out.

Edward laughed, swinging Annie into his arms and leading Katie up the wooden steps to the porch. After introductions had been made Mrs. Sell pushed open the heavy oak door that led into the parlor. Streaks of light marked the wide floorboards of gleaming pine around a braided rug in shades of red and brown. The walls, ceiling, and woodwork were all painted white giving an illusion of spaciousness to the small neat room. A black stove glowed warmly in the corner and shadows moved over the white walls as the branches of a huge hemlock outside the tall six-pane windows dipped in the winter wind.

"Oh," Katie breathed, taking in every detail, her hand squeezing Edwards.

"Would you like to see the dinning room?" Mrs. Sell asked.

"Yes, of course."

Edward smiled. "I believe I'll leave you women to finish the tour of the house. Is Mr. Sell at the mill?"

"Ei, and he's expecting you," Mrs. Sell answered as she led Katie through the door to the next room.

The tour of the downstairs ended in the large, white-washed kitchen, graced by a huge walk-in fireplace, and opening into a back porch that looked out over the sparkling mill pond.

As they climbed the stairs leading out of the kitchen to the second floor, Katie was reminded of her childhood home at

Menges Mills. She held Annie tightly by the hand as the small child manuvered the narrow stairway, her little eyes sparkling with excitement at this new adventure.

"There are three nice rooms up here," Mrs. Sell was saying as they reached the small upstairs hall. As soon as Katie entered the room facing the side of the house facing the pond she knew this was the one she and Edward would share. She walked over to the front window and looked out. An old, gnarled walnut tree guarded the front window but still afforded a view of the appealing little church sitting snuggly on its distant knoll of ground.

She turned to see the kind old lady watching her anxiously.

"Mrs. Sell, I must admit that I was unsure if I could bring myself to leave our sweet little cottage in Jefferson and the memories it holds for me. Our first-born lies there in the cemetery, as does my beloved father. Edward and I have experienced much happiness in the Codorus Valley, but also much sorrow. I know that all things considered, it will be best for us to move to this farm if Edward can strike a deal with your husband."

"Are you sure, dear?"

"Yes. I'm sure. I've already fallen in love with this lovely house and Edward needs to put his sorrows to rest. And we do need more room," she said patting her full belly with a chuckle.

They left the house and walked to the front lawn where they found Edward and Mr. Sell shaking hands.

* * *

Edward lifted Katie and little Annie from the wagon under a warm April sky and together they climbed the three porch steps to their new home. He gently disengaged the little girl's hand from her mother's and swung a startled Katie up into his arms.

"I must carry my wife over the threshold," he said tenderly.

"Laws, Edward, we must be an armful," she said laughing and patting her large belly.

"I'll admit there's a little more there than the last time I lifted you in my arms," he said setting her down gently on the other side of the door.

The next day while Katie and Annie explored the house Edward set about learning to operate a sawmill.

Water to power the saw was diverted from Little Conewago creek into a wide, shallow millpond. From there the stored water was channeled into a millrace which delivered the water to the mill. The sawmill straddled a deep pit housing an undershot water wheel fed by swiftly running water directed from the millrace down a steep wooden trough.

The mill was little more than a long wooden platform, open on all sides, and covered with a cedar shake roof. Edward approached the two hired hands, Jerry and Ludwig, and watched intently as they loaded logs onto a moveable carriage, their motions rhythmical as dancers, the air throbbing to the heavy thud of the up-and-down blade. He was glad he had asked the men to stay. They were good at their job.

Using long hooked poles they canted a fat log onto the carriage. Jerry pushed the carriage forward on wooden rails advancing it into the saw blade and began a cut along one edge of the log.

Edward took a deep breath, drawing the smell of resin running from the fresh cut lumber deep into his lungs. He walked over to a neat pile of finished planks and ran his hand over the smooth wood, stooping to pick up some of the fresh shavings and let them run through his fingers.

"What size planks are you cutting?"

"Eight inch. We're dressing out oak and hickory from Ali Schwartz's back woodlot for his new house," Jerry, the older of two men, replied giving his new employer a careful look. "Want to help turn the rachet wheel back for another cut when this ones done?"

"Best way to learn," Edward replied, striding forward, wiping sweaty palms on his clean overalls.

The first few days were a whirlwind of activity. He and Katie investigated every nook and cranny of the farm and its buildings. Spring planting had to be started and Katie eagerly planned her new garden, pouring over jars of seeds brought from Jefferson. Edward had never seen her so happy, her pregnancy making her more beautiful and desirable than ever.

They were in the kitchen, installing Katie's new stove, when the sound of approaching hoofs made her run to the window.

She peeked through the curtain and let out a gasp. "Laws, Edward isn't that Rev. Sechler from Christ Church?"

"Ei,yi,yi, that it is."

She swept a wild look round the kitchen, still strewn with unpacked baskets and bundles. "We can't bring him in here."

"No. Take him to the parlor."

"But that's in worse shape than the kitchen."

"It can't be helped. He knows we just moved in. He'll understand."

The minister strolled across the wide porch to the front door. Edward had the door open before he could rap.

"Mr. Rebert, so pleased to meet you," Rev. Sechler said extending his hand. "I hope I haven't come at an inopportune time."

"Not at all, not at all," Edward stammered, leading the tall black-clad figure through the hall to the parlor where furniture was piled haphazardly along the walls. He pulled several chairs into a semicircle and Katie perched hesitantly on the nearest one.

After several moments of small talk, a hush fell over the cluttered room. Katie finally broke the heavy silence.

"How long have you been serving Christ Church, Reverend Sechler?"

"Over sixteen years. You know, don't you, that Christ Church is referred to as the "Mother of Reformed Churches" in this area. The first house of worship, a log structure, was built in the shape of a cross way back in the seventeen hundreds."

"Over one hundred years ago," Edward said in awe.

"Yes, and the first service was six years earlier than that. It's a very inspiring story of faith, Mr. Rebert. Great spiritual destitution prevailed among the earliest settlers in Pennsylvania and when their plight was made known to the brethren in Holland they sent a young minister across the ocean to break the bread of life and to organize them into congregations. His name was Reverend Michael Schlatter and after organizing congregations in Philadelphia and Germantown he traveled on horseback across the whole of southern Pennsylvania, stopping here in the Conewago Valley at a school house where Christ Church now stands. When he saw the great need of the people for godly care he arranged at once to observe Holy Communion. People came from far and near. The school house was too small to accommodate the spiritually starved people so he offered the Holy Eucharist under the open heavens. After that he baptized over twenty-one infants. When he announced that the object of his coming was to organize them into a congregation they wept openly."

Katie brushed her hand across a wet cheek. "How proud we shall be to worship there," she said quietly.

Edward, deeply moved, rubbed his hand across the cleft in his chin. He missed his comfortable beard and was still uneasy with the feel of bare skin. He cleared his throat and addressed Reverend Sechler in his best English. "How sad it must have been to be without a pastor to administer the sacraments of Holy baptism and the Lord's supper—or to have someone to comfort the sick and dying. But you said the first church was of log. When was the brick church built?"

"Fifty years ago under the guidance of Reverend Gobrecht who served the Littlestown congregation for over twenty-eight years. The first church was very uncomfortable I venture to say. It was built of rough unhewn logs with no plastering between them and the seats were slab stools with no backs to them. And, of course, there were no stoves to provide heat in winter."

"We're hoping to make Christ Church our place of worship," Katie confessed, with a warm smile at the earnest minister.

"I must say I'm delighted to hear that. When is your baby due, Mrs. Rebert?"

"In June, we believe." Suddenly Katie seemed much more at ease and she jumped up to put her hand on the arm of the sweet man who sat with folded hands beaming at her. "Now come into my kitchen, messy though it is, and share some pie and coffee with us. It's sour cherry, Edward's favorite, baked fresh this morning."

Alexander was born late in June 1854. He was a fat, happy boy and while Annie, fair and blue-eyed, took after the Reberts, Alex, with large brown eyes and a cap of dark hair, was a mirror image of Katie.

In the fall Alexander was baptized at Christ Church. For weeks Katie planned Alex's christening party, her first big dinner in the new house. She invited their new neighbors; the Lohrs, Sells, Groves, and Sterners and, of course, all of the Reberts. Rebecca helped her with the cooking and the tables groaned with food: stewed and roasted chicken, baked ham, mashed potatoes, applesauce, cole slaw, red beets, cheese, pies and coffee.

After dinner, when everyone had left for home and Annie was tucked in for the night, Edward and Katie went out to the front porch and headed for their favorite rockers. He pulled the rockers close together and they sat side by side in companionable silence. As Katie placed Alex to her breast Edward folded her free hand into his. The rockers moved in unison—creak, thump, creak, thump.

Their land surrounded them, heaven and earth bound together. Corn, tall and dark green in the evening twilight, moved gently in the slight breeze. Lightning bugs blinked on and off. Down by the creek a bullfrog barked at regular intervals, and crickets chirped happily in their evening courting ritual. The baby suckled contentedly at Katie's breast. A strand of hair blew across her face and he reached over to tuck it behind her ear.

"Sometimes I feel I must pinch myself to believe this is all mine," he said huskily.

Katie raised her eyebrow. "It isn't really yours, you know," she chided him. "God only put it in your trust to care for until time to pass it on to future generations."

"My grandfather told me that once." Edward said with a grin. "You're right to remind me of that, though." He chuckled softly. Katie always had a way of putting him right. He looked at her and winked. "And . . . as you well know . . . I'm working hard on that next generation."

Katie giggled and the rockers spoke in the gathering twilight. Creak, thump, creak, thump.

"You know, Katie, when I look out over these fields I feel such contentment. Somehow the way of a farmer satisfies a deep yearning in me. In Jefferson I missed the planting and the harvest, the smell of fresh cut hay, the lowing of cows in the evening at milking time. I guess I'll always be a farmer at heart."

"I think you are a romantic at heart, Edward Rebert," Katie answered, love soft in her voice and clear on her face.

"Pa was always afraid I'd turn out that way," Edward said ruefully. He sobered then, adding, "I worry though, about the war talk. Tempers were short enough before they published that danged book, "Uncle Tom's Cabin". They say it was written as an answer to the Fugitive Slave Law the Congress passed to pacify Southerners who were angry at the addition of free territory in California. Now slaveowners can retrieve their property in any Northern state, aided by federal marshals. No slave can ever be free within the borders of the United States. Northern anger is like a smoldering fire, ready to burst into flame anytime."

"I don't like talk of war, Edward. Surely the disagreement isn't enough to cause resistance, is it?"

"War talk is all I hear when I go to town."

"If there is a war you won't be tempted to fight, will you?" she asked in sudden alarm, jumping upright in her rocker and unceremoniously depriving Alex of her nipple. He howled in protest.

"I'm thirty-two already. If war does come I'll most likely be too old to be called upon. Besides I made you a promise." Even as he said it, he had his doubts. If his home was threatened could he really follow a path of non-resistance? Edward shifted in his rocker and looked across his shadow dappled farmland toward Christ Church in the distance. Time enough to answer that question if war ever came.

"I'm sorry I spoke of it. Now let's enjoy this beautiful evening and not talk of war. The north and south will settle their differences if the danged rabble-rousers in Washington will let them be."

Katie said nothing. Edward took her hand and rocked slowly, more content and in love than he had ever dreamed possible.

Chapter
-17-

Sunday morning birdsong issuing from the oak outside his window was less than welcome and Edward burrowed his head under the pillows trying to get another hours sleep. Unable to block out the noise—the birds sounded like a bunch of chattering females at a quilting bee—he finally surrendered and lay there listening to them clamor and greet each other with pulsating song.

Alex had built dozens of birdhouses according to exact dimensions furnished by the Farmers Almanac. A confirmed tree climber, he then proceeded to attach each tiny house to the high swaying tree branches of every tree near the house. Now, it seemed, sparrows, red-throated finches, nut-hatches and birds of every description had set up housekeeping in these houses and every other cozy nesting place the trees had to offer.

Lazily he turned toward Katie, letting his body cup hers, until they fit together like pieces of a puzzle. He moved his hand to the small of her back and then up to her shoulder. As he buried his head in her fragrant hair he felt her stir.

Katie turned onto her other side so that her head rested on the pillow facing him and he leaned down and softly kissed the hollow of her throat. "Good morning, sleepy head," he said softly.

"What a nice way to awaken." She sighed with pleasure, her voice still husky with sleep.

He looked deep into her eyes. "I love, you Katie. More and more every day. Thank you for marrying me."

"Thank you for asking me. Oh, Edward, dearest I love you too—so much it scares me sometimes."

He caught his breath, hearing the emotion tremble in her voice. His mouth met hers, lightly at first, then warming like a flickering candle bursting into flame. His heartbeat quickened, but there was nothing hurried about the long, slow kiss. He knew Katie enjoyed the warm, satisfying closeness as much as he did.

The din from the trees outside their window must have finally reached her ears because she pulled away and chuckled deep in her throat. "Those birds are determinedly cheerful for so early in the morning," she said.

"Forget the birds," he answered huskily.

Although Edward's financial investment at the sawmill did not earn him the return he had hoped for, his affairs did not worsen. He was able to keep his family in comfort, but there were few frills and no surplus funds for investment in other farms as he had hoped. As it turned out this was fortunate, for in 1857 another panic swept the country, and many of his heavily mortgaged neighbors were wiped out.

That he did not lose his business during the Panic of '57, created envy from a few of his less fortunate friends, but served to increase his image as an astute business man among others. Still the sawmill was outdated, no one was building new houses, and he began to think of moving on to something more lucrative. If only the unsettling war talk would stop.

* * *

Katie sat with a basket of mending in her lap as Edward read to her from the weekly edition of the Gettysburg Compiler. Suddenly he moved the newspaper closer to the oil lamp and stopped reading aloud as he pondered the article before him.

Katie laid her mending in her lap and cleared her throat to get his attention. "What are you not reading to me, Mister Rebert?"

"Thought you didn't want to hear any more about the slavery issue."

"Edward, you make it sound like I don't care! Why, Mennonites have always been against slavery. You know they issued the first formal protest against the hateful practice more than two hundred years ago. I'll admit, though, I get angry when I hear men talk of fighting one another with guns to settle the issue. Now what are you reading? What does the paper say?"

Edward's eyes were steady on hers. He was amused by her interest, he had always respected her perceptiveness. He spread the paper on the table and began reading the article aloud. " 'The attention of the entire nation is riveted on the state of Illinois where two men, Republican Abraham Lincoln and Democrat Stephen Douglas, have launched their campaigns for that state's Senate seat with several fierce debates.

The debates were spawned when Lincoln made his

"House Divided" speech at Springfield June 17, 1858. Douglas answered him at Chicago July 9. Some highlights follow:

Lincoln, at Springfield: "A house divided against itself cannot stand. I believe this government cannot endure permanently half slave and half free. I do not expect the house to fall; but I do expect it will cease to be divided. It will become all one thing, or all the other."

Douglas, at Chicago: Mr. Lincoln advocates boldly and clearly a war of sections, a war of the North against the South, of the Free States against the Slave States . . . He objects to the Dred Scott decision because it does not put the Negro in the possession of citizenship on a equality with the white man. I am opposed to Negro equality . . . I am in favor of preserving, not only the purity of the blood, but the purity of the government from any mixture or amalgamation with inferior races."

The redoubtable "Little Giant" (Douglas) and the gawky "Rail Splitter" (Lincoln) are barnstorming across the state in a series of debates which will cover every angle of the slavery question."

Katie had listened carefully, her motionless hands clutching a partially darned sock, her knuckles white. "We're heading straight into war, aren't we?"

"I admit it worries me. Of course, this is only a race for a Senate seat, not the Presidency. I've believed, all along, that after all their posturing and speech making the politicians would reach a compromise."

"But, this sounds like tempers are getting out of control. Every thing you read to me, Edward, seems to show terrible hostility."

"I agree North and South have awfully bitter feelings toward each other. And its not just over the slavery question either. They're competing against each other economically and the North seems to be winning. That doesn't sit too well with the South."

Edward paged through the paper looking for more news. *What would I do if it really came down to a fight?* Then he shook his head. Brother would never fight brother, not in this grand country.

In the midst of this political turmoil Edward was torn with indecision about the future of the sawmill. Larger lumber companies with powerful circular saws were competing in the market with prices he couldn't meet. Jacob Bollinger had approached him with an offer for the farm and he was solely tempted to sell and get out now.

Edward decided to talk things over with Patrick. Patrick had soundly refused his offer of a job at the sawmill and instead was working at Brewster's Tavern near Gettysburg.

Saturday afternoon Edward rode over to Gettysburg, stopping for a time at Abe Heidel's mill, a new turbine operated circular saw. Edward watched in awe while they put lumber over the saw at the rate of four thousand feet per hour. Plainly his old up-and-down could never compete in such a changing marketplace. After exchanging some small talk with Abe he rode on to Brewster's. The bar was busy with Saturday trade and after greeting each other warmly, Patrick suggested Edward wait until his replacement arrived and then accompany him home for supper. Edward killed the next hour wandering around Gettysburg and after Patrick finished up they rode out of town together.

"I'll race you," Patrick shouted, urging his horse to a

gallop.

It had been years since they rode together. Neck and neck they raced down the Emittsburg Road, crossing the pasture at the Rose farm, scattering surprised cows from their path. The wind whipped through his hair, the horses hooves thundered in his ears. He gulped the crisp air, feeling young and reckless, happy to be with Patrick again.

Patrick was living in a small house along Marsh Creek and as they entered his house Inger greeted him in her usual, quiet, withdrawn manner. She had grown thin, almost haggard, and her once pretty blond hair hung in limp strands against her pinched face. She looked at Edward with eyes dull and joyless.

Their home was plain; an old log structure with creaking wooden floors and few windows. Supper, though hearty enough, was a dreary affair and it seemed to Edward that the meal would never end. Inger served the dishes silently and Daniel and Jamie, unlike his own noisy bunch, sat with downcast eyes.

After pie and coffee he followed Patrick to the front porch. As they settled themselves in comfortable rockers Edward reached over and squeezed the hard arm of his friend. "I've missed you Patrick," he said bruskly.

Patrick ran a meaty hand through his tangle of hair and squinted at Edward from blood-shot eyes. "Adams County agrees with you though. 'Tis a mighty fine horse you're ridin'."

"Ja, and I've two fine trotters stabled. I'll admit my horses are a source of real joy to me," Edward said squaring his shoulders.

"Are you racing them?"

"Only at county fairs. I've entered them at York and Lancaster. Took a blue ribbon at the Adams County fair last year."

They discussed family and friends for several minutes before Edward steered the conversation to the matter concerning him.

"I'm thinking of selling my saw mill, Patrick. It's either that or put a lot of money into improvements."

"You're water powered, aren't you? All the big mills nowadays are going to steam."

"I know and that means a big investment. I'm not sure I want to go that far. I did go from a single blade operation to a gang saw which lets me slice a whole log into planks in a single run. But the circular saws are much superior and much more expensive. I stopped at Heidel's on my way over to see you and looked at his new turbine. Couldn't believe my eyes."

"What would you do if you gave up on lumbering?"

"I don't really know. I still dream of raising trotters and I like farming. It's important to me to stay near Christ Church. I'm an elder now."

"Is there still much timber on your farm?"

"Not really. A lot of the land's been cleared for wheat. I don't have more than thirty acres still in hardwood."

"A big steam operated mill would gobble that up fast," Patrick said, looking at Edward shrewdly. "A profitable mill has to be sure of a close supply of timber. Then, of course, you gotta think of the coming war."

"What do you mean?"

"Sure as hell these northerners and southerners are going to have a go at one another. Won't nobody be building new houses then—all the men'll be off shooting at one another."

They sat quietly while Edward pondered Patrick's words.

"I keep hoping it won't come to actual war," he said finally breaking the silence.

"You're sticking your head in the sand then, friend. The business I'd wanta be in is making gunpowder."

"President Buchanan seems to be steering a middle course though, Patrick. He's not a warmonger."

"He's a doughfaced, namby-pamby. Can't decide whose side he's on. We should have elected that California glamour boy with the pretty wife—young John Fremont."

Edward grinned. "A little sex appeal in an election never hurt. If they'd put his wife on the ticket with him he probably would've won."

"Aye, he scared the hell out of those fancy Wall Street bankers who were afraid the South would hold to their threats to secede. Just wait'll the election in sixty. I'll bet the Republicans are gonna run that fellow Lincoln against that fireball Douglas and then you'll see some fireworks."

"Sometimes I don't know whose side I'm on either," Edward said wryly. "I sometimes think the northern abolitionists are a bunch of hypocrites. They have no qualms about their sweat shops; women and little children working at slave wages in inhuman conditions. To me that isn't much better than owning slaves. I don't think I'm on either side."

Patrick looked at him through narrowed eyes. "You've always been too intellectual. Hell man, you gotta be on one side or the other. What about the moral issue? Either you think slavery's wrong or you don't. You're a bookish man. Didn't you read that book by the Stowe woman called Uncle Tom's Cabin?"

"Yes, and part of the story tells of kind Southerners who take good care of their slaves. Besides, is war any more moral than slavery?"

"But it's that part about Simon Legree with his whips and bloodhounds and little Eva's death that get the people's blood boiling." Patrick rocked furiously. "Tell me, do you believe in the Union?"

"Of course I do. But I also believe in States rights and I don't think we have to go to war and kill one another to settle our problems. Besides, I didn't come here to talk politics."

"It's hard for two men to sit talking together without talkin' politics. Whether it's about slavery or preserving the Union or States rights. It's topmost in every ones mind. And a possibility of war does affect your decision about the mill."

"Ei, you're right about the probable slump in the need for building lumber. A grist mill would probably do better. If there's a war the army will need flour and everybody still has to eat. I've heard of a few grist mills for sale at a good price. I'm tempted to take Bollinger's offer. It's a good one."

"Atta boy. Never knew a Rebert to let a good thing get by him," Patrick said, his voice tinged with sarcasm.

Edward winced, though Patrick's envy was understandable. He was more successful than Patrick, but he'd tried hard never to flaunt it. "You've given me something to think about. It always helps to have someone just to talk to. Now all I have to do is convince Katie to move again. She claims I'm never satisfied. But she does seem set on having a large family and we could use a bigger house."

"A nicer, bigger house usually gets a woman's attention," Patrick commented ruefully.

Edward felt uncomfortable. He knew Patrick was unhappy in his marriage, might even blame him for talking him into it, but he was unsure how much he could say. "If I find a going business maybe I can talk you into coming in with me?" Edward questioned.

Patrick threw back his big head and gave a hearty laugh. "Aye, old pal, I may just surprise you and take you up on that. Then if war does come we can march off together."

They laughed and Edward felt the oneness of an old and faithful friendship.

Part
4

❧

Adams County, Pennsylvania

_1860 - 1864_

Chapter
-18-

A breeze pushed at the fresh lace curtains in the large, airy dining room of their new home, and Edward looked down the table past the chattering children, where his eyes locked with Katie's. A smile turned up the corners of her mouth and tiny laugh lines crinkled the corners of her brown eyes as she returned his gaze. Joy in their family and the realization of their dreams flowed between them, a happiness too deep to need words.

It was purely by luck that he had been able to purchase the beautiful grist mill along South Conewago Creek. Rolling fields perfect for grazing horses, a large two story brick home, a massive bank barn and a prosperous grist mill, all adjoining the land of Hostetter Mennonite Church, were the answer to a prayer. Patrick had heard about the grist mill property, midway between Hanover and Gettysburg, just south of the Bonnaughtown Road. Farmers were still reeling from the Panic of '57 and the rumor was that this valuable property could be bought from the Sneeringer family at a bargain price.

Edward was anxious to tour the farm and he urged Patrick to go with him. They rode over the fields to the highest hilltop and sat quietly astride their horses, sweeping every inch of the one hundred twenty seven acres with a critical gaze. The farm had been badly neglected, fences fallen to the earth, roofs on several of the dependencies damaged by a recent storm, the apple orchard behind the house overgrown. But the land was perfect. It was well drained loam, free of rocks, producing substantial corn, wheat, barley, and beans. Edward sat astride Brandy, his eyes picturing white board fences enclosing paddocks where mares and foals grazed contentedly under graceful shade trees. The fields, gently rolling, would help strengthen the legs of growing foals and the soil was rich enough to produce plenty of quality grass for grazing and good hay. His heart bumped against his chest. He could live and die here in perfect harmony with this earthly bounty.

But sparkling little Conewago Creek pleased Edward most of all. Sneeringer assured him that the mill had never been idle for lack of water and large willow trees lined the creek's banks, providing shade and a look of serenity to the land.

The grist mill was perfectly situated to serve the nearby communities of Hanover, McSherrystown, and Brushtown. It would provide a steady income while Edward developed the horse farm. The house was sturdily built, four bricks thick at its base, with large airy rooms and a beautiful central stairway.

At Katie's insistence Edward first repaired the out-buildings used for a summer kitchen, butchering, and laundry. Edward chafed at the necessary repairs, impatient to begin construction of shelters for the horses. Daily he rode to the highest elevation of the farm, looking over the fields, planning his paddocks and stables and dreaming of the future. They named the farm "Rebert's Choice" and together, vowed that from its loins would spring generations of fine Standardbreds—harness horses to rival the best in the state.

On April 22, 1858, just a month before they moved, Emma Lucinda was born. April had become a busy month for birthdays; Annie, J. Edwin, and now Emma, all appearing every two years, along with the promise of spring. Only Alexander had missed his debut in that glorious month, his birthday was in June.

The grist mill required Edward's full attention, repairs had to be made to neglected fences and buildings, wheat had to be planted to supply the mill, and pasture land developed if he were ever to graze horses. Alexander was only six, a big help with the farm work, but not old enough to be much help in the mill. Edward didn't mind working from dawn to dusk, but he was afraid of failure—afraid he wasn't up to the monumental task he had laid out for himself.

He quickly realized that additional hands had to be hired. He wanted to be free to develop the breeding program and began looking in earnest for someone to run the grist mill and help with the farming. Patrick had shown a lot of interest in his search for the farm and with determination Edward sought him out at Brewster's Tavern.

"I need you to run the grist mill for me," he announced without preamble and what he hoped was a proper mixture of conviction and supplication in his voice.

Patrick raised his bushy red eyebrows in mock surprise. "And what makes you think I'll consider doing that."

"I'll pay more than you're making tending bar, there's a fine tenant house on the property, and I'll train young Daniel to work with me in the breeding operation. He loves animals, you've said so yourself, and would be a natural with the horses."

"Still trying to save me, aren't you?"

Edward was temporarily at a loss for words. Patrick was testy—always had been. But he needed his help and that of his two sturdy boys. "That's not it at all. I need someone I can trust to run the mill. I can't manage it and develop the horse farm, too. I don't need an answer today. Think on it, Patrick." It was true that Edward worried about Patrick working at the tavern, with a plentiful supply of hard liquor to feed his weakness, but it was just as true that he had always needed Patrick's strong presence in his life.

Patrick frowned. "Your offer isn't unexpected. I knew you'd need help with that mill. I've talked the idea over with Inger and she's more than anxious for me to leave the tavern and my drinking buddies here in Gettysburg. The tavern isn't good for me, I know that. Besides . . . ."

Patrick hesitated, wiping beefy hands on a dirty apron before finishing in a voice that was barely audible. "I've missed our friendship."

There was sadness and a hint of desperation in his softly spoken words and Edward knew how hard it was for Patrick to admit his need for help.

Within a month Patrick moved into the tenant house with Inger and his two sons, Daniel and Jamie. Despite Patrick's desire for more children, especially a little girl, Inger had lost two babies, adding to her despair and bitterness. Katie employed her to help in the house, but Inger's joylessness was a burden none of them enjoyed .

With Inger helping Katie, and Patrick running the mill, Edward was free to start construction of his first horse barn.

He and Patrick poured over his plans, arguing over every detail. Edward wanted to build to accommodate sixteen mares, but Patrick felt a stable that large was too ambitious an undertaking. Edward finally compromised by constructing twelve stalls out of sturdy oak with a generous twelve foot aisle running down the center of the spacious barn. He knew even twelve stalls were more than he needed, but he was optimistic and wanted room to grow.

Today Daniel was working in the south pasture, liming and fertilizing where they would sow both clover and timothy and he planned to work with Alex cutting locust posts for a three acre paddock. Since Edward planned to pasture his yearlings outside, summer and winter, they had built only a simple three-sided shed, adequate for shelter during bitter cold or extremely hot weather, and Jamie was helping Patrick put the finishing touches on the shake roof.

Now, as he looked down the table and smiled at Katie, he was ready to announce his next step.

"I want to attend the yearling sales at Harrisburg next month. We need more mares of good breeding. Clear Spring's proving uncertain as a brood mare. She hasn't conceived for the past two years."

Alex frowned, lathering a thick slice of bread with apple butter, and spoke in a halting voice. "You won't get rid of Clear Spring, just because she hasn't foaled, will you? She's my horse."

Edward chuckled. Alex had learned to ride on the bright bay filly out of Brandy and had been named by the children when she unceremoniously dumped Alex into the creek after seeing her reflection in the clear water. Edward was grateful for the one foal they had gotten from her, but this year he thought he'd try to breed her to Bay Hunter. Fortunately Dolly had given them two fillies that were already racing well at the local fairs and was due to foal again in February.

"No, son, I don't intend to sell Clear Spring. We'll try her with a different stallion. She's so gentle tempered she makes a good riding horse even if she doesn't conceive."

Alex took a big bite of bread, smearing apple butter over his nose. "Bet she'd get with foal if'n you put her to that beast they call Ebony, over at Grove's." He blushed when he saw his mother attempting to hide a smile.

"Don't talk with your mouth full," Edward reprimanded, also trying to hide a grin. He pushed away from the table. "I plan to take Daniel with me to the sales. He has a good eye for horseflesh and it's time he got a feel for the business end of running a breeding operation."

Edward did not miss the thunderclouds in Alex's eyes at his announcement. There was no doubt that the boy resented his training of young Daniel, but Alex was still young and Edward needed him to help with general work around the farm. Alex was a good rider, showing a firm seat and steady hands, but with his stocky build he promised to be too heavy to drive a sulky and Edward doubted he would ever have the patience necessary to train horses. Daniel, on the other hand, was a natural, born with an uncanny instinct for handling young animals.

Edward and Daniel attended the January sale in Harrisburg where they bought three fine brood mares and then traveled to Lancaster where Edward picked up a five year old stallion named Bay Hunter, who had strong, clean lines and a proven track record of slightly more than two minutes for the mile. Brandy was still doing well at stud, but he was twenty-five and Edward needed the infusion of fresh, young blood into his stable. He had always been against cross breeding with his fillies and two of Daisy's offspring by Brandy were ready to be bred.

The euphoria of the yearling sale and Bay Hunter's purchase stayed with Edward, making him impervious to the escalating talk of war by impassioned farmers as they gathered and gossiped at the mill. His thoughts were of long legged foals soon to scamper through tall timothy, not of slavery and states rights. Perhaps he was closing his eyes to the problems plaguing the land, but his dream overshadowed all else.

February blew in with a vengeance. Roads were drifted shut, skies leaden, the temperature hovering at five below zero. On a moonless, frigid night, Daniel arrived on their porch and pounded on the door. "Mr. Rebert," he gasped, "come quick. Dolly's about to foal."

Inside the barn all was snug and warm. Dolly was lying on her side in the large roomy stall. She was doing fine and appeared to need no help. "Let her do it on her own, son. We'll watch from outside the stall," Edward said.

Within an hour the membrane sack presented. "There it comes, Mr. Rebert. It looks perfect. Both feet are forward like they should be."

The foal, encased in a thin membrane sack, kicked free and Dolly began to clean him. Daniel couldn't contain his excitement any longer and he rushed into the stall, kneeling beside the little foal. "Ain't he the perfectest thing you ever saw," he cried cradling the wet head in his skinny arms. Edward grinned foolishly, feeling like a proud father. The long hours spent with his horses were rewarded each time a healthy, newborn foal struggled to its feet. He was glad Daniel felt the same way he did. "I think you should have the honor of naming this one. What do you want to call him?"

Daniel thought carefully as he watched the little foal nose Dolly looking for her milk.

"Winter Promise?"

Edward watched the little colt, all head and wobbly legs standing beside its dam as it began to nurse. "I can't think of a better name," he said, tousling Daniel's red hair fondly.

So far he and Katie had done well with their small stable. Breeding was a chancy business; a stallion with a good track record was not necessarily a good breeder and mares could come up barren or the foals might show none of the promise of their sires or dams. He had not yet attempted to train his own trotters. The best racing stables were owned by the extremely wealthy and the money required to buy fine bloodlines would probably always be beyond his means. He was content to breed and sell the offspring of trotters who had proved themselves on local tracks and all of Dolly's foals had been sold and were doing well in harness.

He would keep Winter Promise. He liked the pure lines of the young foal; if he was any judge of horseflesh, Winter Promise should develop into a fine trotter. The colt had all the marks of a magnificent future with long sturdy legs and a deep chest.

Then in May, Cold Spring showed that she was in season. It was time to breed her to Bay Hunter. Bay Hunter had never been used at stud, and Edward felt it was about time he learned his new duties.

Edward led Clear Spring into the end of the breeding shed and positioned her for breeding. He hobbled her, just in case she decided to act up and start kicking, then pulled her tail to the side with a length of rope and fastened it to the breast strap of the hobble. Daniel led Bay Hunter into the shed. This was the young stallion's first introduction to the business of breeding and he looked at the hobbled mare with curiosity. On the race track he had been trained to behave himself around mares in season. Now his owner seemed to expect something different from him and he seemed puzzled.

Edward walked him slowly up to the waiting mare, then away, then back again. Cold Spring showed interest, pricking her ears instead of pinning them back and lashing out. Bay Hunter approached the mare's head and they exchanged noises. Edward led him in a circle until her scent triggered the stallion's response. After a few clumsy attempts he mounted her successfully.

To watch Bay Hunter mount a mare was to see a normally tactile, well behaved horse completely change in appearance and temperament. His neck swelled, his eyes gleamed fiercely and he drew his lips back exposing bared teeth. Screams and growls filled the shed as he gathered himself into a mass of bulging muscle intent on achieving the act for which he had been created.

Edward watched carefully to make sure he actually completed the sex act and bred the little mare. Sure enough, Bay Hunter flagged—moving his tail sharply up and down—an indication that he had ejaculated.

With a surprising reaction of his own, Edward admitted to himself that this was sex in its purest form, and suddenly he wanted Katie intensely. This reaction was pure folly. He had seen the breeding of farm animals all his life, but something about the brute force and savage music of this coupling penetrated Edward's soul. Surely a foal of this union would have to be a very special animal.

March was an extraordinarily cold, blustery month, but April was sweet and warm, and the summer that followed was mild with ample rain, turning pastures lush and green. All summer Katie stood at York market with produce from their bountiful garden. The vegetables—rhubarb, spring onions, asparagus, sugar peas, cabbages, corn, beans, and potatoes—came in orderly progression, one following the other.

Edward loved the flow of crops and orchards; he had always found satisfaction in one season following another, a blueprint for life, never changing.

Fall came and with it the county fairs and more importantly the sulky races. He took the entire family to the Adams County fair where one of Brandy's colts, running as a two year old, won every event he entered. Success on the track was necessary to add prestige to Brandy's line and everything was going so well for them, Edward sometimes wondered if he was dreaming. Even the growing talk of war did nothing to dispel his excitement in the moment. Katie was pregnant again, the baby due in April. Patrick had stopped drinking and had become an excellent foreman at the grist mill, and Cold Spring was due to foal in February.

Every day during the fall of '60 Edward listened to anxious talk as men brought their grain to the mill:

"Honest Abe is his nickname. Got it by a lifetime of fair dealing."

"Just what this sorely swindled nation needs—born in a log cabin and spent his youth splitting fence-rails."

"Addressed a meeting of striking shoemakers. Believes in the right of labor."

"The Democrats can't make up their minds which side of the fence they're on. They've gone and nominated two men—Stephen Douglas of Illinois and John Breckinridge of Kentucky."

"Southerners hate Lincoln. Say he looks like an African gorilla and talks like a third-rate slang-whanging lawyer."

"If all the ugly men in the United States vote for him, he'll surely be elected!"

"If he's elected the South will secede."

"Best to let 'em go."

"Never! Anything would be better than to let 'em go. They'd break up the Union, the best government in the world. Everyone will be called on to do their duty."

"You mean we'd have war?"

"Of course we'd have war."

And so it went, talk and more talk, everywhere men gathered. Then, early one cold November morning, Edward's neighbor, Joseph Kindig, rode into the yard waving a newspaper in his hand. "Lincoln's got elected," he yelled, jumping to the ground, his voice cracking with excitement. "Look at this."

Edward grabbed the paper and read the glaring headlines. 'Republican Lincoln carries the Solid North and wins the Electorial College.'

Edward scanned the paper as Joseph commented, "the Democrats carried the popular vote, but damned if they didn't split the ticket right down the middle between Douglas and Breckinridge. This'll make the Southerners furious. Mark my words, Edward, war's coming!"

Lincoln's election did indeed set the nightmare in motion. The Union began to break up. South Carolina was the first to go. By February Florida, Mississippi, Alabama, Georgia, Louisiana, and Texas had all seceded and formed a new union — the Confederate States of America — with a President of their own, Jefferson Davis.

Edward followed the news with mounting dismay. President Buchanan sat in the White House wringing his hands, waiting anxiously for Lincoln to take office. On March 4th Lincoln delivered an Inaugural Address which was conciliatory, but perfectly firm. Two days later President Davis called for 100,000 Confederate volunteers and at 4:30 A.M. April 12, 1861 a dull boom and a spurt of flame broke the misty silence at Fort Sumter, South Carolina.

War had come.

Chapter
-19-

Breakfast over, Edward hurried across dew-wet grass toward the mill. It was April twenty-second, ten days into the war he had never believed possible, and the sun, golden against a pale blue sky, promised a glorious day. Through the hemlocks and pines separating his place from John Lehman's farm he could see a lamp burning in the Lehman kitchen. Today, their oldest son, Luther, was going to war. The New Oxford National Guard, hurriedly organized by Dr. Michael Pfeiffer, was scheduled to leave the Square at ten o'clock. He thought of the mothers all over the valley fixing hearty farm breakfasts, trying hard to hide tears of anxiety as they fussed over their young sons dressed in showy blue jackets, red trousers and caps, their young faces glowing with excitement.

How could there possibly be war in a land so grand? Here on his farm cherry trees were in full bloom, filling the hillsides with fleecy white blossoms and beside the path he was traveling there stretched a carpet of violets and anemones. The water wheel splashed softly in the soft morning peace. April was color and bloom, not blood and killing.

As he sauntered across the meadow his mind relived the events of the past two weeks.

Fort Sumter had touched off a wave of patriotic excitement and boys recruited from New Oxford, Hanover, Littlestown, Gettysburg, and East Berlin rushed to join the Union cause. Daniel was one of the first to join and Patrick watched with pride as his young son drilled in the New Oxford Square.

Now that hostilities had commenced, the entire community was in a state of ferment. Rumors flew, but no one really knew what was going on. Bridges were burned on the line of the Northern Central Railway, interrupting communication between Washington and the North. Newly recruited troops moving to the front were assailed by a mob on the streets of Baltimore and just last Friday a rumor had thrown the entire populace of Hanover into a panic when they believed the Baltimore rowdies were coming to destroy their town. Villagers had gathered at the mill to talk and laugh sheepishly about the excitement and Edward smiled, imagining their anger and confusion although he probably would have been as terrified as they. He heard variations on the story over and over.

It seemed that Massachusetts troops, on their way to Washington, were assailed by a mob on the streets of Baltimore and several soldiers and civilians were killed. The news threw Hanover into a frenzy; Baltimore was only forty miles away. Then when a Captain Jenifer, recently arrived from Texas, rode into Hanover on his way to visit friends in Maryland, a set of bizarre circumstances was set in motion. Someone started the false rumor that the good Captain was deserting to the Southern secessionists and a Hanover burgess was ordered to detain him in the town jail.

A cry soon spread through town: "To arms! To arms! The

Baltimore rowdies are coming to destroy the town and Jenifer is to lead them."

This was like applying a lighted match to gunpowder. A panic ensued, the unfounded rumor spreading through the town like wildfire. Horsemen galloped to and fro warning people of impending danger. Stores and dwellings were closed. Women and children, terror stricken, began firing alarm guns and tolling bells. One woman seized a large feather bed and fled from her house to the country, leaving her silver and jewelry behind. A young mother snatched up her child and ran several squares before its screams attracted the attention of persons less excited, who discovered that she was carrying the poor child upside down. One old gentleman was short of ammunition. Mounting his old horse, with his gun in hand, he dashed up and down the street shouting in Pennsylvania German, "Wo kann ich koogla griega? Wo kann ich koogla griega?" (Where can I get bullets?) Another one got down his flint-lock shotgun and in his haste to load it, and light his pipe to calm his nerves at the same time, he put the tobacco into the gun and the powder into his pipe. Having occasion to use the pipe first, he discovered his mistake by the explosion which seriously damaged his eyes.

The market house in the center of town was the rallying point and here the excitement and confusion were intense. Calm finally prevailed when Rev. Dr. Zieber, who had ascertained the unfounded origin of the rumor, mounted a meat block in the market house and counseled calmness, or Hanover would be forever disgraced as a community.

These and other stories were told time and time again as men passed the time of day at the mill, waiting for their flour.

Edward sighed deeply, entering the mill by a side door. He had spent a sleepless night, thinking about today and the departure of Daniel and other local boys. He'd get the grinding stones started, then he could leave the mill in the hands of Annie and Alex and ride into New Oxford to say good-by to young Daniel.

An hour later things were running smoothly and he left the mill for town, following a trail close beside Conewago Creek. He passed Brushtown, descended one hill and climbed the next. There were few homes here, but all showed activity. Up ahead he saw two riders, and as he gained on them he recognized Patrick's burly frame. He hailed them with a shout and they pulled up to wait for him.

"Don't you wish you were going?" Daniel called, his face flushed with excitement.

Patrick gave a wry chuckle and fixed Edward with a quizzical stare while trying to quiet his prancing horse.

It had become a wearisome question and Edward frowned as he answered. "No, I don't."

"You're gonna miss all the excitement. Poppa says he'll be joining up if things don't end before he can get his affairs in order and Jamie will be coming in soon as he's sixteen."

Edward looked at Patrick with raised eyebrows, though the comment shouldn't have surprised him, knowing Patrick as he did.

They rode on together, Daniel chatting easily showing none of the sorrow that plagued Edward. Leaving the Conewago at Brushtown they followed the smaller Plumb Creek north. Their trail took them past Conewago Chapel and Edward pulled up for a minute to admire the lovely brownstone church.

"I hear that's the oldest stone Catholic church-house in the United States," Daniel said.

Patrick chuckled at Daniel's interest. "Sure, an' it's a contradiction for us today, lad. The Jesuits who founded the chapel back in the 1700's farmed its one thousand acres with the help of *slaves*."

Edward shook his head. "Slaves are no novelty around here although many Northerners don't want to acknowledge that fact. Even today I know of a number of landowners in these parts with household slaves. Why just last week a gent in Gettysburg was advertising for his runaway." He dug his heels into Brandy's flanks to resume their journey. They climbed a steep road into Irishtown, passing a dozen or more houses and a church with a handsome spire. The village streets were lined with oak and chestnut, the yards lush and green.

In the distance they could smell the smoke belching from Diehl's tannery on the outskirts of Oxford. It reminded Edward, none too favorably, of his years in Jefferson. The horses picked their way across the Gettysburg Railroad tracks and they turned up Main Street toward the square and the gathering crowd.

Edward left Patrick and Daniel to themselves so they could say their goodbys in private. He tied up one block from the Square and walked back slowly. He would miss Daniel; the boy had become like his own son. Edward's throat felt dry.

Bands were playing as the Volunteers formed into ranks and Edward spotted J.J. leaning against a wall outside the Washington House. He walked over to join him.

J.J. was unalterably opposed to the Civil War. He noted

frequently to Edward that he could not bear the thought of "shooting at his own countrymen." Edward suspected that he didn't want them shooting at him either.

"I see young Daniel among the recruits," J.J. said.

"Ei, he looks handsome in his new uniform doesn't he?"

"Handsome an' happy. Like he was going to a party or something. They're headed for a training camp at York, I hear. That'll wipe the cocky smile from his face."

A drum roll interrupted their conversation as the formation of new recruits began moving down the street behind their streaming regimental flag. Patrick marched proudly beside Daniel and the crowd fell in behind the band of Volunteers, following them to the edge of town. Everyone was cheering and singing "Yankee Doodle" and every hand waved a flag or a bouquet of flowers.

The boys were soon out of sight and Edward found Patrick at his side. Patrick looked at him soberly. "The lad will be all right. This war'll be over in a coupla weeks, long before I get a chance to join."

Several days after the departure of the New Oxford Volunteers Katie gave birth to another little girl. They named her Ellen Catharine.

Edward tried to hide his disappointment from Katie. They had five children now, three girls and only two boys. Much as he loved his daughters, he had hoped for another son; a farm needed boys.

The summer that followed was almost festive, a time of preparation for what everyone felt certain would be a quick and decisive spanking of the south. Edward wasn't so sure of that. He attended a large rally in Littlestown where orators on platforms draped with yards of red, white and blue bunting, gave eloquent speeches to the accompaniment of brass bands and enthusiastic cheers. Large quantities of barbecued pork and chicken were consumed and the crowd was inflamed with patriotism, singing lustily and waving their flags.

It was a summer of rousing parades, tearful goodbys, boys marching behind their drummer in new uniforms and jaunty caps, prayers, optimism, sadness, and fog.

Edward had never seen such fog before. Day after day, it hid the brightness of the sun. It was hard to crawl out of bed in the morning; easier to lay cocooned in sleep and fog, wrestling with his conscience while two of his nephews marched off to defend his precious Pennsylvania.

Katie couldn't abide the fog. Every morning it invaded the house, creeping through the window sills and under the doors. She pushed rags into the cracks under doors and around windows but still the fog crept in. The swirling fog was a living thing, giving the house a fusty smell, disrupting her careful routine, shrouding the land in ghostly secrecy.

Boys, waiting at the mill for flour, talked eagerly of their plans to join their state regiment the minute they could be spared from their farms, but Edward's thoughts warred with one another as he listened quietly. In July came disappointing news of the Union loss at Bull Run. Edward read accounts of the battle with dismay—how congressmen and their ladies had driven out in fancy carriages to watch with curiosity, in an almost picnic atmosphere, young men butchering one another. These same carriages and spectators clogged the roads as the Union troops, confused and bewildered, scurried to retreat.

In this summer of 1861 Annie was almost nine years old, tall for her age and slender, with golden hair the color of autumn corn. She was a regular little mother to baby Ellen and a real help to Katie in the kitchen. Alexander was seven, with huge brown eyes and chestnut hair; a perfect replica of his mother even down to the freckles she had sported when she was young and which Alex hated with a passion. Jonas Edwin had just turned five, a laughing, carefree child with apple-red cheeks, and Emma, a regular little tom-boy with plump pigtails and bright blue eyes, was three. But despite happiness with his growing family Edward worried about the progress of the war. The north still hadn't won a major engagement and the south was riding high.

By fall Edward's neighbors were no longer prophesying an easy victory, of ending the whole affair in one decisive swoop. The grist mill became an important gathering place where farmers had an hour or so to exchange the news while they waited for their flour. The men began to talk of a war that might go on for a year or longer; the south just might be stronger, more full of piss and vinegar than the northerners gave them credit for. Edward listened to the men brag of their sons, proud young Union soldiers, and he became more troubled, but he remained silent and offered no comment. He was no longer certain he could keep his vow to Katie — or his commitment to himself.

The days and weeks seemed interminable, but summer dragged on. Despite their outward bravado men were fearful. The Maryland border was a few miles distant and an invasion seemed more than possible. Edward worried about his horses and considered sending them further north, like many of his neighbors were doing.

One foggy evening, after bidding the last customer goodnight he closed the mill and, brooding and lonely, made his way to the stable. The Pennsylvania countryside lay misty and bleak under grey skies. Barren hardwood trees stood like silent sentries along the roadside, their naked branches a pattern of dark lace against the low clouds. He shivered in the raw cold, buttoning his blue woolen jacket to his neck. His moods had always been sensitive to the weather and   tonight a deep sense of foreboding filled him with sadness.

What he wouldn't give for the comfort of Duke beside him tonight! His horses filled a need, but they would never replace Duke.

From various places in the barn came the soft rustle of hay and the chomp of horses eating. He walked directly to Brandy's stall, feeling in his pocket for one of the apples he always kept handy. Brandy immediately stuck his handsome head over the half door, the soft brown nose investigating Edward's shirt pocket for sugar. Edward scratched the underside of Brandy's jaw, talking to him softly, savoring the tangy scent of horse and hay.

In the depths of the stable a horse whinnied and stamped in alarm and Edward looked up to see Patrick walking toward him.

"Evening, Patrick. Sit yourself down," Edward said, waving toward a nearby mound of hay. "What brings you out on a night like this?"

Patrick gave him a weak smile. "Let's walk down to the millpond. I've something I want to talk about."

They walked through the swirling fog to the pond, ghostly in the murky light. Patrick leaned his back against an old split-rail fence separating field and water and looked across the meadow while Edward placed his foot on one of the rails and stared into the water, chewing on a piece of straw.

Patrick finally spoke. "I've come to tell you I'm joining up. I'll be leaving sometime next week."

They stood staring at each other, the fog deepening the silence of their thoughts.

Edward threw the tattered piece of wet straw on the ground. "I thought the local militia had its quota."

"Aye, they do and I could wait till there's another recruitment drive from here, but I'm anxious to go. Inger's brother, up in Potter County, wrote that the Pennsylvania Reserves are recruiting lumbermen who are good shots and can bring their own rifles into service with them. They're nicknamed the "Bucktails". Each recruit brings the tail of a buck he shot to prove his skill with a rifle. Aye, an' you know that kinda appeals to me; they wear the deer's tail on their hats."

Edward was silent for a long minute, before answering. "I thought it would be enough, with Daniel serving."

"Aren't you worried about the Union, Edward?" Patrick asked softly.

"Of course I am. Worried and troubled."

"The tide of things'll shift soon. The North will win. We're in the right and right always wins out."

"That's what troubles me so, the right or wrong of it. War is so senseless . . . and stupid, Patrick. Killing one another isn't the right way to settle the problem."

"Our grandfathers helped create this country, Edward. It can't survive if it's broke in two. That's worth fightin' to save, don't you think?"

"Maybe the states don't have enough in common to stay together as a country. The North, with its factory system based on free labor is far ahead of the South both economically and politically and the South is so involved in its slave and cotton investments it can't change even it wants to. Maybe they would be better separate, with trade agreements between them. The North and the South. Maybe even the West would be better separate."

"Tis a bunch of nonsense you're talking. It'd be just like Europe, each section always fighting one another for political superiority. Surely, you don't want to see that in this country."

"I'm not saying that is the answer," Edward said hastily. "But it could happen. I only wish there were an easier way than war to find a solution to our differences."

"Ain't no other way. Hate between north and south has been fanned into flames so strong only a war kin put out the blaze."

"You know, Patrick, there are many families as divided as we seem to be. Take the Shriver family over by Union Mills. Andrew Shriver lives in the old homestead and is for the Union, with a son in the 26th Pennsylvania, while William Shriver was so upset he built himself a mansion just across the road and is a Southern sympathizer with seven boys in the Confederate Army."

Patrick grinned. "And the funny part of that story is that Andrew owns slaves, but William doesn't."

"I know—its a mess isn't it? That's another thing troubling me, Patrick. You know of my feelings about fighting and my promise to Katie. We've talked about it often enough. I guess I never really believed I'd have to make a choice. I thought I'd be too old to serve, but they're talkin' about a national draft if this thing goes on much longer. The recruitment act won't be able to supply enough men once this first flush of patriotism is over."

"You're what—forty or forty one?" Patrick asked with a frown.

"Forty, last month."

"Well, you've got five little ones. That'll probably exempt you if your age don't. That is if you don't want to serve."

"I don't know if I care for the way you put that."

Patrick's jaw tightened. "Well I don't know as I ever understood your reasons for refusing to defend your home, except for some sentimental pledge you made to Katie."

Edward flared. "It's a heck of a lot more than that and you know it. Defend is one word—killing is another. I simply could not serve as a soldier and remain true to Katie and my God."

"Still seems like a coward's way out. Try explaining this non-resistance thing to me, once more."

Edward took a deep breath and let it out slowly. It was terribly important that he make Patrick understand. "Loyalty to my wife and a vow I made to her is part of it. To dishonor that vow would be a betrayal, surely. But Mennonites place strong emphasis on Christian love, Patrick. It's not just mere sentiment, it's a way of life for them. That's why they hold that the use of violence in dealing with others is against the Bible. Patrick, you do not kill people simply because they believe differently over an issue, no matter how big."

A wave of dull crimson moved up Patrick's face with each word Edward uttered. "Bullshit! Wartime calls for another kind of thinking. This war is tearing our country apart and you spout Christian love. I think you're using those fancy bible phrases as an excuse. I think you're a coward. Hiding behind a woman's skirt, an'. . ."

Edward jumped to his feet, his fists clenching. "Those are fighting words," he shouted. Heart-burning acid rose like gall in his throat.

"Thought you only believed in love!"

Edward swallowed and fought for control. He'd just talked about love and values. He must return hostility with kindness. It was the hardest thing he'd ever had to do.

"It often takes more courage not to fight than to join the parade, Patrick. Katie hasn't ever tried to change me on matters of religion, but we both feel deeply about conscientious objection to bearing arms."

"Conscientious objection? You saying your conscience keeps you from fighting to preserve the union?"

"Conscience? Just what is that? I won't get into a war of words with you. You are not my conscience, nor is Katie. Some men will fight from a misguided conscience, some with a hardened conscience, and still others will go into this war driven by a sense of guilt. Some honestly believe they are doing God's bidding. Every man confronts his conscience from his own perspective and every man should make his own decision. And Katie has always understood that and let me make my own choice."

" 'Tis a fact, though, fear of war is a weakness most women share," Patrick said with exasperation. "Inger's been moaning and wringing her hands ever since I announced my intentions."

Edward leaned heavily against the rail. "I'll not break my

vow or go against my moral convictions. I've always tried to be loyal to our friendship, Patrick, but I have to listen to my inner self which tells me it's wrong to kill another. I remember an old veteran from the Revolutionary war once telling me about his first killing. It was a haunting tale. He was only a lad of sixteen when he came up against a Redcoat, no older than himself. He remembered looking straight into that young boy's eyes when he pulled the trigger. Said war was more than killing—it was downright murder. I never forgot his story. I can serve the Union in some other way. I'll run the mill, day and night, if I have to; I'll give every barrel of flour we turn out to the army. But I won't kill, Patrick . . . I can't," he said, his voice dropping to a whisper. He felt very helpless and frightened.

The silence stretched between them. Patrick blinked and watched the fog. "We've shared too much over the years to part enemies," he said, so softly Edward had to strain to hear him. "I'm not sure I understand you, but I've always loved you as a brother."

They stood side by side, leaning slightly on the rail fence, staring across the misty fields. Edward laid his hand on Patrick's rigid arm. "Our roads, then, must finally fork. You must listen to your conscience; I must listen to mine."

They turned to look at one another. Patrick held out his hand and Edward clasped it tightly, the dampness on his cheek more than the wet fog hanging over the land.

Chapter

-20-

White drifts of snow blanketed Adams County, farmers coming to the mill carried the hard news of battles lost, and there was no longer talk of an easy victory. Edward listened with fascination to talk of places he had never heard of—Ball's Bluff, Oak Hill, and Wilson's Creek. He learned to recognize the names of the new heros in the north—McClellan, Seward, and Pennsylvania's own Thaddeus Stevens. The south proclaimed heros named Stonewall Jackson and Robert E. Lee. And he became more worried about his own status in all this turmoil.

Then in February 1862, the North rejoiced in its first real victories and Ulysses S. Grant's name was on every tongue. Ft. Henry, in Tennessee and then Fort Donelson fell to the Union and farmers laughed with pride and congratulated each other on the bravery of their boys. Everyone believed again. The war would soon be over.

"What do you think, Katie?" Edward asked, putting down the paper he had been reading aloud. "Doesn't it sound like it's about over?"

"Do you really think so?" she said, in a tone that surprised him with its sharp edge. "Do you actually believe this senseless war is over?"

"No I don't," he admitted quietly. "It's what I want to

think, but in my heart I know better. Tomorrow will be another battle and young boys will go right on killing one another."

"Don't talk of killing, please. Little pitchers have big ears," she said, nodding toward Alex, sitting at the kitchen table, pretending to be engrossed in his school work. "And why is all the talk about Grant. Isn't General McClellan in charge of the Army of the Potomac?"

"He seems to be just sitting in the East doing nothing. I imagine President Lincoln is pretty upset with him. Grant's the one winning battles down south."

"The President seems so sad every time I see his picture in the papers. In the midst of all this trouble he must be devastated over the death of his son, Willie, from typhoid."

"Lincoln doesn't have an easy time of it," Edward agreed laying the paper aside. "People everywhere make fun of him and criticize him . . . north and south alike. They blame him for the failures of the army and they call him ugly and ignorant."

"Well, I can't explain why, but I have a great deal of faith in our president—he looks as though he really feels the pain of the people, black and white alike," Katie said, softly.

Edward nodded slowly in agreement. "I think you're right Katie. Someday I believe, Mr. Lincoln will be a great man in our children's history books."

Late in June Edward had a letter from Patrick. The Bucktails had seen their first fighting at Mechanicsville and Gaines Mill, both in Virginia. Alex poured over the letter, a look of hero worship in his brown eyes, a look Edward noticed was absent when Alex turned his gaze on him.

That summer was the busiest yet at the grist mill. Jamie enlisted the minute he was sixteen, so Patrick and both of his boys were gone. All the young men were gone; hired help was impossible to find. Edward had to rely on Alexander, who was only eight, to do a man's work. Even Annie helped when Katie could spare her.

On a hot, sultry day early in July Alex was busy feeding grain into the hopper poised above the grinding stones and Annie was controlling the angle of the shoe, which fed the grain from the hopper to the runner stone, when the string attached to the tip of the shoe broke causing severe damage to the grinding stone.

Edward felt his temper flare and yelled at Annie. "Now what will I do? A stone dresser will be impossible to find. They're all in the Army." With chagrin he remembered Pa's attempt to make a stone dresser out of him when he was still a boy. His memory hurtled back to Grandfather Johann's old mill and the distillery. He hadn't thought of the distillery in years.

"It weren't her fault," Alex said, in defense of Annie who was standing with tears brimming in her bright blue eyes. "The danged string let go and they's so much noise in here we couldn't tell somethin' was wrong."

"And I think your English is mighty bad for a young fellow attending school on a regular basis," Edward said, sternly. Seeing Annie's tears he put his hand on her shoulder and attempted to smile. "It seems like everything's been in need of mending lately and I can't get help or materials with this war still going on."

Alex glowered at him. "Yah, all the men are off fighting for their country. Men with guts and courage that is."

Edward gripped the lever controlling the grinding stone until his knuckles turned white. "It often takes more courage to abstain from fighting than to fight, son." He released the lever and wiped his hands on his pants. "I'm sorry. I don't mean to take my anger out on you children. Come now, we'll tie off the sacks of flour and middlings and, Annie, you can go back to the house and help your mother. Alex and I will see if we can't fix the damage."

Annie wiped the tears from her face and grabbed a handful of ties. She finished in no time and hurried toward the door.

Katie had just finished baking bread and she wiped little drops of sweat from her upper lip and chin. She smiled at Annie and handed her a fresh apron with a quick hug. "I missed my best helper this morning," she said. "Emma tries, but she's too little yet to be of much use."

Annie smiled in gratitude, then cocked her head to one side, listening intently. "Isn't that a wagon I hear," she asked, running out to the porch.

In a minute Katie heard her calling in excitement. "Mama, mama, come quick. The huckster wagon is coming."

A buggy clattered down the lane from the Hanover Road and stopped in front of the house. It gleamed in the sun—bright yellow with red wheels—pulled by a spanking team of black horses, their harnesses studded with bright brass fittings.

Katie hurriedly tied on a clean apron, smoothed her hair, and went out to the front gate. The children appeared out of nowhere and the dog was barking furiously, his tail wagging in excitement.

"Edwin, run out to the mill and tell your Poppa that Jacob is here from McSherrystown. Annie, go to the hen house and bring me those six culled hens I set aside and the egg crate," Katie said, hurrying to greet the huckster.

"Morning, Jacob. You're early today."

"Your farm is my first stop this morning, Mrs. Rebert," Jacob said as he rolled up the canvas sides of the wagon to reveal shelves laden with merchandise.

Katie felt a flush of excitement as she viewed the treasures displayed in the crowded interior. Bolts of muslin and calico, stockings, overalls, straw hats, candy, hardware items, horse collars, dry beans, corn meal; drugs such as Epsom salts, castor oil and cough syrup. One entire side of the wagon was given over to sugar, flour, spices, salt and precious coffee.

Jacob climbed nimbly into the back of the wagon and pulled out several large boxes filled with Mason jars, lids and rubbers. "Had a right hard time gettin' these for you, what with the war and all," he said.

"I thank you for your trouble, Jacob," she said. "The peaches are ready for canning and we have a good crop this year." She gazed at the sundries arranged on a shelf. "I think I'll take two of those pretty hair ribbons for the girls. Times haven't been as bright and happy as they should be lately."

"Now that's a fact, Mrs. Rebert. Used to be picnics, square dances and candy-makings at all the farms. Now-a-days you never see a laughin' crowd of young people. All the boys are off fightin'."

Katie picked out some sugar, rice, a sack of coffee beans, and a tin of soda crackers and was busy looking at a bolt of calico when Edward arrived with both boys in tow.

"Good to see you again, Mr. Rebert. Last time I was here you was over at the Hanover auction," Jacob said extending a thin hand in greeting.

"Good to see you, Jacob. Ja, I was buying a few horses. Brandy is getting pretty old now, about due to be retired. Say, I heard your boy was in the fighting at Shiloh. He's alright isn't he?"

Jacob Brightner slumped just a little more and fixed Edward with a tired, haunted look. "We had a letter from him. Says it was a terrible battle, never seed so many men and boys laid low. It was worsen Ft. Donelson and he thought that bad. Somedays, the Missus and I despair of ever seeing him again. More'n thirteen thousand were kilt at that there Shiloh."

"Thirteen thousand!"

"Ja," Jacob spat. "And neither side could claim winning."

Katie saw Edward's face cloud with dismay. He quickly leaned over to take a nice ax-handle from the wagon. "Guess I could use this, Jacob and a gallon of kerosene if you have some." Then, seeing shy little Emma peeking from behind Katie's skirt he added, "and a penny's worth of candy for each of the children."

Annie had returned to the wagon with the chickens and eggs and Katie noticed her quietly eyeing a little shelf of toiletries. "If my eggs and chickens are pay enough for my purchases, Jacob, I think I'd like that small, pink bottle of toilet water," she said.

She saw Edward's smile as his gaze dropped to the hair-ribbons in her market basket. She didn't believe in spoiling the children, but there was so little gaiety around them these days. Let the girls have their toilet water and hair ribbons.

Edward looked at Edwin and Alex standing quietly at his side. "And I think maybe the boys could use a few of those marbles you have in that big jar, Jacob."

* * *

News from the war front continued to filter in from the capitol and was discussed at the mill or wherever the citizenry of Adams County met. Fears were growing stronger that the Confederate Army would begin to move north and into Pennsylvania. Uncertainties mounted and Edward knew with a suffocating sense of dread that there was no longer any doubt about it. War was about to explode on his doorstep.

Then in September, after a victory at Bull Run, Lee began his march toward the Potomac. By moving into Maryland, a border state deeply divided in its sentiments, he hoped to swing the people of that state to the side of the Confederacy and to relieve Virginia for a time of the ravages of war.

In Littlestown, only a few miles from the border, the invasion of Maryland hit like an exploding shell as a Maryland farmer rode into town shouting the news. Days later the Hanover Star and Banner carried the chilling story. Lee had split his forces into two wings, Jackson and six divisions converged on Harpers Ferry on September 15th, and two days later Longstreet with three divisions enroute to Hagerstown engaged the Union Forces at the tiny town of Sharpsburg, Maryland. In "the bloodiest single day of the war" fighting raged along the Antietam Creek. Badly outnumbered Lee withdrew into Virginia and Edward and Katie gave a great sigh of relief.

The Antietam Campaign was the victory for which Lincoln had been waiting to announce his controversial "Emancipation Proclamation."

When the war began, Lincoln had proclaimed it a war only to prevent secession; the South was to keep her slaves after rejoining the Union. Now the President saw that a more motivating force was needed to bolster flagging Northern spirits and he began to outline a plan to extend basic human rights to every human being. This plan would outlaw slavery in all states that continued to rebel against the Federal Government and changed the entire aspect of the war from a political affair to preserve the Union to a crusade to free the slaves.

Edward sat on a rail fence gazing quietly at the peaceful scene before him. The red brick walls of his mill rose in quiet solitude beside the narrow stream, covered with ice and pristine snow. Water from the millpond above, leaking through the sluice, was frozen in place, like a frothy waterfall; the giant overshot waterwheel silent on this cold February morning in 1863.

He had never seen anything quite so beautiful—the winter sun sparkling on the ice, the snow glinting like sparkling jewels, his breath drifting like fog before his face.

In years past the frozen millpond might have been covered with laughing teen-aged boys and girls as they flirted and courted one another on ice skates. The boys were gone now—fighting on unfamiliar soil far from home. Only his young children could be seen gliding around the pond's frozen surface.

If only his thoughts could be as tranquil as the scene

before him. But instead his mind raced in tumultuous circles, destroying his sleep and making him short tempered with everyone. Here under the clear sky, with the cold stillness and space about him, maybe he could untangle the knots of his conscience.

The state recruitment act now included men from eighteen to the age of forty-five. He was forty-one. Unless one had the money necessary to hire a substitute, which was common practice among men with means, service was no longer voluntary. Three hundred dollars was what it took for a substitute. *I can afford that,* he thought, *but do I want to?*

Aside from the religious views he shared with Katie there were other more practical reasons to take advantage of this system of substitute-hiring. The law had been passed, he felt sure, for men like him with large families of small children. Katie was five months pregnant and having a very difficult time carrying this child. She was sick morning and night and her ankles and legs were swollen grotesquely. He was terribly worried about her and feared that she might miscarry. Besides, Alexander was only eight, certainly not old enough to take over the responsibility of the home and mill. Patrick was gone, there was no one at all he could call on for help, and flour was desperately needed by the Army.

Still, he cringed at the very idea of hiring another man to fight in a war for him. It was almost unthinkable. Could he pay someone to fight in his place, just because that option was open to him; pay someone to die in his place? Could he ever live with himself if that happened? But could he live with himself if he was asked to kill another man? And that is what he would be asked to do. The dilemna gnawed at his stomach.

The war was not going well for the North. Stories of the latest Confederate victories, at Fredericksburg and Stones River, brought despair to all who read the news.

The fighting was getting closer to Pennsylvania, that was certain. The Confederate invasion of Maryland last September, terminating at Antietam Creek, was only forty miles away. And Jeb Stuart's cavalry had caused havoc in the western part of Adams County, seizing horses, cattle, wagons, and even seven unlucky citizens they used as hostages.

All of his neighbors were frightened; no one ventured far from home, especially after nightfall, and despite Katie's protests Edward kept his old flintlock with him at all times. Could he even think of leaving a pregnant wife and five little children to fend for themselves when there was an alternative?

He had talked for hours with Reverend Sechler and, of course, with Katie, but he knew the decision rested squarely on his shoulders. And he could put it off no longer.

Slowly in the peace and quiet of this snow-swept countryside he found part of his answer. His strength had always come from God. He would ride over to Christ Church and there in the comforting peace of its little chapel he would pray for guidance. He should have known before that his answer could only come from there.

He went to the barn, saddled Brandy, and headed across the snow covered field separating the barn from the church. As many times as he had approached the church from this angle the sight of it sitting serenely atop the slight knoll still stirred something deep within him.

He entered the small vestibule, which smelled of lemon oil and candle wax, and climbed to one of the three galleries high on the end wall where he would be unnoticed by anyone entering the church. He sat quietly letting the peace of the church quiet the turmoil in his soul before dropping to his knees.

He would pray and then he would make his decision.

* * *

Excerpt from the Star and Banner,

Hanover, Pa. The following is a list of substitutes for drafted men in Adams County, Union Township.

Philip Kretz for Philip Sterner
Jacob Groff for Andrew Sell
George Winters for John Rife
Jacob Bollinger for Henry Bollinger
John A. Gerrick for Andrew Gerrick
Emanuel Sell for Adam Lease
Anthony Kerch for Abraham Rife
John Waller for George D. Basehoar
William Sickle for Edward Rebert

Chapter
-21-

For months refugees from Virginia, fleeing from the Shenandoah Valley, passed through Hanover, coming by way of Harpers Ferry and Frederick. Wagons, loaded with bedding, furniture and household utensils, often stopped over night in Hanover's Center Square.

In early May 1863, Edward and Katie heard that there had been a terrible battle at a place called Chancellorsville, Virginia. This was a great Southern victory, but here the Southerners lost Stonewall Jackson, accidentally shot by his own men. This battle had followed another great Southern victory at Fredericksburg and from all reports General Robert E. Lee had now decided the time was ripe for an invasion of the North.

By the beginning of June the Confederates had fought their way up the Shenandoah Valley of Virginia, then moved through Maryland by way of Hagerstown, and were now approaching Pennsylvania.

Then late in June, just as wheat began turning the countryside into glorious shades of gold, Confederate forces entered Pennsylvania and Edward's world narrowed totally to the region of his own inner self. His home and family were threatened. This changed everything.

The final days of June approached with the delightful

warmth of May rather than the heat of mid-summer. Days were warm, but nights were cool enough for a blanket. Edward sat with Katie on the front porch during long summer twilights, listening to the sweet song of the wood thrush and watching fireflies sprinkle the darkness with light. Life was once more quickening within Katie; their sixth child was due next month.

Earlier in the summer Governor Curtin had ordered all citizens of Pennsylvania along the Maryland border to move their valuables north for safety and protection. A general stampede had started and for weeks roads throughout the valley were clogged with cattle, horses, sheep and hogs hurrying to cross the Susquehanna River at Harrisburg. In addition to the livestock there were long lines of wagons loaded with grain and whiskey, and scores of frightened families running from the threatening danger. Banks were urged to transfer their money to Philadelphia and by the end of June there was hardly a bank open in all of Adams county.

So far Edward had not moved his horses. Spring was an especially critical time for new born foals, and if he were to relocate them he would have to move them with their dams. But daily he became more apprehensive. Being close to the border they had lived with the threat of invasion since the outbreak of the war, but there was something different this time, something that made him uneasy . . . as uneasy as the stallions pacing in the barn. Shadows were moving over the land and fear was in the air—the horses sensed it.

* * *

Edward found Katie in the yard hanging clothes on the line. Annie was helping by reaching into the wicker basket to hand her mother each piece of wet clothing, while two year old Ellen was playing nearby, trying unsuccessfully to keep a kitten, dressed in doll clothes, confined to a toy carriage. Emma and Edwin were playing tag, Emma squealing loudly each time she was caught. Edward plucked a sun-warmed apricot from a tree and leaned back against the rough bark, watching Katie. She had no idea how lovely she looked, a floppy white sun-bonnet framing rosy cheeks, her body large with child.

Slowly he let his gaze wander. Chickens ran freely around the yard and summer vegetables stood high in Katie's garden. Along the garden path spires of hollyhocks swayed while hummingbirds vied with butterflies and honey bees for the flower's sweet nectar.

The wealth of his land lay visible in the golden fields and grazing cattle. Field after field of ripening wheat flamed brass and copper, while high on a hill Alex was working a team of horses along rows of knee-high corn.

Hard to believe that scarcely twenty miles away Confederate troops were advancing on Pennsylvania soil and that he was waiting here to talk with Katie about his fears for the safety of their home. In disgust he threw the apricot pit across the lawn. Katie looked toward him, startled by his angry motion. After lowering the clothes prop to put the line within Annie's reach she came to stand in front of him, hands on her hips, head tilted.

"You look angry, Edward. Is something wrong at the mill?"

"No, not at the mill, but I just heard some worrisome

news. The Rebs are headed into Pennsylvania, confiscating horses from every farm they pass. The governor is again urging everyone to move their stock north, if they haven't already done so."

"What will you do?"

"Samuel is sending Sam Jr. north with his horses. He offered to take mine along. He can be ready to go by morning."

"But you can't send the foals, they're only three months old, much too young to be weaned, and that's way too far for them to travel."

"I'll leave them here. I doubt the Rebs will bother taking mares with young foals. They're interested in mounts for their Cavalry. I'm thinking only of Brandy, Cold Spring and Winter Promise. Maybe the work horses . . . I haven't decided about them yet."

Katie's brown eyes turned black with anger. She whipped her bonnet off her head and slapped it against her apron. "Oh, I hate this war! I hate it! Everything we've worked so hard for, threatened by those southern hotheads."

Katie seldom displayed anger and Edward stared at her in surprise. Little Ellen, alarmed by her mother's outburst, came running to her side and wrapped her fat arms around Katie's skirt. Edward's throat clogged with emotion.

"Ei, Katie, but danger is coming and we have to act quickly. I'll get the stock ready to move, but I must trust you to do something else. I'm going to send Alex in from the fields. Take him and Edwin to the garden and have them dig holes to bury our valuables—your silver and china, Ma's pocket watch, and all our cash. Be sure each of the children see where it is buried in case something happens to one of us."

He had to turn away from the fear he saw in Katie's eyes. Dear God, she was in her eighth month of pregnancy. What would happen if soldiers invaded their farm? A flat, bitter taste filled his mouth—a taste of anger, a taste of apprehension. He started to run toward the barn. He would ride up to the north field and get Alex right away, then he and Edwin would start getting the horses ready for their journey. He'd send only the trotters. Wheat would be ready to harvest in a week or so and he'd need the draft horses. He'd take a chance on keeping them.

The sun was sinking behind the western horizon when a farmer pulled his wagon up to the mill and jumped to the ground. Edward walked over and ran his hand over the graying muzzle of a dispirited looking nag.

"This looks like a different horse, Joseph. Where's Tom?"

"Dang Johnny Rebs stole Tom," Joseph spat, with an oath. "Did'ja hear of the ruckus over in Hanover today?"

Edward shook his head. "Nein."

"I was in town when a whole battalion of Rebs came riding up Carlisle Street, four abreast. They was riding slow-like and every man of them had his finger on the trigger of his carbine looking mean as a bull in heat. In the center of the column rode an officer, a large man of ruddy complexion."

"Do you know who he was?"

"A Colonel White, I heared someone say, of the Virginia Cavalry. He put guards at the ends of all the streets and the whole battalion assembled in the Square, then he rode over to the Central Hotel to talk to a bunch of us men standing there. He said they was *gentlemen* fightin' for a cause they thought right and would harm no one."

Joseph whipped his hat from his head and spat on the ground. "Gentlemen! What a lie that were! Within the hour they was raiding all the stores, waving their pistols about and terrifying everyone with dire threats. Then after about an hour of putting us all in a panic they rode off toward Jefferson, swaping their worn-out mounts for fresh horses wherever they found them. They took poor Tom an' left me this worthless plug. Ain't worth the powder to blow him up with."

Edward shook his head. "Hope they don't give any of my brothers in Jefferson trouble when they pass through."

"They're trouble, all right." He glared at his horse standing with drooping head. "Can't hardly bear to think of my Tom doing duty for the Johnnie Rebs."

For the next few days all the news that could be relied upon proved favorable to the Confederates. From all directions came reports of raiders. General Early was at York and Wrightsville, Ewell's troops near Harrisburg, the Cumberland Valley was filled with Confederates, and on the mountains above Gettysburg Rebel campfires could be seen. The entire country seemed to be in the grip of the enemy.

Then on June 29th a rider arrived with welcome news of the approach of the Union Army; scouting parties of cavalrymen were reported advancing from Westminister, Maryland toward Littlestown.

Early the next morning Edward began some long overdue repairs to the grinding wheel in the mill. He had just finished dressing one of the stones when he heard sounds of gunfire from the direction of Hanover. He listened intently. That was definitely musket fire he heard and it was growing in intensity. Suddenly the ground shook as a cannon joined the fray.

He threw his chisel to the ground and ran outside. The noise was louder there and, frightened now, he ran across the pasture to the house.

Katie was sitting in the kitchen talking quietly to the wide-eyed children. She looked at him, her face drawn with anxiety.

"It sounds as though the armies are fighting nearby," Edward said, struggling to keep his voice calm, "but no riders have come by to say what is happening. I'll stay here with you until we get some news."

Katie had just put the children down for an afternoon nap when Samuel came galloping into the yard and hurried to the kitchen.

Katie settled him at the table with a cup of coffee and he launched into his story.

"I was in Hanover, buying nails at Gitts' Store when hundreds of Union Troops came riding up Frederick Street. I couldn't believe my eyes, Edward. Never saw so many soldiers at one time. And such a wonderful sight it was. Uniforms of blue, and prancing horses, and regimental flags a-waving in the breeze. The men and horses was awful tired and bedraggled looking, but people ran out of their houses and greeted them with cheers and songs. Those soldiers perked right up. Their commander was a young fellow called General Kilpatrick. Ain't never heard of him. Right behind him came General Custer, a real dandy with long flowing curls dressed up in a velvet uniform. Katie, you never seen such a sight as that General Custer."

She laughed. "And how about General Kilpatrick. Was he a dandy too?"

"No, he was right ordinary looking . . . long nose, big ears, and a straggly looking beard. Not near as pretty as that fellow Custer. Ja, well anyhow, Kilpatrick and Custer dismounted and was directed to Jacob Wirt's house, where Rev. Zieber and some other men from the Citizens Safety Committee had gathered, and when Kilpatrick mentioned that his men had had no breakfast Rev. Zieber went out to the sidewalk and told the people of the need for food. Everyone scrambled to their homes to collect coffee and cold meat, and anything eatable the womenfolk could put together fast. In no time there was a regular parade of old men, women, and girls bearing trays and dishes and pans of food while more an' more soldiers came pouring through the square and out Abbottstown Street. Ei,yi,yi, it did my heart good to see such a pouring out of good will by our people. I, myself, went over to Shirk's store and bought as many cigars as I had money for, and passed them out to the men."

Samuel took a gulp of coffee and wiped his mouth on his sleeve. "Some of the regiments stopped and the men dismounted, mingling with the people, but others ate their food sitting on their horses. The halts were short, though, and as soon as one brigade had been given their lunches they moved onward toward Abbottstown to give place to another brigade. By ten o'clock the last bunch, our own 18th Pennsylvania boys, were coming into town.

I was still in the Square when firing was heard coming from the direction of Littlestown and we all began peering down Frederick Street. Then a cannon boomed and a shell flew over the town. A Union officer came careening by on his horse shouting out to the people to run into their houses, as a fight was on, and within minutes the 18th Pennsylvania came dashing pell-mell up Frederick Street followed by Rebel cavalry who had come into town through fields and alleys, shouting and cheering as they charged."

"Oh dear, what did you do?" Katie asked wide-eyed.

"I wanna tell you it scared the daylights outa me. The Square was a mess of yelling, fightin' men, their sabers clashing and revolvers firing. I ran into Gitt's and dove behind a counter. Screaming folks were running everywhere. Awfulist thing you ever seen."

Samuel stopped for breath and wordlessly Katie filled his coffee cup. Samuel took a huge gulp and continued. "Dead men and horses was falling everywhere. Our soldiers got pushed out Abbottstown Street to the railroad, but they soon got their wits about them and came riding back through the markethouse hot on the tails of the Rebs. They was fightin' all over town, dismounted soldiers jumping fences into yards and gardens, cavalrymen slashing at each other as they galloped at full speed, shells screaming and bursting everywhere. Noise you wouldn't believe! What with the fierce yells and the clatter of iron hoofs on the wooden floor of the old markethouse, you knew there was a war on for sure."

"Were any townspeople killed?" Edward asked.

"Nein, but an artillery shell crashed into the balcony of Henry Winebrenner's house just minutes after Misses Sarah and Martha had gone inside. And I helped dress the wounds of a Miss Lizzie Sweitzer. She was helping to distribute food among the soldiers and was struck in the ankle by a pistol or carbine ball. It looked to be a serious wound."

"I know her; she's a domestic in the family of Rev. Alleman. A quiet, shy, young thing," Katie observed.

"Go on, Samuel. What happened next?" Edward asked impatiently.

"Someone had hoisted an American flag in front of the Hanover Spectator newspaper office and several Rebs were trying hard to cut the halyards with their sabers and get the flag for a trophy, but our men chased them off.

About noon time, when there was a lull in the fightin', I got my courage together and went out into the square. Ambulances were creating awful confusion trying to get through the streets and one almost knocked me to the ground. I joined a group of soldiers and townspeople throwing up barricades at the ends of Baltimore, York and Frederick Street. We used store boxes, wagons, hay ladders, fence rails, barrels, bar iron and anything else that would keep the Rebs from dashing back into town.

Kilpatrick and Custer took up headquarters in the Central Hotel and, mind you, Custer tied his horse to a young maple in front of Gitt's and left his colored servant to stand nearby to guard the animal."

"Wonder how that sits with the Confederates," Edward muttered.

Samuel took his spectacles off and rubbed his eyes, squinting at Edward with an amused smile before resuming. "In the middle of all this terrible fighting and yelling I saw a funny thing. I had just finished carrying a wounded man to the sidewalk, so he wouldn't get trampled by all those surging horsemen, when I heard laughter, of all things. I turned to see General Kilpatrick and two of his brigadiers examining a Rebel officer being held prisoner by a young sergeant of the Fifth New York. You wouldn't believe that officer's appearance, Edward. His gray uniform with its fancy velvet facing and his white gauntlet gloves and his face and hair had been completely stained with an ugly brown liquid. I moved closer to hear what they was saying."

Samuel chuckled. "It seems like the sergeant had been taken prisoner by that same Colonel. . . a Colonel Payne . . . and was being taken to the rear. They was passing Winebrenner's tannery, you know his vats are never covered and they stand close to the street, and the sergeant saw a carbine lying on the ground. He snatched it up real quick and fired, killing Payne's horse, which threw Payne head-first into one of them vats, completely under the tanning liquid. The sergeant fished the colonel out and made him his own prisoner." The corners of Samuel's mouth turned up in amusement. "He was a poor sight for sure."

Edward's face creased in a smile then quickly sobered, chagrined that he should find humor at such a sorry time.

Katie refilled Samuel's cup and he resumed his story. "A shell came hissing and crashing into the street only yards from where I stood and I high-tailed it down Frederick Street where I ran into young Herbert Shriver, William's boy, from over at Union Mills. They're Southern sympathizers, you know. He told me that he was serving as a scout for the Confederates. Said the Rebs spent the night in his Pa's meadow along Pipe Creek and Jeb Stuart and his men had breakfast with the Shriver family in the morning."

"This was Jeb Stuart's regiment then?" Edward asked.

"Yep. The General led the charge through town in person. Big handsome man with a full black beard. Herbert said that one of Stuart's generals, Fitzhugh Lee, captured over a hundred fifty Union supply wagons at Rockville and they had 'em in tow. They were slowing Stuart down or he would have been through Hanover yesterday and this battle probably wouldn't have happened."

"Herbert isn't in the army, is he?"

"No, he's too young, but four of his brothers are serving the Confederacy. Strange war, isn't it? It was Herbert told me one of our own boys, young Corporal Hoffacker from West Manheim Township, was killed on the first charge. They knew one another."

Katie gave a gasp and sank into a nearby chair. "I know his mother. Oh, how sad. To die within sight of one's own home."

Samuel nodded his head. "I wished Herbert well, despite his role, and found Rev. Zieber and Doctor Hinkle. They had decided to use Marion Hall, over near the public school house, as a temporary hospital and I helped carry a couple wounded soldiers there. The bodies of twelve Union soldiers had been taken to the Flickinger Foundry over on York Street and Henry Wirt ordered caskets made. I heard the men would be buried in Emmanuels Reformed cemetary before nightfall.

The doorway of George Walsh's house stood open and I carried a young corporal, whose leg had been shot off and who was bleeding badly, into the Walsh parlor. Mrs. Walsh took over immediately with no thought to the blood staining her velvet couch. I saw lots of folks coming out their doors to carry wounded into their homes. People are really wonderful in times of crisis, Katie. They was treating the wounded Rebs kindly, same as the Yanks."

"The gunfire sounded like it was right next door," Katie said.

"Weren't too far away. Worst of it was on Forney's farm."

"Who won the fight, do you know?"

"Don't know that anyone won. The Rebs headed out of town toward Jefferson and they say Kilpatrick's boys are marching toward Gettysburg. I jest came from the Bonaughtown Road and there's thousands of Union soldiers on the move. It's a darn good thing we sent our horses north. The Rebs are stealing horses from every farm they pass. Talk is they captured a thousand or more in Codorus and York County."

Edward sat his coffee cup down with a loud thump and glanced at Samuel. "I guess you heard the Rebs were in Jefferson a few days ago. Some of Colonial White's Virginia cavalry ransacked Jacob's store and knocked in two barrels of whiskey, then burned a car load of bark intended for Henry's tannery."

"Ei,yi,yi. I hadn't heard. Bet Henry was madder then hell!" Samuel's face turned beet red. "Sorry Katie, in my excitement I forgot there was a lady present."

"Under the circumstances you're to be excused," she said with a grin.

Edward looked at Samuel with anxious eyes. "Did you happen to hear which Union regiments took part in the fight?"

"I spotted the flags of the First Vermont, Fifth New York, and Eighteenth Pennsylvania and I know Custer was leading parts of the Michigan Cavalry. Why?"

"Someone at the mill this morning said the Pennsylvania

Reserves were bivouacked over on the Sell farm. Do you think Patrick's unit might be among them?"

"Can't say. I'd surely think if he was this close he'd try to get in touch with the family."

"Think I'll ride out there tomorrow afternoon and see if the Bucktails are among them."

Katie carried the empty coffee cups to her wash basin. "Take the wagon, Edward, and drop me off at Marion Hall. I might be of some use to the ladies that are ministering to the wounded."

Edward looked at her sternly. "You're too close to your confinement; it isn't safe for you to go!"

"I'm in a lot better shape than most of those poor men who may be missing an arm or a leg. I'm only having a baby!"

Chapter
-22-

Alex crouched on the milking stool, head resting against the cow's flank, pulling on its soft teat. White jets of milk hissed and frothed into the bucket held between his knees and with a mischievous grin he directed a warm stream into the face of the tabby waiting nearby. The cat feigned outrage, stalking on stiff legs to the corner of a nearby stall to sit quietly, wiping his whiskers of the sweet warm milk. The barn was warm and the cows, Primrose, Aster, and Violet, stood docilely swishing their tails to ward off troublesome flies. Thunder grumbled in the east and heat lightning flashed occasionally in the sultry June sky. Edward, Alex and Edwin were milking this evening, although it was a chore usually considered women's work. Katie was baking extra bread and pies to take to the wounded soldiers in Hanover and Edward had sent Annie to the kitchen to help her.

The barn door burst open and Emma came running in, blond pigtails flying, breathless with excitement. Her blue eyes were wide and animated as she ran to Edward and clutched his sleeve.

"Papa, Papa, there's soldiers in our orchard an' they're wearing grey uniforms."

Edward's stomach lurched and he moved quickly to the

corner of the barn where his old flintlock was leaning against the wall. He must remain calm; he didn't want to scare the children. Grey uniforms? That meant they were Rebels.

"How many are there, child? What're they doing?"

"Not many, Papa, about six I guess, and they're just sitting on the ground resting." Emma turned to Alex and Edwin who were watching her with open mouths. "They seem nice and friendly and they asked for water. They look awful tired and dirty. I told 'em I'd come ask my Papa about water."

Edward rose from his milking stool, struggling to gather his wits. The fierce battle fought at Hanover, with its crackling gunfire and smoke filled air, had scared everyone badly. These soldiers in his orchard must be scavengers, looking for horses.

And what about his own horses? Brandy, Cold Spring and Winter Promise should be well north by now, but he still had the mares and two draft horses in his stable. Were the Rebs after them?

Good heavens, Emma had actually walked up to the enemy soldiers and talked with them. The thought terrified him. But, if Emma in her six year old wisdom, had decided they were nice then maybe they meant no harm to the family.

He fondled his flintlock. *Shall I carry it for protection or will that only cause conflict?* Carefully he turned the question over in his mind. *A man carrying a gun can only cause animosity. I'd better leave it here.*

"Alex, you come with me. Edwin, you and Emma stay here in the barn till we come back. Primrose still hasn't been milked, and when you're finished with her fill the tins with milk for the cats. And don't either of you dare move out of this barn!"

Edwin looked mutinous. "I wanna go too . . . it ain't fair that I hafta stay here with a girl like I'm some kind'a baby."

"I'm not treating you like a baby. I need you to protect my gun as well as your little sister. If you both stay in the barn we won't have to alarm your mamma. You listen to me, Edwin. Come, Alex."

"Aren't you taking the gun?" Alex asked, his brown eyes dark with alarm, his young voice vibrating with urgency.

"I hope to reason with these soldiers, Alex, not fight with them."

"But they have guns. They're the ENEMY!"

"Only if we treat them that way. Now come."

They walked from the barn at a rapid pace and headed toward the orchard, Edward's back straight, his head erect, his gut tight with fear.

Alex scrambled after Edward, his brown eyes questioning, his forehead puckered. "Pa, it just ain't right. Many's the time me and Edwin pretended we was soldiers shooting at those dirty Rebs. Now we got those Rebs in our own apple orchard and we don't even have a gun. Ain't right!"

"War isn't right, Alex. Now you be quiet and let me do the talking."

Five Confederate soldiers lounged in the shade of the orchard, their horses tethered nearby, and several more were eating green apples they had garnered from the heavily laden trees. They were the dirtiest men Edward had ever seen, like a mangy pack of wolves, and their smell made him gasp.

One of the men, a young officer, arose as Edward approached and eyed him in weary defiance. Gauntleted hands held the dusty reins of his nervous horse. The officer was of medium height, but thin to the point of emaciation. Long brown hair, that must once have been rich and wavy, hung to his shoulders in dirty, oily strands. A straggly beard covered a life-weary face, young in age, but battle old. His tattered woolen uniform was soaked with sweat from the hot sun and he spoke in a voice raspy from lack of sleep, but strong and bold.

"We're needing water and food for ourselves and our horses. Rains comin' and we'd like to sleep the night in your barn," the officer said, standing tall in the fading light.

Edward stood silently and surveyed the men in Grey, guessing their hidden purpose. For weeks hungry Confederates had been pillaging local farms for food and replacement mounts. As Alex had so aptly put it, this, after all, was the enemy! Yet, except for their ragged appearance, they looked no different than his own brothers. If Alex were several years older he might have been pitched in battle against these same men. But fellow men they were, fighting for their own cause, and although Edward feared them he could not hate them.

His gaze swung back to the young officer. "If I give you what you ask will you leave us in peace?" he asked with a worried frown.

"We make war only against armed men."

Their eyes locked and held and something about this man's face made Edward instinctively trust him.

Edward finally broke the heavy silence. "Come, then," he said reluctantly, but firmly. "You can bed down in the hay loft. You should be safe there. I'd appreciate it if your men stayed clear of the house. My wife is expecting a baby and I don't want to alarm her. We'll bring food and water out to you." He glanced toward the ragged group of soldiers and his expression softened. "Better not eat too many of those green apples, though. They'll give you the runs and a fierce belly ache."

The soldiers untied their horses and followed Edward and Alex through the gathering dusk toward the barn. Edward leaned over and whispered to Alex, "Better run inside and tell your brother and sister to stay put, that everything is all right. We'll be with them shortly. And bring out some oats for these horses."

Alex's face, puckered in disapproval at this show of aid to *the enemy*. Nevertheless he assumed an air of importance as he scurried to fetch buckets of oats and bran for the hungry horses. After leading the men and their mounts to the creek to drink, Edward directed the weary soldiers to stow their bed rolls in the hay loft and then took them to a watering trough near the barn where they could wash away some of the sweat and grime.

Edward took Alex aside. "As soon as these men are washed up we'll go the barn. You get Edwin and Emma to help you draw some extra drinking water. I want to keep the soldiers away from the kitchen well." Then he added firmly, "but see you keep your brother and sister right by your side. They're probably bursting with curiosity."

Alex gave him a sullen look. Edward sighed in exasperation; he'd have to have a talk with the boy when this was all over.

The last of the soldiers dried himself on one of the feed sacks Edward had thrown on the ground beside the water trough and walked up the barn bridge to the upper level of the bank barn.

Edward and Alex entered the lower half of the barn where an impatient Emma was poking her head from the nearest stall. Edwin sat in a corner firmly holding onto the flintlock. Alex sauntered up to them and said in a voice as mature as he could muster, "Papa says you kin help draw some buckets of water for those ole Rebs. Guess they get thirsty jest like we do. You gotta mind me, though."

"Are they mean?" Edwin asked, placing the gun carefully in the corner.

"Naw, just dirty and smelly. We could sure wup 'em if we had a mind to!"

When four buckets of fresh well water had been collected Edward carried them up the ladder to the Rebels with the promise of food to follow as soon as his wife could get some prepared, then he returned and collected the milk. He and the children carried the foaming buckets to the milkhouse and strained the milk into cans before placing them in a trough of spring water to cool.

Their chores finally finished they began walking toward the house. Edward's feet lagged. How in the world could he tell Katie that Confederate soldiers were spending the night in their barn? And how would she react to his request for food to feed them? It was only last week that she had learned of the death of her nephew, Jethro, a lad of only sixteen, fighting for the Union at Chancellorsville.

He need not have worried how he would broach the story to her. Emma, bursting with excitement, ran ahead of them and had the tale half told by the time he and the boys arrived in the kitchen. Stumbling over her words in her haste to tell her mother all of her story Emma concluded in a matter-of-fact voice: ". . . and they asked me for water so I went to get Papa."

"I got oats for their horses," Alex supplied importantly, "and . . ."

"And I guarded Papa's flintlock," Edwin broke in.

Emma had finally caught her breath. "One of the soldiers smiled at me and asked my name. They seemed nice, Mama, but I think they're awful hungry."

Edward stood by the door, quietly watching Katie and the emotions, reflected one-by-one, on her face. First, fear for Emma, then anger that the act of war, which she hated so much, was being brought to her very door step. Now, compassion for hungry men, even though they were southern soldiers. Her eyes glistened with tears. What a wonderful woman she was. Wonderful, warm, loving, and brave.

"I think we have enough extra to feed a few hungry men," Katie said, directing a tremulous smile at the children who were standing quietly, watching for her reaction.

Alex's face turned red and he clenched his fist. "Mama, they're stinkin' Rebs!"

"And God commands us: love your enemies and pray for those who persecute you."

"But, Ma, they're killing our soldiers. They killed Jethro."

"Remember your bible, son. Love keeps no record of wrongs—we are taught to have faith, hope, and love—but the greatest of these is love." Katie smiled softly at the look of bewilderment on Alex's young face. "You're thinking as a child, reasoning as a child. When you become a man, like your father, you will understand."

Edward walked over and kissed her cheek. "The officer in charge assured me they mean no harm. They only want food and a place to spend the night."

"Do you think they're after our horses? I don't want our horses to be part of the war any more than I want you to be," Katie said.

"I'm sure they are. Thank God we sent the trotters north and kept only the mares with foal and the draft horses. I'd hate to lose them, though."

Annie had been sitting quietly, rocking Ellen in her lap. "Oh, 1 do wish this horrible war was over," she said.

Katie pushed a wisp of hair under her cap and gave a sad smile. "But it isn't, dear, and right now we have Confederate soldiers in our hay loft expecting to be fed."

Edward carried a big crock of cold milk, Katie had two sour cherry pies still warm from the oven, and Alex carried the picnic hamper filled with hot stew and homemade bread as they entered the hay loft where several of the soldiers already lay in exhausted sleep. Katie's face mirrored her dismay as she gazed at their tattered appearance and Edward shared her anguish. He had always pictured the Southern soldiers as arrogant young aristocrats, but these were young boys, no different than his own sons, except for what they believed was right. He looked at the hollow faces. Gone was their bravado and rhetoric, the thrill of donning the smart new uniforms and setting the cap jauntily on the head, the rapid beat of the heart as they shouldered their muskets and marched into battle. Now, blistered feet poked through broken boots. What Edward saw was the true reality of war—bone numbing weariness, hunger, and dirt.

Katie's eyes traveled over the blanket of a young boy lying on the floor close to her. It was crawling with vermin.

"Oh, Edward," she whispered softly, tears swimming in her eyes.

He took the hamper from Alex and set it on the floor, earlier anger dissolved. These men had taken arms to fight against his family and neighbors, but he could feel only sympathy for them. "It's all we can spare," he said gruffly. "I trust you'll be gone in the morning. Folks could take our helping you an act of treason."

The officer nodded in understanding. "Thank you. We'll not harm your family or property."

Edward felt Katie's soft hand on his arm. She spoke to the Confederate officer in a quiet, yet firm, voice. "If you'll give your blankets to Edward I'll wash them first thing in the morning." Then with a half smile, she added, "a trip to the bake oven will dry them and kill the wild life."

The next morning Katie arose before dawn and with Annie's help, prepared tubs of boiling water. They washed the blankets in strong lye soap, then placed them on boards in the hot bake oven where Edward had a brisk fire going. The blankets were soon dry and vermin free and the soldiers gathered around the barn where large black kettles and skillets simmered over open fires. Katie and Annie tossed flapjack batter on hot griddles and loaded their plates as they filed by.

With clean blankets and a full belly the Rebs mounted their horses and made ready to leave as crimson streaked the early morning sky. One by one they rode down the lane toward the Bonnaughtown Road.

Only one boy stopped to speak to Katie, the youth whose innocent face had stirred her to tears.

"It was a kindness I'll remember Mam. Somethin' my own Ma might'a done."

Katie smiled. "God be with you! What direction are you headin' this morning?"

"Gettysburg."

Chapter

-23-

After the Confederate soldiers left Edward hurried to the mill where men had already gathered anxious to talk of the previous day's fight in Hanover.

"A Union officer was heard to say there will be a heavy battle somewhere nearby, but no one can tell where," Emanuel commented with a worried look on his sunburned face.

"Last week them damn Rebs stole the horses right outa the lot behind the church in Fairfield while folks was a prayin' inside," Will Shivley said, slapping his thigh in disgust.

Charles, a young neighbor nodded in agreement. "Eb and me skedaddled with our horses as far north as we could git. Let 'em with my wife's folks till after this mess is all over."

An old German farmer with a heavy Dutch accent broke in with a tale of his own woes. "Vell I tell you, dey jost take my prize Percherons. Dey take em avay. Missus she's crying, say's ve'll be ruint. Now how ve pull the vagons mit no horses?"

"Did ya see the red flaring in the sky from over near Gettysburg, coupla days ago?" Will asked. I heard they burned the big railroad bridge over Rock Creek."

Edward wiped a dusty hand across his face and threw a

sack of flour into the bed of Emanuel Slagle's wagon. "Not just the blamed bridge, Will. They burned all the railroad cars and the railway engine house too. They're burning all the railway bridges hereabouts, to cut off supplies. It'll take us years to recover."

Charles nodded in agreement. "My Pa said that was Jubal Early's Division. They been in Gettysburg trying to buy shoes and hats. Heard tell they was brash enough to play Dixie right in the town square,"

"Well, we got us a new General now name o' George Meade. Bet he'll kick Bobby Lee's butt back down to Virginy," Emanuael said with a sly grin.

About ten o'clock on that first day of July, a rumble, like distant thunder, shook the floor of the mill. The noise seemed to be coming from the west, near Gettysburg. Edward stopped the heavy grinding wheel and went outside to investigate, but he heard only one sound, the rush and rumble of the water wheel and the sound of rushing water invading the millrace from the Conewago, swollen by recent heavy rain. He was confused; the sky was clear with no sign of an approaching storm. He listened intently, looking across the road at the peaceful woods, and then toward his house, the pale brick warm in the soft sunshine. Was it possible that what he heard was the distant booming of cannons?

Every dog for miles around seemed to be barking and Katie's chickens were running excitedly around the farmyard. Chickens always sensed trouble and suddenly Edward felt weak with fear. The booming of cannon and the rattle of musketry shook the hot, still air. Something was terribly wrong. A low boom echoed and then another, and another. Boom, boom, boom—the earth shook.

Edward hurried into the kitchen where Katie, her face creased with alarm, was preparing breakfast. "I think we may be in for trouble, again," he said, knowing it was foolish to try to fool her. "It sounds like artillery fire nearby."

Katie nodded. "I don't want to scare the children. We'll go about our chores in a normal way. Today is cleaning day, and that's what we'll do." She sighed, and her eyes darkened with concern. I worry so about our neighbor, Mrs. Hostetter. She has two little ones, and her Mister is quarantined with typhoid fever. What ever will she do?"

"The soldiers won't bother her with quarantine signs posted, but if danger from cannon fire comes close I'll go over and move them to the cellar."

Katie took Edward's hand and drew it to her lips. "You'll expose yourself to terrible danger from the typhoid, Edward, but I love you for your compassion. Now come with me. I believe you and I should go into the parlor for a short prayer."

The noise continued all morning and as farmers began coming to the mill a tale of heavy fighting at Gettysburg began to unfold.

"They's tens a thousands Johnny Rebs come down outa the South Mountain west o' Gettysburg, over near Cashtown," old Mr. Kindig said, shooting a stream of tobacco juice to the ground. "My wife's brother lives jest south o' town and he brung the whole family over ta stay with us till the fightin's over. Scared shitless, they was."

"Must be just as many Union soldiers in Gettysburg,

from the sound of things," Edward commented, glancing at the western sky now filled with tiny puffs of black smoke."

"The whole damned Northern army and the whole damned Southern army is meetin' head-on over there at Gettysburg. Must be hundreds of thousands of soldiers. I never expected a big battle to be fought this close," observed Jacob Hostetter who was patiently waiting for his order of buckwheat flour. "My cows jest won't settle down this mornin'."

The next day was the same. Except for a few riders stopping to tell of a gigantic battle being fought at Gettysburg, few folks showed up at the mill. It was maddening not to know what was going on. Edward couldn't work, couldn't think of anything but what was happening in the normally serene little village only ten miles away. He walked to the millpond and looked about. Ducks floated peacefully across its surface, the water sparkling in the warm sunshine, the creek murmuring softly. Yet, just beyond that peaceful creek and those fir-clad hills, men were being slaughtered by the thousands.

It was close to four o'clock when volleys of cannon fire erupted near the farm. The ground reverberated and every window in the house shook, the sound deafening.

Edward hurried to close the shutters on the first floor of the house. Gunfire was getting awfully close. Maybe he should move the family into the root cellar. In the darkened kitchen Katie was reading to the frightened children. Edwin was peering through the slatted shutters, his thin shoulders hunched in excitement.

"Maybe that's the end, like the 4th of July when they set off all the firecrackers at once," Edwin said running to

Edward. "The whole sky's fulla smoke."

"1 most certainly hope that's the end. I didn't get a single egg from those chickens today," Katie said rocking furiously. "Nor, any milk from the cows!"

But it clearly wasn't the end. The noise gained in intensity and Edward led them to the root cellar for safety. They huddled together on the dirt floor in the damp and darkness, hushed and frightened until Katie began to sing an old German lullaby and soon Annie's clear young voice joined hers, their voices covering the sound of the distant battle. Edward pulled his harmonica from his pocket and the other children joined the singing as Edward led them in lively folk ballads: We'll Kill an Old Rooster, I Can Dance So Flashily, Maiden, Will You Marry?, and Edward's favorite, Hawwer Reche (Raking Oats).

When all was silent in the distance they left the cellar and crept through the sultry, starless midnight to their beds.

The worst part, Edward thought, tossing sleeplessly on his bed-tick, was not knowing what was happening and how real their danger was. He looked down at Katie, as much in love with her as he had been as a young boy. *Suppose the fighting came here! I would have to take up my gun to protect her,* he thought wildly. He ran a hand over her distended belly, and she sighed, as awake as he.

"Are you alright, dear? No early pains or anything?"

"I'm fine. This will be all over before "little Thumper" puts in an appearance."

Edward grinned in the darkness. Katie claimed that this baby kicked more viciously than all of her others combined and the whole family had taken to calling it "Thumper." This time it must surely be a boy.

Shortly before dawn, three days after the disturbance had first begun, bombarding cannons rocked them awake. Edward rolled over with an oath. Would it never stop? How many men and boys had to die on the battlefield to satisfy the warmongers? He put a strong arm around Katie and pulled her close.

She buried her head on his chest. "I keep seeing the face of that young soldier as he lay sleeping in our hay loft. Do you think he is dead now?" she asked, her voice choking on a sob.

Edward found he couldn't answer. He simply pulled her closer and closed his eyes, distressed at his own hot tears. And what of Patrick? Was he at Gettysburg, fighting in this terrible battle. And what of Edward's replacement, William Sickle, willing to serve in his stead for money. Was he at Gettysburg?

"Such folly, such awful folly," Katie whispered.

* * *

A light haze covered the farm during the quiet morning as the temperature climbed toward one hundred degrees. The sun burned in the cloudless sky on fields unnaturally still.

Katie moved about the house with a slight feeling of nausea and a dull backache. Tomorrow would be the 4th of July and although she doubted they would be having their annual church picnic she baked several pies and set them to cool on the deep window sills.

Suddenly a thundering blast shook the windows and the ground shook as an unbelievable noise reverberated through the air. Katie's entire flock of chickens and guinea hens flew into nearby peach trees and began making an ungodly noise. Artillery fire streaked the western sky with great streams of black smoke hanging in the blue sky like thunder clouds. Salvo after salvo roared through the air. Occasionally a huge boom, from exploding ammunition caches, rocked the ground and the combined crack of rifles, roar of heavy musketry and boom of cannon sounded like heaven and earth were crashing together.

Edward came running toward the house shouting, "to the cellar. For God's sake get the children in the cellar."

Katie grabbed little Emma's hand and started to run for the cellar door which Alex had already thrown open. Edward was herding the children who came running from all directions, down the ladder. Katie entered last, just as a loud boom shook the earth, and Edward flung the door down, shutting out the sunshine. "I'm clasping it shut until the danger is over," he shouted through the heavy oak door. "I'll stay in the barn, with my musket in case we are attacked."

When Edward pulled the door shut over their heads the cellar was pitched into total darkness. Katie had no time to light the lantern she was carrying, and she was only a few steps down the ladder, slippery from the dampness of the earthen basement. Carefully she felt for the next rung with her bare toe and just then Emma screamed in fright. Katie was startled, her foot missed the rung, and she fell heavily to the dirt floor, the unlit lantern smashing on the hard ground.

Stunned, she lay there. Dimly she could see Annie feeling her way through the murky darkness. "Jest lay still, till you catch your breath," Annie crooned, cradling Katie's head in her lap.

Emma was screaming in terror. "I'm afraid, Mama, I'm afraid," and Katie could hear all of the children sobbing as she tried to sit up. "The lantern is broken, but your eyes will soon get accustomed to the dark. There's nothing to be afraid of. We're safe here in the cellar and Poppa is outside to protect us."

"Will the soldiers come here to fight in our orchard?" Edwin asked in a quivering voice.

Alex spoke out in derision, "of course not, dummy. They're fighting a big battle in Gettysburg and when its all over they'll be tired of fighting and go away from here."

Emma started to cry again. "I don't like those bangs. I want this war to be all over." Katie had managed to crawl to Emma's side and she pulled the child onto her lap. "Hush now Emma. We're safe here on the farm. You remember how nice the soldiers were to you when they rested in the orchard." As she spoke, a sharp pain convulsed her stomach. She gasped and clutched Emma tightly.

"You're hurting me," Emma yelped in surprise.

"Is something wrong, Mama. Are you hurt," Annie asked in alarm.

"Just a little pain in my stomach, honey. I'll be alright soon as we can get out of this cellar."

The din went on for over an hour and a half, audible even in the earthen cellar. Katie put her hands over her ears to shut out the awful noise and her pains increased. This little one was ready to come, war or no war.

Unable to hide her distress any longer she pulled Annie to her side and whispered in her ear. "The baby is coming, Annie, and you must help me."

"Mama, I don't know what to do."

Katie could hear the terror in her young voice. Annie was only eleven and had never seen a birthing. "You must be calm and listen to me carefully. Talk to Alex and explain to him that he must keep the younger children in the far end of the cellar where they can't see us. Then go over to that pile of potatoes in the corner. I believe you'll find some old burlap bags. Bring them here, they'll have to serve to wrap the baby. And on that shelf built into the wall there is a knife. Bring that too."

"Mama we must get you out of here. Maybe if we pound on the door Papa will hear us and unlock the door."

"He'd never hear us in this racket. Besides, it isn't safe, Annie. Everything will be fine if you do as I say." She smiled in the dark and pressed Annie's hand to her cheek. "Mama's been through this a few times before, honey. I just need your help; you'll do fine."

Katie stretched out on the floor. Her pains were coming in rapid succession and this baby seemed determined to make an untimely entrance into the frightful fray taking place around it.

Annie, once she conquered her fear, was efficient as any midwife. As Katie gave a final gigantic heave the baby slid into Annie's waiting hands. "It's a little girl," she cried, laughing and sobbing at the same time.

Carefully she followed Katie's instructions, cutting the cord neatly in the middle and tying both ends with strips torn from her apron. Tenderly Annie wrapped the infant in a piece of cloth Alex handed her and soon the baby was suckling at Katie's breast.

* * *

After hours of the distant bombardment there was a sudden deafening calm, the quiet almost more frightening than the noise.

The day dragged on and all was silent. When Edward felt reasonably sure that there was no danger he ran back to the house to release his family from the cellar. He unclasped the door and pulled it back, surprised to see no light coming from below. "Is everyone all right," he called urgently. He almost dropped the door when he heard the unmistakable cry of a baby.

He stumbled down the ladder to find everyone huddled around Katie looking up at him out of the gloom with big smiles. "Surprise, Papa," Edwin said, laughing, running to Edward and pulling him by the hand toward Katie. "Mama went and had her new baby right down here in the cellar."

Edward knelt beside her, looking in wonder at the bundle cradled in her arms. "Our thumper is a girl," she said, weakly pulling a piece of muslin, trimmed in a frilly green ruffle, from around the tiny red face.

"What ever is she wrapped in?" Edward stammered, his mind tumbling with a thousand questions.

Katie laughed. "Alex couldn't stand to wrap his new sister in a burlap bag so he undressed little Emma and took her petticoat for a blanket." She smiled at Alex proudly and gave a deep sigh. "Now please, Mister Rebert will you get us out of this terrible cellar and into a nice clean bed."

Hours later, when everyone was fed and settled, Edward pulled the big rocker close to the bed and cradled his new daughter in his arms while he told Katie what he knew about the battle.

"A rider came by on his way to Hanover and told me the

battle appears to be over. He didn't know who won, but says there are thousands dead on a big field south of Gettysburg. You better keep the children in the house for a day or so until we know which way the armies are retreating."

"You think there's still danger, then?"

"I don't think we're in any immediate danger. The shelling is over and I doubt either side will be looking for a fight after these last three days. But the armies are both hungry and they lost a lot of horses."

The baby started to fuss and he handed her to Katie. "I'm so sorry I closed you in the cellar. Were you terribly frightened?"

"I was terrified," she admitted. "It was so horribly dark." She stuck her chin out and gave him a stern look. "I know you did what you thought was best to keep us safe, but I was pretty upset when I realized we were locked in that dark cellar."

"I was excited. I didn't know how real the danger might be." He grinned sheepishly. "We haven't picked a name for the baby, yet."

"I'd like to call her Mary Alice, if you approve."

"Of course, Katie, that's a sweet name."

Edward watched the tiny infant pulling on Katie's nipple. On this day of such terrible slaughter a new life had been born. The circle of life—the awe of it made him want to weep.

The next day it started raining. Torrents of rain covered the countryside and columns of Confederate soldiers, drenched, suffering and down-at-heart in defeat could be spotted on most of the roads leading south out of Gettysburg.

And it rained, and rained, and rained.

Chapter -24-

"Pow, Pow, Pow," Alex shouted throwing himself down behind a log and pointing the thick tree limb which served as his rifle at the imaginary enemy. He wiggled into a comfortable position and after a few more noisy bangs, sprang to his feet, mounted a dead tree limb, and galloped behind a tree.

"I'm General Kilpatrick," he shouted to Edwin and Emma, "and I'm gonna capture you.' Edwin and little Emma represented Confederate soldiers.

He squinted down the length of the branch and took careful aim at his brother and sister hiding behind a fallen log. "Pow, I gottcha, you dirty Rebs. " He ran from tree to tree, shooting as he went, stopping only long enough to break a dried twig from a small oak tree. "Come out and fight," he yelled, brandishing the twig as a bowie knife. Edwin rose to his feet reluctantly, but Emma stayed crouched behind the tree, watching with large blue eyes. Alex jumped at Edwin, engaging in hand to hand combat while emitting blood curdling yells and jabbing with more force than Edwin felt necessary. "Fall down, dummy, don't you know I killed you," Alex growled, glaring at Edwin.

"No you didn't. I stabbed you first," Edwin glared back. "It isn't fair. You always win at everything!"

"Then "Pow" I shot you. Now fall dead, dummy!" Alex shouted. He looked up to find his father standing nearby, quietly watching them.

Edward had been standing for some time watching his children playing at war. *How can I make them see the folly of their games,* he wondered. *What does it take to bring the message home to them?"*

"Alex, your Mama needs you at the house," he shouted, his forehead creased with concern.

Alex threw his rifle limb to the ground and brushed twigs and leaves from his trousers with dirty hands. Chagrined at being caught playing war he hurried over to a small basket of ripe peaches and hefted it to his shoulder.

"Sure, Papa, right away. I was jest pickin' some of these early peaches for her."

"Then see you take them to the house right away. Edwin and Emma, you come with me."

Edwin stood with downcast eyes watching Alex walk away carrying the basket of peaches. "He always hasta win, Papa. Just cause I'm littler than he is."

Edward sighed as he patted his young son on the shoulder. "It isn't always important who wins the game, Edwin. It's who is the best sport about losing. But son, aside from who won or lost, you know how your Mamma and I feel about war games."

"I didn't wanna play, Papa. He called me a baby."

"Well you have a mind of your own. I don't want you to let Alexander guide you into doing things you know are wrong. After all, you're seven years old now and I expect you to act grown up. Now come with me. I need your help at the mill."

That evening, after the children had been put to bed, Katie joined Edward on the front porch and sank wearily into her old rocker.

They sat in companionable silence for a few minutes before Edward broached the idea that had been plaguing him since morning. An idea Katie would be sure to disapprove of.

"Gettysburg is truly devastated, Katie. The townspeople are pleading for help. With all the wounded on their hands they're terribly short of food. The railway bridges were destroyed so no supplies have reached the town for days. And they need horses, wagons and manpower to help bury the dead and cleanse the streets. They worry an epidemic might sweep the town if the bodies aren't put in graves, soon. I think I'll take the older children with me to Gettysburg tomorrow. Surely we can be of some help in this time of need."

"Oh Edward, no!" Katie cried. "They're far too young to see all those dead and wounded men. It must be simply awful."

"Well Alex was busy playing war today and having a grand time killing Rebels out in the orchard. To boys his age it's all brass bands and shining horses ridden by brave men wearing fine uniforms. Sure he saw the tired, dirty men who stopped at our farm and heard the thunder of the cannons—he knows some men were killed—but he thinks things like that wouldn't happen to him. And he enticed Edwin into his so-called game. Katie, the boys need to know the truth of war."

"Then leave Annie here. I need her help."

"She'll be awfully put out at being left behind."

"We'll get busy in the morning making bandages. I have spare sheets we can tear up and at least ten yards of muslin." Katie pursed her lips in displeasure, and added, "I'm still against the boys going, though. I hope you know what you're doing."

Edward pulled himself erect to stand tall in authority. "I believe I do. I think I'll ride over to Samuel's and let him know I plan to go to Gettysburg tomorrow. He may want to send some supplies and bandages with us."

The next morning, after seeing that everything was under control at the mill, Edward, Alex, and Edwin packed the wagon with barrels of flour, several gallons of molasses, crocks of apple butter and several hams. Katie had been baking bread since dawn and she and the girls had torn every sheet they could spare into bandages. Just as Edward was ready to leave she appeared in the doorway with some old quilts and pillows. "I imagine they could use extra bedding too," she said. Edward nodded. He didn't know what to expect in Gettysburg although customers at the grist mill talked of unbelievable carnage. Help was needed everywhere.

By ten o'clock they were on their way. It was a little over a mile to the Hanover-Bonnaughtown Road where they turned west toward Gettysburg. Samuel's imposing grey-stone house was immediately on their left and he added butter, eggs, chickens, dried beef, potatoes and pickles to the already heavily laden wagon before they finally creaked down the muddy road toward Gettysburg .

Two days of heavy rain had turned the road into a quagmire of sticky mud and several times the ponderous wagon was in danger of either turning over or sticking fast.

By noon they were passing through the small village of Bonnaughtown and after fording a small creek Edward pulled the wagon to a halt beside a burned out bridge to rest the horses and eat the picnic lunch Katie had fixed for them.

"Papa, it seems awful quiet. Is the war all over?" Edwin asked.

"No son, just this part of the war, this battle, is over."

"Guess it's all over for a lot of dead Johnny Rebs and Blue Bellies," Alex said with a smirk.

Edward looked at him sadly. He didn't think Alex would be wearing that cocky grin an hour from now. "That's enough of that kind of talk," he said sharply.

Edwin looked at his brother with troubled eyes. "I hope those soldiers who were at our farm didn't get hurt."

Edward reached over and tousled Edwin's head. He felt a surge of love, startling in its intensity, as he looked at Edwin, followed by a pang of guilt when he felt Alex watching him.

They returned to the road which was quickly hardening into bone jarring ruts under the hot July sun. Just beyond the Brinkerhoff farm Edward pointed to a small lane leading off to the right.

"Back that road is Rocky Grove School where your cousins Joseph and Elizabeth go to school."

"Bet it's not as good as Centre School," Alex said importantly.

Edward frowned. Alex was definitely getting too big for his britches. He would have to give serious thought as to how to handle the boy. For some reason Alex irritated him. *Just like I irritated my Pa*, he thought with sudden guilt. I must be careful not to show favoritism between Edwin and Alex.

Alex, although physically like Katie, had more of Edward's personality; serious, rather moody at times. Edwin was just the opposite; he looked like Edward and had Katie's laughing, joyful nature. Edward mused about the differences in the two boys. Could it be that he found fault with Alex because of the traits he disliked in himself?

"We should be in Gettysburg in a few minutes," he commented as the horses began to pull a long ridge on the Benner farm. "So far I haven't seen much sign of a battle."

Just then a truly obnoxious odor reached them on a stiffening breeze.

"Wow, what's that," Edwin piped, wrinkling his nose. "Smells worse than a dead rat."

As the wagon breasted the hill they spotted a group of men with picks and shovels working along a long trench on the left side of the road.

Edward pulled off the road and tried to quiet the nervous horses. They were terribly jumpy and upset. Then glancing down the row of sweating men he saw the reason for their distress.

A caisson, blown to smithereens, rested among a heap of dead horses and soldiers. The soldiers looked like rag dolls, their limbs splayed in grotesque positions, their grey or butternut uniforms covered with dried blood. Dead horses, with legs stiff in the air, had puffed up to twice their size in the hot humid air and lay among men and debris.

Edward approached one of the workers, resting for a minute on a shovel, at the edge of what appeared to be a mass grave. "I came from Hanover with my boys and some supplies to help out. We could hear the fighting and heard you had a terrible battle here. Is this where it started then?"

"Naw, this here was jest a little skirmish. Most'a the fightin' was over on that hill on the Culp farm and south of town. Wait'll you see that."

"Where should I take the food and bandages?"

"They got hospitals everywhere. All the churches opened their doors and the wounded can be found wherever they could crawl. The whole danged town's a hospital."

"How may dead do you have here?"

"Bout ten was kilt an' close ta fifty shot up. This was part'a Latimor's Battalion of Ewell's Cavalry. That's why there's so dadblamed many horses. Counted thirty of them poor brutes."

"What'll you do with them?"

"Haul em away I guess, or let em rot. They's too damn big to bury."

Edward could not help gazing at what had once been a beautiful sorrel, with rich saddle and trappings. The man noticed his glance and commented, "That were an officer's horse. Major Latimore was mortally wounded here by Union fire commin' off that hill."

Edward shook his head in dismay. "I better get back to my boys. The team's upset and might be hard to hold . . . guess they can smell the death. We'll be back later and give you a hand with that grave."

"Could sure use it. Trenches don't hafta be very deep. Imagine they'll dig em all up and give em a decent burial later on, but we gotta get these bodies in the ground afore they rot."

Edward found a subdued Alex and Edwin sitting

somberly in the wagon. Without words he urged the restive horses forward.

They crossed the covered bridge at Rock Creek and entered the small town, the sun high in the sky and the heat of the day blazing down on trampled fields. Ambulances rumbled down the road from the battlefields, packed with wounded men moaning in pain as they bounced over the rutted road. Their blood dripped into the dust and great swarms of flies were everywhere.

Edward's team of horses rolled their eyes and snorted at the cloying odor of death permeating the air. He held the reins tight as they traveled up York Street, then turned left onto Stratton Street where they found the German Reformed Church.

Edward tied the horses securely and led the boys into the small church, identified as a hospital by a hastily fashioned white flag.

Never in his wildest dreams could he have imagined the sight that assaulted his eyes. Bleeding and torn bodies, some sitting, some lying, covered every inch of space the little church could provide. Stretched end-to-end along the pews were wounded and dying soldiers, some clutching at gaping wounds that spilled puddles of blood on the wooden floor. Some were screaming in pain, while others cussed in anger, and others cried in agony. Across the front of the santuary doctors worked over the wounded at three tables, made from doors ripped from the Sunday School rooms, as they barked out orders to trembling aids. Scalpels flashed and saws sighed in the fetid air. In front of the pulpit a large wicker clothes-basket held an assortment of amputated limbs. Blood was everywhere and moans and screams filled the sanctuary which until now had been witness only to the quiet prayers of its parishioners.

Edward shuddered and pulled the boys to him, burying their heads against his trembling body. *Gott im Himmel,* he thought in agony, *what had possessed him to subject his children to this inferno of pain and smell.*

A grey-haired lady, holding a cup of water to the lips of a pale youth, looked at Edward inquiringly while he stood dumb-founded in the doorway.

"I brought some bandages and food," he stammered.

"The U.S. Christian Commission has a tent just down the street," she said nodding tiredly. "They can distribute your things where they are needed most. We do thank you."

From across the room a southern soldier was calling pitifully, "Watah, watah, watah!" Blue eyes, looking out from under his grey forage cap, pleaded for help.

The woman pushed a wisp of hair from her face with a shaking hand, and turned toward the entreaty, as Edward took Edwin's hand and led the boys towards the door.

They were just about to leave when Edward's glance happened to fall on a soldier lying on a nearby litter. The left sleeve of his blue uniform had been ripped off and his arm was heavily bandaged, but what caught Edward's attention was the trademark bucktail on the cap lying beside him.

Edward placed a trembling hand on Alex's shoulder and steered him toward the wounded man. "I'm Edward Rebert from over near Littlestown and these are my boys, Alex and Edwin," he said in response to the puzzled look on the soldier's face. " I noticed your cap. My best friend Patrick McPherson is with the Bucktails. I've been wondering if his unit was in the fighting here."

The soldier nodded and gave them a faint smile. "Name's Vance Sheppard, Company K, 13th Pennsylvania. I know Pat. Far as I know he wasn't hurt."

"Did you see much action?"

"We got here the second day of the fighting and was thrown right into the thick of things. The Bucktails are first rate riflemen, you know. We were put with General Barnes Fifth corps and sent to break the ranks of the Confederates who were pushing through a heavy wheat field trying to get to a big pile of rocks they call Devil's Den. We pushed 'em back through a swampy valley on a dead run. When those Confederates saw the bucktail in our hats they knew what they was up against and we made 'em skedaddle clear back across that valley to a little peach orchard. We took up a position behind a stone wall and held their advances the rest of the day." Sheppard's animated face fell still. "We lost our leader, though. Colonel Taylor was killed right at the stone wall."

"What kind of rifles were you using," Alex asked, his voice quivering with excitement.

Sheppard grinned. "We received a shipment of breechloading Sharp's rifles last year that were intended for the Berdan's sharpshooters. That's some rifle . . . loads twice as fast as the old muzzle loaders and it's accurate as hell."

"But you say Patrick survived the fighting?" Edward asked.

Sheppard nodded his head. "Our unit was held in reserve on the last day of the fighting and I saw Pat moving about. He's hard to miss with that red hair of his. We lost two officers and five enlisted men. About thirty of us were wounded and brought here to this church."

"Is there anything we can do for you?"

"You wouldn't happen to have a ration of whiskey with you?"

"Fraid not."

"Well then pray this arm of mine will heal good and proper and maybe get me a dipper of water."

Edward secured water and said a brief prayer before taking their leave into the sunshine of Stratton Street.

They turned west on High Street, past Union School, to the corner of Baltimore Street where women were hurrying in and out of the Presbyterian Church. Across the street Edward spied a tent bearing a white flag with a red cross. He tied the team to a small sapling and on instructions from the officials inside, began unloading their wagon.

Edwin and Alex worked without saying a word. Alex kept glancing toward the Presbyterian Church, also serving as a hospital, with a look of sadness. But he said nothing.

Before returning to the Benner farm to help the men with their dismal task, Edward turned the wagon toward the south end of town, where they had been told the heaviest fighting took place.

Slowly they moved south on Baltimore Street, passing beneath stately sycamore trees, splintered and torn from gunfire, the street still strewn with blankets, knapsacks, cartridge boxes and dead horses; past the Winebrenner Tannery and Waggon Hotel at the intersection of the Emmitsburg and Taneytown Roads where a barricade of furniture and rocks still lingered, blocking their way. Several men were working to disassemble the barricade and they waved Edward over to the Baltimore Pike. He would have to cut through Evergreen Cemetery to get back to the Emmitsburg Road beyond the barricade.

Edward turned his wagon past the large archway at the entrance to the cemetery that also served as living quarters for the sexton and his family. An old sign caught Alex's attention and he read it aloud. "ALL PERSONS USING FIREARMS IN THESE GROUNDS WILL BE PROSECUTED WITH THE UTMOST RIGOR OF THE LAW."

"Guess no one read the sign," Edward said with a faint smile looking askance at overturned tombstones and graves turned up by ploughing shot. A dead horse lay astride a marble monument and abandoned muskets lay everywhere.

A woman and an old man were digging a grave and Edward turned the horses toward them. He pulled up, gasping with surprise when he saw the woman was noticeably pregnant. She straightened up, pushing wisps of hair from her sweating face, and gave him "Good Morning."

Edward jumped down from the wagon. "Let me give you a hand with that grave. You're in no condition to be doing such hard work."

"Thank you, sir. If you'd spell me just a minute while I get a drink I'd be grateful. I must keep on with this terrible task though. I'm Elizabeth Thorn and my husband is the sexton of Evergreen Cemetery, but he's away just now. He took our livestock north, never dreaming, of course, that such a terrible battle would be fought here. I'll do what I can to get these bodies covered till he gets back. A shallow grave is all we need for now."

Edward motioned to Alex and Edwin to grab shovels and give him a hand and they worked for an hour before Mrs.

Thorn insisted she would carry on.

They climbed back in the wagon and drove through the cemetery and finally gained access to the Emmitsburg Road, washed by rain and churned into red mud by thousands of feet and wheels and dripping blood.

He gritted his teeth at the scene before his eyes as they rode south. Maybe this was too much for the boys to see. Maybe he should turn back. His senses were numb, but some force kept him going forward. Wreckage of the three day battle lay everywhere. Shattered wagons, cannon, caisson, and all the implements of two large armies at war with one-another littered the area. Thousands of muskets lay on the open fields beside the animal and human wreckage that still lay in the open. Everywhere lay shell fragments, shreds of blue and grey cloth, and broken muskets. Pieces of paper blew over the open ground and Edward saw that they were letters and photographs, blown from dead fingers.

The heavy rains of the past few days had already begun to uncover bodies placed in shallow mass graves. The air was sickening with the overpowering, awful stench of death and as Edward looked toward Alex he saw him lean over the side of the wagon and start to retch.

Edward stopped for a time and let the boy recover himself before he urged the horses forward again. On both sides of the road he saw wheat, ripe in the fields, trampled flat. Corn, already waist high, was crushed to the ground, fences were gone or scattered haphazardly, and large numbers of stray cows and hogs wandered untended.

They arrived at a small peach orchard, stripped of its fruit, its trees shattered and wounded, witness to the terrible battle. Mounds of earth covering bodies were marked by pieces of fence rail or biscuit boxes, identified only by names scratched with a sharp stone.

As he turned the wagon, to return to town, Edwin spied a musket lying beside the road. "Papa kin I get me one of those muskets to keep?" he pleaded, his blue eyes round with excitement.

"You most certainly can not. Those guns most likely have loaded cartridges in them. You could easily get killed."

"Look at all those buzzards," Alex said pointing to the sky above them.

"I guess that can be expected," Edward said, his brow knitting together in a frown. "Let's get back to town and give those men a hand with that trench. Until these dead are all underground the buzzards and flies will only get worse, more's the pity."

He looked at the somber faces of Alex and Edwin and changed his mind. They had seen enough. Alex might be old enough to assist with the burying, but Edwin was just too young. He'd take the boys home and return tomorrow. Help was needed everywhere.

The next day Edward returned alone, and grimly shouldered a shovel. The men dug shallow ditches and used fence rails to roll the decaying bodies into the trenches.

A week later, after working all day at the bleak task, Edward sat with Katie recounting the sights and sounds of the horror he was witnessing.

"You can't imagine, Katie. I passed one building where they had done surgery and actually threw the severed limbs out the window. Arms and legs were heaped on the ground outside, covered with those awful green bottle flies. Flies are everywhere. When I went back to help the men with the burying I put my hand on a fence rail and it was solid . . . solid mind you . . . with vicious green flies."

Katie shuddered. "I'm glad you brought the boys home that first day and didn't insist they help."

"I knew they'd had enough. Believe me, Katie, it's a sight they will never forget. Me either, for that matter."

"Even this far away, I can smell a terrible odor and the air seems heavy with smoke. What's the smoke from, Edward?"

"They're piling the dead horses into mounds, dousing them with kerosene, then setting them afire. The stench is unbelievable, the horses will probably burn for days."

"Why don't they bury them?"

"You know how stiff a dead animal gets, Katie. Their legs are straight out. . . horses are huge when bloated. . . it'd take an awful deep hole just to bury one. And someone told me they think there must be close to five thousand dead horses around the battlefield."

"Laws, if there are that many animals I can't imagine how many dead soldiers there must be."

"Well over a hundred thousand were said to be in the fight. From the looks of things, half of them must'a been killed or wounded. Katie, every home is a hospital. The women are doing an unbelievable job cooking and caring for them. There aren't many men in town. Most of the young men are in the army and a lot of the older men headed north with their horses and cattle when they heard the armies were coming."

Katie's eyes filled with tears, indecision clear on her face. "Are you going back tomorrow?" she finally asked.

"I must. Those fallen men must be placed in graves."

Katie's eyes cleared, and her face seemed to glow with that inner light he always envied. "I must go with you. I can help some poor woman care for those in her home. Annie is old enough to go with me. Alex and Edwin can be in charge here."

"But they're only children. And what about the baby? You can't take the baby, the smell is unbelievable."

"I'll take a bottle of peppermint, we can wet a handkerchief and put it beside us. Edward, we didn't ask for this war to be fought in our backyard, but it was, and I think the experience can act to strengthen all of us."

"Katie, my dear, you just gave birth. You aren't strong enough to take on the strain of caring for sick and wounded men."

"Fiddlesticks! When have you ever known me to lie abed more than a week. Even if I'm only able to help with the cooking or change a few bandages I'll be doing God's bidding. Never has our help been needed more. I'm going!"

Edward dropped Katie, Annie, and Mary Alice off each morning at the home of a widow on York Street who had lost her son in the fighting in the Shenendoah and was unselfishly caring for three wounded Confederate boys. He then proceeded to a field on the Emmitsburg Road where the worst of the battle must have taken place, and where they were reburying bodies that had been washed out of shallow graves by the insistent rain.

It was the thirteenth of July before the Gettysburg Compiler was able to publish a newspaper. Crowds gathered around Levi Mumper's Confectionary in Littlestown to grab papers as fast as they were unloaded from the delivery wagon. Edward hastily paid for his copy and rushed home to read it to the family.

"Listen to this," he said as they gathered around the kitchen table. 'Our usually quiet and unpretending little town of Gettysburg has become historic. During the last two weeks scenes have been enacted here that beggar all description. War has been raging all around us in its most horrid form.

Two mighty armies have passed through our county and the bloodiest fight of the war has taken place in our midst.

. . . so far as the fight was concerned, neither army can be said to have gained any material advantage. To retreat and leave an enemy in possession is technically a defeat. Still Lee's army was not driven away. it was not routed.'"

"Do they say how many men fought in the battle, Papa?" Alex asked.

Edward turned the paper to page two for more information. "Here it is. It says that there are over one hundred fifty thousand men engaged with fifty-one thousand believed to be killed or wounded."

Katie sighed, glancing toward a silent Alex. "I just can't imagine it. Such a terrible, terrible waste of our young men. And the war's still not over."

Chapter
-25-

On a warm foggy morning late in July Edward rode over to Camp Letterman, a central hospital the U.S Sanitary Commission had established on eighty acres just east of Gettysburg where he found hundreds of tents containing thousands of wounded.

He was directed to the headquarters of the Christian Commission where he volunteered to work under the Commission's direction and was assigned to a nearby tent crowded with Union wounded.

Edward fed, washed and dressed their wounds, and prayed with them and as the day wore on his resolution to become a part of this service took shape. After doing what he could for the wounded, he sought out an elderly gentleman who seemed to be in charge of the Commission and sat down to talk with him.

After introductions had been exchanged with Reverend Russell from Wilkes-Barre, Pennsylvania, Edward asked the question that had been plaguing him all day. "Who are the members of your organization . . . are they all clergy?"

"The Christian Commission is comprised mostly of ministers from churches around the state, but not limited to men of the cloth. We follow the Union soldiers into battle, offering help in the hospitals and ministering to the spiritual needs of the wounded. I have watched you today, Mr. Rebert, and I must say your services would be gratefully accepted."

"I gather it's volunteer service. Is there a required tour of time?"

"We ask for six weeks. Since most of our volunteers serve a home church it is a workable arrangement. Let me tell you more specifically how we operate . . ."

As Edward listened he felt as though a huge weight had been lifted from his shoulders. This was the answer he had been looking for. Nightly, he had prayed that God would show him the way to make peace with his conscience. This was it. He would join the Christian Commission as a lay minister. Katie wouldn't like it, but this is what he was going to do.

That evening, riding home on Brandy, he practiced what he would say to Katie. Brandy pricked his ears, listening to every word just as Duke had done, years ago.

But that evening Edward had to wait, unable to broach the subject of the Commission, while Katie chattered about her charges in Gettysburg. Her "boys" as she had taken to calling them. She was almost tearful because a wagon had arrived that very afternoon for young Johnnie King. "His family sent a black slave, clear from North Carolina, after hearing that he lay wounded in Gettysburg. We were glad that he was going home, but oh, Edward, I did hate to say goodby. He was such a sweet boy, I've grown so fond of him."

"I know, it's hard not to get attached."

"Did you notice how many families are in town looking for loved ones? With all the wounded still in private homes there's hardly room to put the families up overnight, let alone feed them."

"Ei, and I don't mind the families, but it hurts me to see so many that are just curious. They swarm over the battlefield looking for souvenirs, picking up muskets just recently held in the hand of some poor boy, now lying nearby in a shallow grave. It's downright gruesome."

Edward waited until they were in bed and then, unable to constrain his thoughts any longer, he pulled her close and propped himself up on his elbows looking deep into her questioning eyes.

"Darling, I've kept my pledge to you, not to fight in this awful war, but I can no longer sit at home and do nothing. It's tearing me apart."

"But, Edward I . . ."

"Shhh. Let me finish. Today I believe God has shown me a way to help. I can join forces with a group called the Christian Commission, as a lay minister, and travel with them to the battlefields where they minister to wounded men. I need only sign up for a six week tour. I know what you're going to say. Yes, it's dangerous. Any time you're near the lines of battle, it's dangerous. But I'm not a coward, Katie. Patrick called me that once, but that has never been my reason for staying out of the war, you know that. I feel called on to do this."

Katie started to cry. "You're still trying to prove yourself to Patrick—and to your father who has been dead these many years," she said bitterly.

"No . . . no! And you know better than that. Look at me dearest." Roughly he pulled her to him, cupping her chin in his hand, looking deep into her brown eyes swimming with tears.

"Believe in me Katie . . . please believe in me."

Katie did not answer. She slid away, turning on her side away from him. She was definitely not going to help him with this. "You made me a vow, Edward . . . a vow as important to me as our marriage vow. I didn't take it lightly." The silence stretched between them.

Edward had no answer. He twisted and turned on the feather bed trying to get comfortable, like Duke circling to find the right spot on his rug. Katie turned over, her back rigid. Her words echoed in his head. Was he merely looking for an excuse to break his vow to her?

He reached out his hand and touched her hair, breathing in her scent. She moved at his touch, and he smiled into the darkness. He raised up slightly and pulled her over to face him. "Katie, I have kept my promise . . . more importantly, I've come to believe in it. There's no anger in my heart. I'll not take another man's life. But maybe, just maybe, I can find words of comfort to make it easier for those dying young men who followed a different drum. Katie . . . Katie, my darling, don't turn away from me. I wish it were different, but all I know is that I must serve my country, somehow!"

Katie turned to face him and lay looking at him, her eyes dark with pain. She shuddered and pushed her wet face against his rough nightshirt. "I love you," she murmured, tracing the cleft in his chin in the darkness. "I love you so much I think I'd die if I lost you. But I do know the moral battle you've fought and I thank the Lord for giving you the strength to stand by your convictions. I think that is all your father ever wanted of you—to grow morally and spiritually strong. I'm terribly afraid of what you're proposing. I'm not even sure I approve of that much participation in this stupid war—two sets of men killing each other for reasons they no longer know—but how can I object to my husband ministering to them, offering them some degree of comfort. Go, my darling. Six weeks will seem like an eternity to me and the children, but I know my husband will return more at peace with himself. Our prayers will be with you every hour until you're safely back with us."

Tears formed in Edward's eyes and he buried his face in her sweet hair. Tears always came easy to him, too easy, but he had never been ashamed to cry in front of Katie. What a wonderful, wonderful woman she was.

Edward began putting his affairs in order. Jamie had been mustered out of the army after being wounded at Chancellorsville and he put him in charge of the grist mill. Inger agreed to work full time in the house, helping Katie. The congregation at Christ Church took up a special collection for the Christian Commission and over six hundred dollars was collected. Things were falling into place.

By the end of August he was ready to leave, when tragedy struck once again. Mary Alice, barely two months old contacted typhoid fever. The local doctors were still in Gettysburg, tending the wounded, and medicine was scarce. Still, Dr. Seiss came from Littlestown and did what he could. But Mary Alice did not respond and in two short days she was gone.

Together he and Katie washed and dressed the baby and placed her in a tiny pine coffin he hurriedly constructed. Because of the contagious nature of typhoid the casket had to be sealed and the body disposed of quickly.

Was Mary Alice another victim of the war? Had her exposure to the fetid air of Gettysburg proved deadly to her? Edward would never know, but early on the morning of August 27th, during a driving rainstorm, her tiny coffin was lowered into the ground behind Christ Church.

That night Edward walked to the bank of Conewago Creek and sank down on the hard ground. There, beside the quiet water, he gave in to the grief that shook his body.

Slowly the peace and beauty of his surroundings quieted him and he relaxed, gazing out at the water, milky white in the reflected light of the moon. Edward stroked his chin, feeling the slight stubble of a day's beard, letting his thoughts drift with the slowly moving stream. Funny, how important water is in a man's life, he thought. We are born in our mother's water, baptized with water, cleanse ourselves and slake our thirst with water, and look for comfort in water's soothing power.

He rose, and like a small boy, threw a pebble, watching it skip across the water, watching the ripples spread from the center until they were no more.

* * *

Edward's appointment was secure, but with the baby's death he decided to wait until spring to join the commission.

Late in the afternoon of November 18th Edward and Katie, with all the children in tow, hurried toward the Hanover depot where it was rumored President Lincoln's train might stop enroute to Gettysburg for the dedication of the National Cemetery.

About five o'clock in the evening it chugged into sight and to everyone s delight came down a switch and halted at the station. Several hundred people had gathered, all anxious to get a look at the President. Katie had Annie and Edwin firmly by the hand while Edward had hoisted Emma to his shoulders afraid that she would get crushed in the surge of people.

"Poppa, Poppa, do you think he'll come out on the platform?" Annie asked.

"Probably not, honey. But you watch careful now and you might see him at a window."

Just then Pastor Alleman of St. Mathews Lutheran Church stepped out of the crowd and approached the train. "Father Abraham, your children want to hear you," he shouted, in a deep resounding voice.

"Boy is he dumb," Alex said in disgust. "The President of the United States won't talk to small town farmers like us!"

Just then a gasp went up from the crowd as the rear door of the last car opened. Abraham Lincoln removed his high silk hat and bent his six foot, four-inch frame to step through the narrow doorway. He stood on the platform and surveyed the people, then reached down to grasp the hands of several men lucky enough to be close.

"I can't see," Edwin wailed stretching to stand on his tip toes. "Hoist me up on your shoulders, Alex."

Alex stooped down and let Edwin climb on his shoulders.

"I see him, I see him," Edwin screamed.

"Shh," Katie scolded, her own cheeks pink with excitement. "He's saying something."

The President smiled and held his arm high to quiet the

noisy crowd. "Well, you have seen me, and according to general experience you have seen less than you expected to see."

The crowd laughed and cheered. Three young girls approached the train with bouquets and presented them to the President. Little Jackie Melsheimer, held up by his father, handed Lincoln an apple which he accepted with a laugh and a merry twinkle in his eyes.

Lincoln looked out over the sea of faces and held out his long arm as though in benediction. "I trust when the enemy was here the citizens of Hanover were loyal to our country and the Stars and Stripes," he said in his wonderfully deep voice.

"Hanover supports the Union," a voice called out and everyone cheered.

Lincoln was about to say more when the whistle screamed, the brakes loosened, and the train began to rattle out of the station.

"Ach, I wish I'd thought to bring flowers," Katie moaned. "I never thought we'd actually get close to him."

Edward put his hand on her shoulder and squeezed it tight, his heart still hammering with the thrill of seeing the President. "Tomorrow you can take flowers," he said his voice trembling slightly. "We'll go to Gettysburg to hear his speech. I never realized what a man of the people Lincoln is. Why he actually knew we were citizens of Hanover and that a skirmish had taken place here. We'll leave early in the morning, after the milking is done, and find places in the cemetery close to the speakers platform where the children can see him clearly. This is history, Katie . . . we must let our children be a part of that history."

The next morning, true to his word, Edward steered his family through the arch of the two story brick gateway to Evergreen Cemetery and found a spot near the flag draped platform. Most of the crowd was still in town for the planned parade to the dedication ceremonies, but Edward wanted to be certain they had a place close enough to the platform to hear the President's speech.

Katie spread a blanket and began to unpack the picnic hamper. The boys, anxious to stretch their legs, were chasing each other among the monuments while Emma had curled up on the edge of the blanket and was fast asleep.

Edward took a sandwich and leaned his back against a tall fir tree. His gaze wandered around the small cemetery. Directly in front of him was an impressive grey monument to the McLean family and immediately to his left, smaller thin slabs marked the graves of several member of the Plank family - John Plank, Jr. and two smaller children. Sad how many young children died, their frail bodies unable to fight off the dreaded typhoid or diphtheria. He sighed, remembering his own two little girls resting in cemeteries in Jefferson and Littlestown.

He picked up a round stone laying on the ground and turned it slowly between his fingers. It was sun-warmed and smooth, almost like river stone, a relic of wind and weather. Absently he dropped it into his pocket and jumped to his feet.

"I believe I hear drums and cheering, the parade must be coming. Now where are those danged boys?"

"I see them down at the gate, Poppa," Annie offered.

A band was emerging through the arched entrance, flags waving in the brisk breeze and behind them Edward could make out the tall hats of the dignitaries.

The platform was soon crowded with solemn men in black cutaways. Lincoln had been led to a chair in the back of the platform and to Edward's disbelief seemed to be ignored as men crowded around the main speaker, Edward Everett.

Everett took the podium and launched into a speech that droned on and on for a good two hours. Emma fell back to sleep and the boys became restless, but Katie never took her eyes from Lincoln.

Finally it was Lincoln's turn to speak and he moved to the front of the platform. His penetrating eyes scanned the crowd, waiting for them to quiet. For a fleeting second Edward felt the dark intense eyes look into his, then resume their sad sweep of the cemetery grounds.

He began to talk:

"Four score and seven years ago . . ."

As the simple speech unfolded Edward felt paralyzed with emotion. Agonizing memories of death filled his heart as his fingers toyed with the stone deep in his pocket. Memories of the birth and death of little Mary Alice—born too soon and died too soon—an uncounted casualty of this terrible conflict.

His gaze dropped to the ground as Lincoln's simple words hung in the air above him and with the toe of his boot he worried a small depression in the soft earth. He dropped the stone into the shallow hole and then slowly pushed the loose dirt back in place.

"For you, Mary Alice," he mouthed silently.

Chapter
-26-

Over the winter Edward spent much time with his family, for he knew that come spring he would be leaving for the battlefield. The days sped by, turning into weeks, then months. At last winter released her hold on the land and with Katie's tearful blessing, he kissed the family goodby and departed for Philadelphia.

He went directly to the headquarters of the Commission on Bank Street to turn over the contribution from Christ Church. There he was put with a group of ministers, volunteers from many different Pennsylvania churches, and together they set off for the national headquarters in Washington, D.C. where they picked up more volunteers and headed south on the Potomac River.

They were a curious mixture. Most were dignified ministers wearing black broadcloth suits, white shirts, and shiny boots. Edward chuckled to himself. Wait until they saw a battlefield after a rain. Bless their hearts, their intentions were good, but they had no idea what they were getting into.

The boat carried many others besides the Christian Commission: soldiers, officers, doctors and nurses. As they entered Aquia Creek, outside Fredericksburg, a heavy rain began to fall. Edward spread his gum blanket across his shoulders, but by the time they docked and everyone disembarked he was drenched, irritable, and homesick.

They marched, as best they could in the pouring rain, to a large tent designated as Commission Headquarters. Boxes of supplies waiting to be distributed were piled in the center of the tent, leaving little room for the milling men. A long table had been set up containing a sparse supper of coffee and hard tack and Edward found himself seated beside a short, chubby, Scotchman.

"I don't believe I'm dressed properly for the occasion," the minister said running pudgy fingers over his mud splattered clerical garb .

"Perhaps I could loan you a pair of overalls if you've none packed for yourself."

The minister's blue eyes twinkled in laughter, sweeping Edward's tall frame. "I might have to pin the legs up to my knees, but I thank you for the offer," he said in a thick Scotch brogue. He stuck out his hand. Name's George MacIntosh."

"Edward Rebert."

"And what church might you pastor?"

"I'm not a minister, just a lay-person from Christ Church, Littlestown."

"Littlestown? Don't believe I know of it. I'm with First Presbyterian in Pittsburgh. Looks like we've quite a night ahead of us."

Although still early evening, sheets of rain pelted the trembling tent and the sky glowered with roiling thunderclouds. Wounded from the battle of the Wilderness near Fredericksburg streamed into camp. Edward's mission, and that of the Commission members, was to give the soldiers food and drink and try to comfort them while they waited to be loaded on transports to be sent on to Washington. The hills were crowded with tents, long ago filled with injured, and the newly arrived wounded men were lying on the ground with nothing but their blankets for cover. The pouring rain and the red Virginia clay had changed the temporary camp into a hellish mudhole.

"We're to take coffee and food to those that are hungry. We may as well get started. The rain shows no sign of letting up. Want to join me, Reverend?"

"Let's go. And by the way, the name is George."

They placed a large bucket of hot coffee between them, slung haversacks of hardtack over their shoulders and tramped into the wet night.

Their destination was a small knoll separated from the headquarters tent by a deep ravine. Mud, washed down from the surrounding hills, filled the bottom of the ravine, obstructing their forward progress.

"That mud hole must be twenty feet across," George muttered. He peered into the darkness searching for another crossing.

"There's no other way." Edward took a tentative step into the slick clay. "Stay beside me and hold the bucket as high as you can."

Immediately Edward sank into mud over his boot tops and poor little George was in almost to his knees. The mud sucked and pulled Edward's boots and rain pelted his face. "Hold the bucket higher," Edward yelled, almost loosing his footing on the slippery clay.

"I can't. Your arms are longer than mine. If this mud gets any deeper I'll be up to my you-know-what."

Edward smiled at the comic picture they must make, trying to hold the huge bucket of coffee aloft, while wading through red muck in the pouring rain.

Grimly they plodded on. Once across they scrambled up the hillside and placed the bucket on the firmest piece of ground they could find. Edward filled his tin cup with coffee and gingerly approached the first stretcher. The young soldier grabbed it with shaking hands.

Edward's mission had begun.

He and George moved among the wounded, unaware of the incessant rain and the passage of time, until their supplies were exhausted .

They returned to the Commission tent and Edward collapsed wearily on the floor. His blanket was sodden and of no use whatsoever. He buried his head on his arm and let the sound of rain lashing the canvas tent lull him to sleep, Katie's face haunting his dreams.

Early the next morning the wounded were placed aboard a large steamer for the trip north. The Commission was ordered to march to Fredericksburg, a distance of ten or twelve miles. Edward and George fell in together and by the time they reached Fredericksburg they had become fast friends.

They paused for a few minutes on a high bluff above the Rappahannock River, overlooking the city and surrounding Virginia hills. It was a beautiful sight, the valley green and fresh from the spring rain, the mountains in the distance purple in the gathering twilight, the river sparkling in the sunlight. Edward remembered words of John Jay's that he had read in the Federalist Papers; words to the effect that America was not composed of detached and distant territories, but was one connected, fertile, wide-spreading country. He felt ashamed that he had ever thought of a separate North and South.

They descended the hill into Fredericksburg where they marched to the Christian Commission headquarters near the center of town and spent the night in wet, musty smelling tents. The next morning Edward was assigned hospital work at the Old Factory where several hundred Union and Confederate wounded were being cared for.

Happily he and George had been assigned to the same hospital and together they spent the day washing and dressing wounds. The following day, Sunday, George conducted services and Edward led the singing as they made the rounds of each ward in the hospital. That night he wrote to Katie, his first letter since joining the Commission in Washington.

Over the next week he worked tirelessly, washing the faces of the sick men, combing their hair, distributing clean shirts and writing paper, writing letters for those unable to hold a pencil, and praying with those that sought it. He felt as homesick as the weary soldiers he tended and had to fight constantly to present a smile of encouragement on his own face. In the evening he and George often sat together in the large enclosed yard at the rear of headquarters and exchanged confidences.

"I find the hardest part is not to get emotionally involved with these men," Edward confided to George as they sat smoking a pipe on a soft day in early May. "Especially those you know are beyond hope. Did you know Bernard Sinclair died last night."

George reached over and patted Edward's knee. "But you

made his last hours easier. I hear you stayed beside him till the end."

"I did. No man should die alone." A great shudder shook Edward's body. "He was only seventeen. A boy in a man's war."

George shook his head and drew slowly on his pipe. "Be glad your sons aren't old enough to serve. I'm surprised you weren't called up in the draft."

Edward rubbed the soft beard, once more covering his chin, and sat in silence, trying to formulate his answer. It was so complex. But if any man could understand his reasons, this man could. So for the next hour Edward told his story while George listened intently.

A week later, Fredericksburg buzzed with excitement and rumors as artillery fire cracked in the distance. It came from the direction of Spotsylvania and word spread that the hospital would be evacuated of all men able to move across the Rappahannock. The commission wagons were packed, ready to move toward the new lines of battle.

Early the next morning the wagons rolled, following close behind the Union Second Corps, and by mid-day they reached the field hospital at the front. Artillery fire burst all around him and cannon fire shook the earth. The hospital was located on the summit of a hill and Edward stood there for half an hour watching the awful and thrilling spectacle of a battle raging in the distance. He could plainly see the long lines of men, parallel to one another and the visible flight of projectiles through the air, their strange hiss like a smithy plunging a hot shoe into water. The report of the cannon echoed and re-echoed over the hills.

He spent two days from sunup to sundown ministering to

the wounded who were pouring in from the fight around Spotsylvania, before orders came to strike their tents and move forward once again.

They were now deep in the midst of the Grand Army of the Potomac as it advanced on Spotsylvania Courthouse. Once again it was raining.

"Didn't you say your friend, Patrick, was with the Fifth Corps, 1st Pennsylvania Rifles?" George asked as they carried a stretcher into the protection of a nearby tent.

"Ei. Have you heard something of him?"

"Not of him, exactly, but I heard that his regiment is bivouacked in the woods not far from here."

"Do you think they'd let me off long enough to search him out?" Edward's voice trembled with excitement.

"Can't hurt to ask."

Edward's supervisor gave reluctant permission for him to take a one day leave, so early the next morning as pink fingers of dawn touched the dogwood, white with blossom, he hiked across murky, sulphur laden fields, reaking of blood and smoke from the recent battle. Several times he hit the ground as sniper fire rang out from the deep woods across the open field.

It was mid-morning before he found the temporary encampment of the Pennsylvania Bucktails. With his heart in his mouth he approached a blazing campfire where a group of soldiers squatted around a boiling kettle of coffee. One of the men, noticing the Red Cross on his sleeve, held out a tin of coffee and waved to an empty spot by the fire.

"Expect we're keepin' you Red Cross fellows pretty busy. This fight's shaping up to be one of the hardest of the Campaign," a dark haired young man said watching Edward gulp the hot coffee.

Edward nodded. "Heard your men made a grand charge against the Rebels yesterday."

"Yep, we was up against the Stonewall Brigade. We wupped their asses good," a thin pimply faced youth, said proudly.

"What brings you here? I thought the hospital tents were several miles back," the dark-haired man asked.

"They are. I'm looking for a friend, Patrick McPherson, 1st Pennsylvania Rifles. Do any of you know of him?"

Silence settled over the men and they stared into the fire. Edward's mouth turned dry and the cup trembled in his hand.

Finally the dark-haired soldier lifted his eyes and Edward read the awful truth. "Your friend is over yonder on a stretcher waiting to be evacuated. He's close to death, if'n he ain't already gone."

A terrible cold settled over Edward and he sat motionless, as though carved from stone. Several of the men started to talk softly with one another, but the dark-haired soldier reached over and carefully took the cup from Edward's hand.

"Come along, I'll take you to him."

Patrick lay motionless, his red hair matted with blood, his beard caked with mud. His face was bandaged and blood oozed through the linen wrappings. Beside him on the ground lay his tattered forage cap, the bucktail still intact, symbol of his proud regiment. His eyes were closed but Edward saw a slight movement of his massive chest. Praise God, he was still alive.

Edward fell to his knees beside Patrick and reached for

his hand. It was icy cold and Edward pressed it to his cheek. Patrick opened his eyes and slow recognition crept into their green depths.

"Why . . . how . . . ?"

"Don't try to talk, Patrick. I'm here with you, just hold my hand and rest. Let me . . . let me tell you of home and your family."

Slowly Edward told Patrick about his enlistment in the Christian Commission, about Inger and the boys, and about Patrick's parents.

Patrick's face softened, he seemed stronger and began to speak in a voice barely a whisper. Edward bent close to listen, his head almost touching Patrick's.

"Tell Inger I'm sorry for everything . . . I tried . . . I wanted to do right for her, but things just got started wrong." He paused and gave an agonizing sigh. "And Edward, if my boys survive this god-awful war please help them get started on the right path."

"I will, but don't give up, Patrick. I'll get some stretcher bearers and we'll get you to the hospital. It's only a few miles away." Edward pulled a New Testament from his pocket. "Would you like me to read you some scripture?"

Patrick shook his head slowly. "Never held with men who sinned and drank 'an all, and then . . ." He coughed and Edward gently wiped the bloody spittal from his mouth. Patrick took a deep breath and continued. "Then when the time comes to die they cry out for help and try to make up with God."

Edward closed his eyes and sought carefully for his answer. "I don't see it that way, Patrick. Most of us do seek God out of desperation, and it doesn't always follow that it comes only with approaching death. I think when a person knows he needs God, when he stops shutting Him out whatever the circumstances, God is there, patiently waiting. I remember once when I was a young boy I decided to cut through the woods and return home from a church picnic on my own. I didn't account for the lateness of the hour and while I was deep in the woods darkness fell and I couldn't see my way. I stood for what seemed an eternity, afraid of the dark, afraid to go forward and afraid to go back. Then in the darkness I saw a light move toward me. I was terrified for I didn't know who held the light. And then without a word my father reached out his hand, took mine, and led me from the darkness. That's all the Savior asks of you. To take his hand and let him lead you from the darkness."

Edward took Patrick's cold hand in his and held it tightly. "Cry out for the help you need. Trust Him . . . He is there!"

Suddenly Patrick began to cough and a spittle of blood frothed at his mouth, running into his matted red beard. Edward wiped his mouth tenderly and brushed his hair back from his broad forehead. Patrick lay with his eyes closed, his mouth moving silently, then he tried to move his hand toward the pocket of his shirt. Edward saw what he wanted and reached over to remove a blood stained prayer book. Patrick's lips worked once more, but no sound issued from his cracked lips.

The small prayer book fell open at Psalms 46 and Edward began to read aloud:

> God is our refuge and strength, a tested
> help in time of trouble. And so we need

not fear even if the world blows up, and
the mountains crumble into the sea . . .

A spasm of coughing interupted Edward's reading and he waited for it to subside before he resumed:

He maketh wars to cease unto the end of
the earth; He . . .

Patrick pressed his hand and gave a deep sigh. The massive chest stopped moving and the hand went limp.

With a deep keening cry Edward rocked back and forth cradling the shaggy head against his chest, his grief too great to bear.

Several of Patrick's comrades moved to his side watching silently until finally Edward was able to bring himself under control. He eased Patrick's head back unto the scorched ground and reached up to close the sightless eyes, then placed the blood-soaked prayer book into the pocket of his trousers and stuffed Patrick's bucktail cap into his tunic.

Several of the soldiers helped him dig a shallow grave and after covering it with dirt Edward constructed a crude cross from several pieces of fence rail and scratched Patrick's initials on it with a sharp rock. He impressed the location of the grave on his memory. Someday, after the war, he would return and take Patrick's body home.

Somehow Edward managed to stumble his way back across the fields to the hospital, filled with wounded and dying men and he was able to keep his mind blank, moving about them, caring for their needs.

Quiet finally settled on the camp. Edward made his way

to his cot and fell on his knees fully clothed, unable to hold back the flood gates of tears.

The past was still intimate, the memories as powerful as if they had happened yesterday. As adults, their lives had moved in different directions, but he and Patrick had shared the antagonizing, intense relationship of youth, when they were most carefree, most idealistic, and most innocent. He loved Patrick. Oh, not in the same way he loved his parents, and not in the same way he loved his children. Certainly not in the same way he loved Katie. But love nevertheless.

The fighting continued for several more days before the Union withdrew and headed north once more, pursuing General Grant's policy of "relentless hammering". They next faced Lee on the North Anna River.

Edward's six weeks were about up. Six weeks! It seemed like a lifetime. His inclination was to follow the troops to their next engagement, but when the Commission wagons arrived at Fredericksburg to replenish their medical supplies a letter was waiting for him from Katie, his first since leaving home. She was expecting another child.

That night he boarded the steamship "Highland Light" bound for Washington, D.C., his tour of duty ended.

The reunion with Katie was unbelievably sweet and he looked at each of his children as though seeing them for the first time. Annie, petite and pretty with her mother's smile; Alex, standing tall with shoulders flung back, his huge brown eyes serious and proud; Edwin, handsome and laughing, his blond hair falling into his eyes; Emma, in a starched blue cotton shift covered by a flower sprigged, pinafore apron, with fat pigtails and bright blue eyes, and bashful little Emma peering at him from behind Katie's billowing skirt.

That night the children were allowed to stay up late and they donned sweaters and gathered around him on the front porch listening to his stories. The October evening was soft, the wind quiet, the fields all around silent. An early frost had hushed the grasshoppers and crickets and frogs. A pheasant crowed from the gloom of Katie's garden with its mums and honesty and arching bittersweet. He was truly home.

Katie rose finally, to lead the children into the house and prepare them for bed. Edward smiled, thinking about the pleasures of the night ahead. But first there was something he had to do.

He strolled across the field to the millpond where he and Patrick had parted three long years ago and leaned on the old rail fence looking into the water . . . remembering . . . thinking of the past.

Edward felt stronger now, at peace with himself. He had stayed on the land as his father and grandfather before him had done, he had remained true to the vow he made Katie, to his God and to his conscience. And despite their divergent views on many issues he had been true to Patrick and their friendship.

They had gone in different directions, he and Patrick, but they had parted friends. Patrick had listened to his drummer, Edward to his.

A faint clanging, clamerous sound from high in the silent autumn night interrupted his goodby prayer and he raised his eyes upward in irritation, then a smile settled on his heart. Edward stood in his tracks, his face turned toward the heavens, his breath held. On the horizon a dark wedge of Canada geese, speeding along their starlit highway, were outlined against the darkening sky and as he watched, the point bird dropped off and settled back to rest in the draft of others. Another bird moved to the head of the column, to battle the buffeting breeze, and lead the flock onward.

THE END

Afterward

A tall grey granite monument marks the grave of Edward Rebert in Christ Church Cemetery, just off the Pike running between Littlestown and Hanover. His final resting place lies high on the crown of a knoll from where one can see the sawmill property, and not far in the distance, with a little imagination, the grist mill property where he died. The monument reads, fittingly enough, "Gone But Not Forgotten."

Katie lived for twenty-two years after Edward's death, dying in 1908, and is buried beside him. Despite her wishes that her name on the monument be recorded as "Katie" it is inscribed more formally, Catherine, probably thought by one of the austere Reberts to be a more fitting epitaph.

Mary Alice is buried beside her parents, Sarah Jane rests in Jefferson.

Edward's brothers all did well for themselves. Samuel owned two large farms, and a house in Littlestown, and fathered seven children. Henry remained in the tanning business at Jefferson all his life. Jacob operated a store at Jefferson Station and his children married and settled in a community known as Jefferson Station. Charles became a very prominent business man in East Berlin, operating the feed mill there and owning several large tracts of land. The old Eyster homestead was farmed by J.J. until his death in 1894. Michael remained at the tannery in Jefferson, working for Henry, and Andrew moved to Ohio in the late 1800's.

The whereabouts of John is uncertain due to missing courthouse documents.

Jonas was laid to rest in the burial ground at Emmanuel Reformed Church in Hanover, Pennsylvania beside his beloved Maria. The small graveyard can be found off a narrow alley near York Street. The monument's inscription, worn smooth by time and weather, is barely discernable.

During his lifetime Edward became a prominent citizen of Littlestown and Adams County. He served several terms as Tax Assessor, was Judge of Elections, worked diligently on the building committee at Christ Church and owned several farms.

The contribution of the Pennsylvania Dutch to the culture of our great country cannot be denied. They were never a people to brag of their accomplishments, but we are indebted to them for so many things we take for granted; the Tannenberg organ and hundreds of church hymns, Hershey candy, Santa Claus, the Christmas tree and candles of Christmas eve, the Easter Rabbit and dyed eggs, and the uniquely American habit of driving on the right side of the road.

William Rittenhouse, a Mennonite preacher began the first paper mill in the colonies. John D. Rockefeller, H. J. Heinz, John Wanamaker, Herbert Hoover, and Dwight D. Eisenhour all lay claim to a Pennsylvania German heritage.

As does the author!

About The Author

Dolores H. Myers

Dolores H. Myers, affectionately called Dody, is married to James M. Myers, a licensed battlefield guide. Her interest in genealogy and history led her into a writing career.

Dody, a direct descendant of German ancestors who came to this country before the Revolutionary War, brings years of historical and genealogical research to her work.

She studied writing at Dickinson College, Carlisle, Pennsylvania and holds membership in the Kittochtiny Historical Society and the National Society of the American Revolution (D.A.R.).

She and her husband live in Chambersburg, Pennsylvania.